AF262911

DREAMER'S DAUGHTER

SURVIVING MY CHILDHOOD
AND RAISING MY FATHER

LORI THICKE

PUBLISHED BY SIMON & SCHUSTER

New York   Amsterdam/Antwerp   London
Toronto   Sydney/Melbourne   New Delhi

SIMON &
SCHUSTER
CANADA

A Division of Simon & Schuster, LLC
166 King Street East, Suite 300
Toronto, Ontario M5A 1J3

For more than 100 years, Simon & Schuster has championed authors and the stories they create. By respecting the copyright of an author's intellectual property, you enable Simon & Schuster and the author to continue publishing exceptional books for years to come. We thank you for supporting the author's copyright by purchasing an authorized edition of this book.

This Simon & Schuster Canada edition April 2026

SIMON & SCHUSTER CANADA and colophon are trademarks of Simon & Schuster, LLC

Simon & Schuster strongly believes in freedom of expression and stands against censorship in all its forms. For more information, visit BooksBelong.com.

For information about special discounts for bulk purchases, please contact Simon & Schuster Special Sales at 1-800-268-3216 or CustomerService@simonandschuster.ca.

Interior design by Wendy Blum

Manufactured in the United States of America

10   9   8   7   6   5   4   3   2   1

Online Computer Library Center number: 1519923491

ISBN 978-1-6682-0449-8
ISBN 978-1-6682-0452-8 (ebook)

So long as men can breathe or eyes can see,
So long lives this, and this gives life to thee.

William Shakespeare (1564–1616), Sonnet 18

Barn's burnt down—now I can see the moon.

Mizuta Masahide (1657–1723)

CONTENTS

CONTENTS

PROLOGUE

KIRKLAND LAKE, 1972

By the time we got home to our little farmhouse, the embers were cold, but the smell of smoke still hung heavy in the air. At fourteen, I was no stranger to loss and starting over—you could say it was my family's normal. Pieces of our life were always dropping away, as if we'd forgotten them someplace. This time was different. Everything had been wiped out at once.

I felt a tug. My father was gathering me and my little brother into his burly, tattooed arms. The three of us were silent—a rare event. I stared at the pile of charred planks until I could make out the clump of metal that must have been our freezer, filled with butcher-paper packets of moose meat, and fish from Kenogami Lake. Beyond, my room with the princess bed was now all cinders and collapsed beams from the attic, where my father and brother used to sleep on mattresses on the floor.

"Maybe we took a wrong turn." My nine-year-old brother's voice ached with wanting—wanting to believe that our house was still standing down some other country road. Skinny but with chubby cheeks, he held on to our father like he would crawl inside him if he could. Being younger, he had it harder, but I didn't try to make him feel any better. I had my own shit to worry about. Like guilt, because more than anything, I'd wanted to get the hell out of Kirkland Lake. My desire alone could have set that house on fire.

The whole place must have ignited as sparks to tinder. Like most homes in the North, it was made of wood; even the red bricks were papered on. We'd been down south when it happened, so the fire had burned undetected. Neighbors raised the alarm only when the flames climbed high enough above the scrub pines to lick the sky like Northern Lights.

Our farmhouse had already gone up in smoke by the time the town's fire truck peeled out past the Mile o' Gold.

Suddenly, I heard a crackle. Brad and I jumped back as something settled in the remains of our kitchen. Just the week before, a long wooden table had been right there, its vinyl tablecloth partly melted where someone— probably me—had left a hot pot. Now it was all gone—along with a pile of letters, and one large brown envelope from the insurance company, stamped in red: FINAL NOTICE.

Remind me to pay that, won't you, Lor?

I hadn't reminded him.

"Dad, the fire insurance!" I said, like we still had time to pay it.

I watched the realization dawn across his face: No insurance. No nothing.

My father surveyed the pile of rubble and ash that used to be our home and then turned back to us with a bright look in his eyes. He stretched his arms out, thrusting them skyward.

"Well, kids," he said, "now we're free!"

Brad and I exchanged a look of panic. Where our father saw *free*, we saw *homeless*.

"Come on. Don't wear that face." My father poked me with his elbow. "We still have each other. We only lost stuff."

"But it was *our* stuff!"

Brad grabbed hold of our father's hand. I didn't. I was damned if I was going to admit to needing anyone. I crossed my arms over my chest, resentment growing with every breath of that scorched air.

"So, where are we supposed to live now?"

"Anywhere we want."

"Sure, Dad." It seemed so simple, if you could just forget the part about our family having no money.

Behind us, the engine of our Volkswagen van was clinking as it cooled down. My father cocked his head in the direction of the sound.

"Lucky we still have our clothes, eh?"

"Yeah, Dad, so lucky."

He raised his eyebrows at me.

Our things in the van's back seat were all we had left now; the clothes we'd gone away with, plus some of my books, my brother's chessboard, and my father's war medals, saved only by being mixed in with my jewelry. I wished I'd thought to pack my grandfather's poems. But how could I have known that our house would burn down?

My father shook his thick finger at me. "You worry too much."

"Well, you worry too little."

"Dad, Dad!" Brad, his long hair falling over one freckled cheek, was tugging urgently on our father's sleeve.

"What is it, son?"

"If we don't live here anymore, how will Mom find us?"

CHAPTER 1

LAND OF HOPE AND DREAMS

KIRKLAND LAKE, 1968

MY FATHER WAS WHISTLING at the wheel of our Valiant. The tires were making a pleasant thrumming noise as they slipped through the bed of snow. The car, with its boxy yellow body, vinyl seats, and push-button gears, was cozy and familiar. I'd snagged the front seat—an easy victory when you're ten to your brother's five—so Brad was stuck in the back scowling, arms crossed. I scooted over close enough to take in my father's Old Spice. He'd just come home for the weekend after working down south for what felt like forever to a daddy's girl like me.

That winter morning, as diamonds of ice twinkled in the trees, we were headed for hot chocolate at a local restaurant called the Golden Palms, its name embodying all the hopes of our little mining town: Get rich and go somewhere balmy.

In a few years, a fire would render the three of us homeless, but today we were a family of four, with a warm apartment awaiting our return and our mother at the kitchen table clutching her cup of Maxwell House.

To get a rise out of Brad and me, my father began steering the car with his knee. With both hands free, he reached into his breast pocket for his battered old harmonica and put it to his lips. In 1968, the Age of Aquarius was dawning, but my father was playing a forties show tune about what a beautiful morning this was. I was so happy he was here that I sang along at the top of my voice.

He took hold of the wheel again, his sleeves riding up to reveal the tattoos on his forearms. An anchor and a lady with a floppy hat: they looked like they'd been drawn on by Magic Marker. The tattoos were one of his contradictions.

I can't stand people with tattoos.

Daddy, you have *tattoos.*

That's different. I was young and stupid.

I couldn't imagine him as stupid, or young. His hair was salt and pepper—his goatee more like salt, his sideburns more like pepper. I knew from photos that his hair used to be black, like mine, while Brad had inherited his freckles and reddish hair from our mother's side.

What happened next would stay with me forever. We had just turned onto the street that rounded the Teck Pioneer nursing home, my father drumming his fingers on the wheel, hot air blowing from the vent at our feet, when the town's garbage truck lumbered into our path. In that space between my first thought and the other, nobler one, I waved. We were close enough that I could see the driver's grizzled face weighing what to do.

He waved back.

My father stopped humming. "Who was that?"

"Mommy's boyfriend."

He slammed on the brakes.

We swerved on the ice, and our back end fishtailed. Brad slid to the floor with a *whumpf.* We came out of the skid in the middle of the road. My father whipped his head around to make sure neither of us was hurt. Then he turned his full glare on me.

"What the hell do you mean 'Mommy's boyfriend'?"

I clamped my lips shut. Brad, clambering back onto the seat, gave me a reproachful look. Our mother had sworn us both to secrecy. But her boyfriend, Art, suddenly crossing our path like that in his garbage truck, moonlighting while working as a bartender, had provided me with the excuse I needed. I wouldn't have to admit how much I'd wanted to hurt my mother and get rid of Art. Not if *the words just slipped out.*

I felt the Valiant drifting. My father was stepping on the gas, staring through the windshield but seeing nothing. We were heading into a snowbank.

"Daddy!"

He turned the steering wheel just in time. I could barely breathe from the guilt and the fishtailing. I hadn't meant to hurt *him.* I just wanted him back home to stay.

Our life was supposed to have been better up in Kirkland Lake than it had been down south in Toronto. No more deals gone sour, my father had promised. No more *rat bastard crooked son-of-a-bitch partners* to steal his ideas and leave us in debt.

"The Mile o' Gold starts here," he had said when we first drove into his hometown, just nine months before. I believed him. I always did.

Did my mother? The day we moved here from Toronto, she had kept her face turned toward the window for what seemed like the whole four hundred miles.

"Kids, your mother's giving me the silent treatment again." He'd used his stage voice, lifting his eyebrows theatrically.

"Oh, Dacker," my mother had said, sighing.

Dacker wasn't even his real name, but we didn't know that then.

Now, looking through the Valiant's windshield at the bleak white landscape, I realized how bad it must have been down in Toronto for Kirkland Lake to seem like a land of hope and dreams.

"Let's go back home, kids."

His broken voice made me wish I could take back what I'd done.

He straightened out the car, angling the wheels into the transparent tracks between snowbanks splashed with mud from the last thaw. Beneath was black ice, slippery and treacherous. In the car, the heat was blasting, but I felt cold with dread. What would my mother say when she found out I'd betrayed her? What would my father say to her?

It's not like she hadn't warned me. The first time I met Art, my mother had pulled me into the kitchen and whispered, "Don't tell Daddy. He wouldn't understand Art coming for dinner." If my heart wasn't hurting so much right then, I would have told her that I didn't, either. Art was the opposite of my father. He was tall and sinewy, with veins popping out of the muscles in his arms. He smoked and drank and swore—*tabarnak, câlice*—like the toughs on the Catholic side of town. Before the mines shut down, Art had worked underground, so when he laughed, it sounded like he was excavating chunks of silica from his lungs. The *horking* made me want to throw up.

In Siberian silence, Brad, my father, and I drove around the front of the IGA grocery store to the side entrance on Prospect Avenue. It was a gray concrete building with a bank of glass on the front. On the sides it was as windowless as a bunker, except for the top floor, where we lived. We shopped in that IGA for the only food you could get up north: meat, anything canned, a few wizened vegetables. At the time, I gave no thought to what it must have been like for my mother, going from a two-story maisonette in Toronto to living above a grocery store in Kirkland Lake. Or for my father, who'd come back to his hometown so full of dreams—*Helen, this time I've got it*—only to find out it was hard to make a killing on a population of 12,000, most of them poor. One business after another failed, and the only solution seemed to be for him to go back to Toronto—alone. There, to support his family, he'd sunk to the worst depths he could ever imagine. He'd had to get a job.

"You kids stay in the car," my father said. The minute he was out the door, Brad ran to catch up with him, the swaddled legs of his snowsuit making a swishing sound. I followed, walking in the footprints my father had left in the snow.

He waited until I reached him outside the street door before wrenching it open. Inside, piano notes cascaded down the stairs: my mother's beloved *Moonlight Sonata*. He took the steps to the landing two at a time.

My mother was still playing when he burst into the apartment. When she saw the look on his face, her fingers froze. My father smacked the wall. The sound was like a shot. She jumped up. Her piano bench scraped the floor.

"I'm away from my children, working a goddamned *job* to send you money," he cried, his voice cracking. "And you—you've got some guy on the side?"

My mother squeezed back against the wall. I avoided her eyes, pretending to study the linoleum where the snow from my boots was puddling. She would know it was me who tattled on her; Brad always did what he was told.

My father stormed into their bedroom and began pulling out drawers. My mother went in after him and shut the door. From the hallway, Brad and I could hear our father's angry voice. Our mother's replies were so quiet, they were like ghosts of words. After what seemed like hours, my father came out. On his shoulder was his duffel bag from when he was in the army.

"Daddy, don't go." I wrapped myself around his legs. My heart was aching so bad I thought it would stop beating. "Please. Don't leave us."

"I'll be back"—he peeled me off him and turned to my mother—"to see my kids." Then he was gone.

The top door slammed, then the street door. After that, all was silent.

I would relive that moment many times, my mother slumped at the kitchen table, the flat look in her eyes hiding feelings it would take me a lifetime to understand. She would never mention what I did, not once. Neither would my brother, despite what my betrayal cost him.

Even if Brad didn't hate me, after my father left that day, I hated myself. It never occurred to me that I had been given a secret too big for a ten-year-old to carry. All I knew was that I had broken my mother's trust, and instead of getting rid of Art, I'd lost my father.

CHAPTER 2

THE LETTER

KIRKLAND LAKE, 1968

MY MOTHER CHECKED THE fine gold watch on her wrist for the third time. It was the week after Art's garbage truck crossed our path, and to my relief, he hadn't been back. On Fridays, my father always left work in Toronto early to make the eight-hour drive home, and today, sure enough, my mother had set an extra place at the table. Butterflies of excitement danced in my stomach at the thought of seeing my father again. One week apart from him was like a year.

"We should start," my mother said after checking her watch again. But she left her fork lying by the side of her plate. Brad looked at her with eyes too solemn for a five-year-old.

My mother tilted her head toward the street, listening. With one delicate finger, she flicked the volume wheel higher on the beige crescent nestled behind her ear. Then she smoothed down her curls to hide her hearing aid. Suddenly my heart flip-flopped: footsteps were thudding up to the landing.

Arms aflutter, my mother flew down the hallway. Her heels clacked on the linoleum.

At the sound they made, I crumpled back down into my chair. She was wearing high heels, not slippers: it wouldn't be my father at the door.

The next afternoon, with my heart still bruised from seeing Art and my mother cuddled together on the couch, I trudged through the snow to Mrs. Chenette's for my music lesson—because, for my mother, we were never so poor that we couldn't afford a music teacher.

Mrs. Chenette let me in. I took my usual spot on the hard piano bench. All of a sudden, the skin on the back of my neck began to prickle. I looked around. The room where I took my lessons no longer held Mrs. Chenette's worn brown furniture. Covered in protective plastic was *our* French provincial love seat. Next to the window was *our* marble table, *our* globe lamp, and *our* blue velvet sitting chairs. We'd bought them all in Toronto that one time we were rich. They were supposed to be in storage for when my father's ship came in and we could get a bigger place.

Mrs. Chenette tapped her finger on the staff where I was to start. I turned to her, too shocked to speak, and tried to remember what we were doing.

"Every Good Boy Deserves Fudge," she reminded me, setting the metronome. "Only two weeks to your recital."

My mother picked me up after my lesson. Walking home with her, I wanted to ask why our best furniture was in Mrs. Chenette's living room, but I didn't. I was afraid she'd say it was because of what I'd done.

Suddenly, there was a blur of movement: a woman bounding toward us. We leapt out of her way. I felt myself tumbling back into a snowbank. My mother fell next to me. The woman advanced until she towered above us.

"You leave my 'usband alone."

My mother struggled to her feet. She gave me her hand and hauled me out of the snowbank. I hid behind her.

"You've got the wrong person," she said. But as she brushed the snow from her coat, her hands were shaking.

"Wrong person, my ass." *My hass* is what it sounded like.

"Mom." I tugged on her sleeve. "Let's get out of here." I knew that accent.

"We're not going anywhere." Indignant, my mother pulled her fur collar up around her neck. "I don't know your husband."

"Did Art say he 'ad no wife?"

My mother gasped.

"And six children. *Six.* 'Ow many do you 'ave?"

My mother grabbed my hand roughly. "Come on." She hurried me down the sidewalk, away from Art's wife.

Later, my aunt Dixie, who seemed to know everything that went on in town, told me that Art got a black eye that night. I fantasized about telling his wife where we lived, so she could give him another. Then maybe he'd stay away for good.

One morning not long afterward, I was leaving for school when I saw my mother's camel coat draped over one of the two wingback chairs we had left. Since my father had returned to Toronto, I'd been resenting her, but I still loved her coat, the way it tucked in at her small waist and flared out around her ankles. The way the white fur collar enclosed her neck like a cloud. I wished I were delicate like her, instead of husky like my father.

It was only when I was sitting in my fourth-grade classroom that I realized how odd it was for my mother's coat to be on the arm of the chair and not hanging up.

The camel coat was still gnawing at me as I walked home for lunch. I pulled the street door open. There was no *Moonlight Sonata* drifting down from the piano to greet me, no lunch dishes clattering. I climbed the steps, bits of ice sluicing off onto the treads. Removing my boots on the landing, I stepped into my own melting snow. The cold was seeping through my wet socks as I turned the door handle.

"Mom?" I felt my heart beat faster as I waited to hear her voice. "I'm home," I called, louder.

My words bounced back to me, echoing the emptiness of our apartment. Dread pounded in my chest. She wasn't there. The prior week I'd come upon her staring out at the back laneway, where tendrils of brown grass poked through the crust of snow. I looked now to the spot where she had stood. The breakfast dishes were put away, the lunch dishes were nowhere to be seen. The table was wiped clean, a dish towel folded in thirds. It was as if Brad and I hadn't been there at all.

Just then I heard the street door open. I ran out to the landing.

"Where were you?" I cried. But it was only Brad, trudging up the steps on his little legs. Behind him was the babysitter, who came when my mother played piano at the nursing home. The babysitter's pale face was spidered with red veins from the cold as she ushered Brad upstairs. She hoisted him to the top of the chest freezer we kept out on the landing to store what my father brought home from hunting and fishing: moose meat and partridge, pike and pickerel.

"Let's get your boots off, little man." She reached out for one of Brad's mukluks.

"Where's Mom?" I demanded.

"The nursing home," the babysitter replied.

Brad kicked his heel against the front of the freezer, making a pucker in the white metal. "She left."

He was the only one who'd seen our mother leave. Over the years, he would forget what he said that day. But I wouldn't.

Let it go, Lor, Brad would say today, though it's been many years since I've seen him. And he's right: I should let it go. But I can't. And now my brother's memories have become mine.

He's playing hide-and-seek under the staircase when our mother comes out onto the landing. Through the wooden slats, he sees her camel coat swirling around her ankles. Down the steps she comes. Stifling a giggle, he waits for her to look for him. Instead, she tightens her scarf under her chin. Then she slips outside. Brad crawls out of his hiding place to follow her. He opens the door to the street just as our mother approaches a car at the curb. She sweeps up the bottom of her coat and lowers herself into the passenger seat. "Mommy!" he calls. The car begins to move. He runs after her, into the street. *Mommy!* The car accelerates. Our mother doesn't look back.

"Now, Bradley, you sure you seen your mommy drive away?" The babysitter put her hands on her hips. "When I came down, I didn't see no car. She always walks to the nursing home."

"I *did* see a car." He squirmed away from the babysitter. "I called, but Mommy didn't hear me."

"Well, I'm sure she'll be home by tonight."

Back at school, I ignored the bell for afternoon recess. My classmates were already taking their coats and scarves off the hooks and their mitts from the cubbyholes, but I was craving warmth.

"My mom drove away with a man. I think it was her boyfriend." I used Brad's story, which I didn't believe at that time, as a pretext to stay inside with my teacher.

She immediately stopped putting the atlases away. "You don't have to go out for recess," she said, squeezing my shoulders.

I'd gotten what I wanted, but her pity made me feel worse. Until that moment, I hadn't considered that our mother might not come back from wherever she was. Now I felt a sense of panic. No matter how mad I was at her for hurting my father, I didn't mean for her to leave us, too.

After school, my father's younger sister, Dixie, came over. She must have been on her way to work, because she was dressed in a pastel pantsuit. Her nurse's cap covered her short dark hair, so similar in color to mine that people often mistook her for my mother. That is, if they didn't notice her total lack of affection toward me.

Aunt Dixie went straight for our phone. "Why should *I* pay for the long distance?" she asked, as if I'd dared question her.

My father lived in a boardinghouse in Toronto. He didn't have his own phone there, so she called him at his job. "Helen's gone," she said into the receiver. She didn't sound surprised, or sorry. She didn't like my mother. Probably because my aunt's husband, my uncle Stan, had always had eyes for her.

Beside me, my little brother twisted the legs of his green Gumby. My aunt handed me the receiver. "Here, talk to your father."

"Daddy!" I didn't tell him what Brad had seen. Anyway, everyone knew mothers didn't leave their children. She'd come back.

"Darling, don't worry. I'm sure your mother won't be away long. It'll all work out."

"Okay, Daddy." I sniffled. It was what he always said, and what I'd longed to hear.

Until our mother returned, Brad and I were to stay at our aunt Dixie's. Under the sink, our aunt found a brown paper bag, neatly folded like everything in our home. "Here, put your toothbrushes and your clothes in this."

I crossed my arms. "We don't need to pack any clothes. My mom'll be back soon." I had started making up a story in my head: my mother was in the hospital and was keeping it a secret so we wouldn't worry.

"Suit yourself."

At bedtime over at Aunt Dixie's house, I was forced to borrow a nightgown from my cousin Bev, who was also ten and my best friend. When Bev moved over to make room for me in her bed, her face showed the same pitying look my teacher had given me.

"My mom's only at the hospital." I yanked the covers over to my half of the bed.

Bev gave me another of her compassionate looks. Then she yanked the covers back to her side.

On the fourth day, my father called from Toronto to say a letter had come in the mail. My mother had addressed it to the company where he worked selling cable TV. The receptionist had opened the envelope by mistake.

I imagine that receptionist holding my mother's open letter, her face red as she delivered the news:

"I'm sorry, Mr. Thicke, but your wife has left you."

The letter would not survive the upheavals of the following years, but my father told Brad and me what it had said, refusing to hold anything back—as if secrets were a poison he had to expel.

Dear Dacker,

You'd better sit down before you read this.

Our mother had written that he should come and get us. But she didn't say why she'd left.

Deep inside, I knew why. Because I'd told on her.

There was no personal message for Brad and me, no goodbye. Instead, she closed the letter by writing:

You always wanted the children. Now you can have them.

CHAPTER 3

NIGHT TRAIN

KIRKLAND LAKE, 1968

MY AUNT DIXIE BOOKED us on the night train to Toronto. Before we left, she took us back home to the apartment above the store to collect our things. Instead of packing my clothes like I was supposed to, I slipped into my mother's bedroom. Along with everything else, she'd left behind her hope chest. Now I lifted the cedar lid. Its woody smell wafted out like a sigh, spicy and soft. Inside were our family photograph albums. I flipped through the pages, looking for gaps to show she'd taken something of me with her. Not a single picture was missing. I dumped the albums back into her hope chest. Four years later, they would burn up in the fire.

That night, shuffled into our aunt Dixie's car, I felt lost and confused. What kind of life were we going to? Why hadn't my mother tried to take us with her? Would she still be here if I hadn't waved to Art?

The closest railway station was in Swastika. The town, which had refused to surrender its name, even after the Nazis appropriated it, had once been a busy hub, transporting mine workers north and gold south. Now it was deserted; the platform where Brad and I stood bundled in our winter coats was nearly empty. Next to us, Aunt Dixie stamped the snow off her mukluks. Her cushioned nurse's shoes were back in her car. She'd left the motor running, and it sent white puffs of smoke out the exhaust pipe. She scanned the brown-brick station for a clock, wearing an expression that said she was eager to be getting back.

The train pulled into the station.

"Off you go," Aunt Dixie said to Brad, who'd been gripping her hand. She passed him off to a porter in a blue Northlander uniform. "You, too," she said to me, then hurried to her car without a backward look. The porter lifted my brother up the metal steps to the train. Brad, who must have forgotten his scarf in the back seat of Aunt Dixie's car, gave a little cough. We followed the porter down the train's corridor, then waited while he took a key from his pocket.

"If you need me, ring the buzzer," he said, unlocking the door of our tiny couchette.

Inside, two bunk beds had been made up with neat white sheets and scratchy-looking blankets. Fitted into one corner of the space was a small triangular sink. A big window streaked with grime looked out onto the snowy platform. I locked the door, and the whistle blew. The train began to chug away from the station.

Brad was waiting for me to tell him which bunk to take. I would always balk at filling in for our mother, even later, when it would become clear how much he needed me to. It's hard to forgive myself for that. As he looked to me for guidance, I said nothing. After a minute, he shrugged and climbed up onto the top bunk.

I stared out the window at the moon reflected on the snow. I didn't know where we'd live or go to school or who'd take care of us while our father was working. I didn't know anything except that all this was my fault. I heard Brad cough a few times before he settled down, then all went silent except for the creaking of the train and the occasional blast of its whistle.

We woke up in the city, snaking along tracks that curved around Lake Ontario. The ice was breaking up; it made the surface of the Great Lake look like porridge. Wheels squealing, the train slid into Toronto's Union Station. While Brad and I waited for the porter to come get us, we heard doors opening and a bustling up and down the train's corridor. I pressed my face against the window. Travelers who had been invisible the whole trip were spilling onto the platform. When they all dispersed like water down a drain, I looked for a sign of our father. The platform was empty.

There was a sharp rap at the couchette door, and I opened it. The porter took Brad's bags, and I took mine. Brad and I half-ran to keep up as the porter led us down the platform to the station's main hall. When he finally stopped, we found ourselves in a cavernous space with an arched bank of windows and a ceiling as high as a church.

I scoured the hall for my father, expecting him to walk over and collect us. When I didn't see him, I thought, *What if he doesn't want us, either?* I glanced down at Brad to see if he was worried, too. Suddenly, our father was striding toward us, haloed by the light streaming through the station windows.

"*Daddy!*" Brad and I yelled in unison, running to him. He squatted down to hold us. I pressed my face into his buckskin coat and breathed in the earthy smell.

He kissed our heads, one after another. "I love you kids more than a whole herd of Shetland ponies. Don't you forget that."

Beside me, Brad coughed hoarsely. He let go of my father and bent over, gasping for air. His cold seemed to have gotten worse overnight.

"Are you all right, son?" my father asked, kneeling in front of him.

Brad's cheeks had turned red, but he nodded, and after a few moments his breathing returned to normal.

"Okay, then, let's go." Picking Brad up in his arms, my father took us outside the station. I recognized our Valiant, keys still in the ignition, idling by a fire hydrant. A parking ticket was tucked under the windshield wiper.

"Just throw it there," my father said to me, pointing to a pile of tickets on the dashboard.

Our mother would never have let him get away with that stack of traffic tickets. All at once, it hit me how different our lives were going to be. What would happen to us now that we no longer lived in her orderly realm of hot lunches and weekly piano lessons?

CHAPTER 4

AFTER THE SILVER RUSH

THE NORTH, 1924

MY FATHER WAS BORN in a silver rush and raised in a gold rush. That explains a lot.

My father's corner of Northern Ontario was once known the world over as the Silver Sidewalk and the Mile o' Gold. At the turn of the twentieth century, the hard rock of the Canadian Shield was ready to yield some of the richest mineral deposits on earth. But unlike the Klondike and the California gold rushes, its rise and fall was never immortalized in a bestselling book. The spectacular gold and silver finds, the rip-roaring boomtowns, the extraordinary wealth won and lost—these were the biggest events you'd never heard of.

In 1903, my great-grandparents Stanley Edward Thicke, known as S.E., and Isabella Cowie, known as Belle, boarded the brand-new Temiskaming and Northern Ontario Railway for Cobalt, sixty miles south of Kirkland Lake, which was as far north as the tracks had been laid. But it wasn't gold that beckoned them—those rich veins, buried deep in the uncharted bush, were yet to be discovered. It was silver. And the rush was on.

It's not hard to discern where my father got his optimism. I can see his grandfather now, an unlikely prospector by any measure. S.E. is a small-framed man with a big mustache. Prior to coming north, he clerked in an office in the city and sang in a barbershop quartet; Belle, his wife, managed a bakery. They are nothing like the other passengers on the train that day: young, single men out to make their fortunes with a miner's pick. Yet here they are, S.E. and his wife, heading off to the silver fields along with their six children, who at that very moment are clambering over the carriage's wooden benches, with Lily, the oldest, trying to contain them while taking care of William Henry, S.E.'s bitter, aged father.

Coming from Toronto, where trolley cars clang between buildings ten stories tall, S.E. and Belle are shocked. The train has left them in a muddy slash of woods. It is the mining camp of Cobalt—named, as it will turn out, for the wrong metal. Trees have been chopped down so tarpaper shacks can be thrown up among the bleeding stumps. No plan has been made as to where the streets should go, nor how to dispose of the sewage—the "night soil" that will freeze in winter and then thaw, stinking, in spring.

In just five years, Cobalt will explode. Silver floats as big as cannonballs and as wide as stove lids will be discovered. The spot where my great-grand-parents have landed will be known as Canada's Silver Sidewalk. At its height, this area will yield one tenth of all the silver in the world.

The wealth will come so suddenly that before a boardwalk is laid down to protect long skirts from dragging in the mud, the foundations will be poured for a stock exchange and an opera house, and the future British king Edward VIII will come sniffing around for opportunities. But right now, Cobalt is a rowdy, lawless bush camp.

My great-grandfather decides this is no place to raise his sons and daughters. *Silver be damned.* Unlike the women in my family, the men will always put their children first.

S.E. hires a horse and wagon to haul them to where the packet boat the *Meteor* is anchored. It will take them to a farming settlement up Lake Temiskaming. On the opposite bank of the Wabi River, they will open a bakery. From then on, the only silver S.E. will seek will be in dimes and dollars. *Leave the prospecting for the dreamers.*

Twenty-one years later, when my father is born to S.E. and Belle's second-oldest son, Charles, and his war bride, Dorothy Dacre, Cobalt's air is still reverberating with the clangs of claim stakes being hammered into the ground. The area is attracting so many dreamers that when the mine-owners transport workers from down south, they have to handcuff them to the rail-cars so they won't jump off to stake their own claims. If ever there was a place to make you believe anything is possible, it's here.

As the silver rush winds down, my father's parents move their young family to Kirkland Lake—just in time for the gold rush. My father's new hometown is the site of one of the largest and richest gold veins on the planet. As an impressionable young man, he watches mineowners strut around town in full-length mink coats; he skirts scruffy Roza Brown, who is sitting on a fortune in mining stocks while sharing her hovel with assorted dogs, cats, and chickens; he sneaks in to drink at Charlie's Hotel, whose owner, Charlie Chow, is making so much money by getting paid in mine shares that when a blizzard holds up the town's payroll, he will loan the bank $250,000 in cash.

By the time my father is a teenager, most of the silver mines have closed, and the gold mines are heading the same way. At the tender age of fifteen, my father walks into that very same Charlie's Hotel determined to join the war and make his fortune abroad.

CHAPTER 5

I WANT TO HOLD YOUR HAND

TORONTO, 1968

OUTSIDE UNION STATION, MY father bundled my brother and me into the yellow Valiant. Brad clutched his hand so tight, my father had to extricate his fingers to settle him inside the car.

"Son, if you're tired from the train, you can lie down in the back."

"I'm okay," Brad said, but he immediately laid his head down on the seat cushions.

My father looked over his shoulder and pulled a U-turn across two lanes of early-morning traffic. As we bumped over the streetcar tracks, Brad sat up coughing.

"How long has he had that for?" my father asked.

"I don't know." Thinking back, I realized that in the five days since our mother left, I hadn't paid Brad much attention—which meant that no one had.

"Son, I've got some cough medicine in my room. Just hold on a little longer." Without taking his eyes from the road or slowing down, my father reached his hand back and felt my brother's forehead.

I turned away from that tender gesture. I see now that I was trying to hold myself together by shutting out any emotions. If, at that moment, my father had so much as asked me if I missed my mother, I would have broken into bits so small no one would have been able to put me back together again. But he didn't ask. It was like everything had already worked out for the best.

I faced the window, where the passing neighborhoods were changing like our family's fortunes. Solid brick buildings slid by, replaced a few blocks later by cheap wooden storefronts, then by narrow houses with postage-stamp yards. Then the lawns became larger, the trees bigger and older, until finally my father parked the Valiant in front of a large Victorian house.

Wheezing slightly, Brad knelt on the back seat to look outside. "That's where we're going to live?"

"That's our room in front." My father pointed out a turret with rounded windows. He took his scarf off and passed it behind him. "Here, Brad, wrap this around your neck. I don't like the sound of that cold."

Toronto is half a season warmer than Kirkland Lake, so instead of ice on the front steps, there was slush. As my father pulled out a clutch of keys from his pocket, I tried to see through the door's leaded-glass panels. It was black inside. When we entered, a dim shaft of light illuminated a red carpet with bald patches. Then the door closed behind us, and we were in the dark. I heard voices coming from down the hall, and I looked up.

"We have to share the kitchen with other people," my father explained. He sounded apologetic as he ushered us into his room and locked the door.

When the light came on, I took in our new home. The rounded wall of windows had made it awkward to fit in the furniture, so everything was crowded in the center of the room. There was a double bed, the mattress concave, above which a single bulb was suspended. Against the one straight wall was an old-fashioned wooden wardrobe with a mirror, and beside that, a suitcase on the floor spilling out clothes. On the unfolded ironing board were a couple of wrinkled shirts, an iron, and a small television set. The knob was gone from the front of the TV, so my father had clipped on a pair of pliers to change the channels.

"I'll sleep there." My father pointed to a clear spot on the thin brown carpet. "You kids can take the bed."

"Daddy, don't you have to go to work today?" I knew the money he had sent to my mother came from knocking on doors to sell cable TV, which was still a novelty in 1968.

"Work?" His forehead creased as if he had forgotten he had a job. "No, my darling. I'm not going to work today."

"But what if you get fired?"

"Don't worry. It'll all work out."

That evening, my father tucked Brad, solemn and obedient in his sports car pajamas, under the covers. Brad's eyes closed, and all was quiet except for the television, turned down low. For the first time since my mother left, we had stopped moving. The sudden stillness filled me with panic. I jumped up between my father and the program he was watching.

"When do we go back to school?"

My father sighed. "Lori, shush. Brad needs to sleep."

"We have to go to school!"

My father's concerned face was bathed in the blue light from the TV screen. "We'll figure something out."

Brad sat up and began coughing. Soon tears were running down his cheeks. Patting Brad's back with one hand, my father gestured with the other for me to hand him the Vicks. Using the lid as a spoon, he held some cough syrup up to Brad's lips.

"Take this, son. It'll calm you down." Cradling my brother in his arms, my father turned away from me; I knew he blamed me for waking Brad.

A couple of mornings later, my father stood at the ironing board in his baggy underwear—grayish rather than white because he never separated colors in the wash—ironing the clothes he would send me to school in. At forty-four, he was just beginning to get a dad belly; there was no fat on him anywhere else. The iron hissed, so he held it away to leak water onto the rug instead of my clothes. While he ironed, he checked on Brad, who was lying with the covers up to his nose, wearing the same lost look he'd had since our mother left.

Because of his cold, my brother didn't have to start kindergarten yet, so I went alone. That afternoon, when my father picked me up at the gates of the school I wouldn't attend long enough to remember the name of, Brad was sitting in the front seat. His cheeks were a hot red. When I got in beside him, it sounded like a toy whistle was embedded in his chest.

"Brad can't seem to shake his cold," my father said. Worry added more gravel to his voice. "Let's go see what your uncle Brian says."

My father had two brothers, one rich, one poor. My rich uncle was a doctor who lived in Brampton, less than an hour from Toronto. After the war, my father, on his waiter's salary, put him through his first year of medical school, but their relationship soured when my father started sending the money late. If we were asking Uncle Brian for a favor, it meant Brad was in bad shape.

My uncle's stately house was arranged like a horseshoe around a circular driveway. We parked directly in front. As we got out, a faint burning smell came from the Valiant. My aunt Joan opened the front door of the house with a highball in one hand. Her dark, shoulder-length hair was thin and tousled. She wore a purple velour tracksuit; gold chains adorned her winter-tanned neck.

"Come on in," she said. She had a blurry look, like she couldn't focus on us, but then I realized she had locked her eyes on our car as if fearing it might leave a grease stain on her elegant paving stones. (It would.)

Gripping her drink, she led us inside. Alan, my oldest cousin, was already working in television, and his sister, Joanne, was off at swim practice, but I could hear Todd, the youngest, practicing his drums in the basement. I yearned to hang out with my cousins, but we were the poor relations, and they were too good for me. This feeling was reinforced by my aunt. Whenever we came over, she handed me a cloth to buff the silverware.

This was the first time we'd set foot in the second living room, reserved for guests. Brad immediately curled up into a ball on the alabaster sofa. We'd never had any furniture that color: you had to have money to afford white. After a few minutes, my uncle strode in wearing a clean polo shirt and tan pants. He was wiry and fit from golfing. He set his drink on a coaster and opened his leather doctor's bag. My uncle always had a medical kit in his house—as well as a treasure trove of prescription drug samples, which would be a welcome discovery in my teen years.

Taking out his stethoscope, he put the metal disk to Brad's tiny chest. After a moment, he folded the stethoscope and put it away. "This kid needs to be in a hospital." He snapped the lock on his bag. "It sounds like bronchitis on top of asthma. It's probably the stress, but that doesn't mean it's not real."

My uncle's hospital privileges in Brampton meant Brad went straight from emergency to a private room. While the orderlies were wheeling him in, somewhere down the hall an alarm rang and rang. They placed Brad inside a clear oxygen tent that covered most of his body, making him seem even smaller than he was. He twisted his head to look at the machines that beeped and whirred beside him. Through the oxygen tent, his freckles seemed paler.

A nurse bustled in wearing a pastel pantsuit like my aunt Dixie up in Kirkland Lake. "That girl's too young to be in here," she told my father.

He already knew I wasn't allowed in because of the sign we saw when we came up. "She's mature for her age."

"I'm sorry. She'll have to go."

My brother's eyes widened in terror as we walked to the door. Down the hall, the faraway alarm was still ringing. "Don't leave me, you guys."

"Son, son." My father went back to his side. "I'll be back tomorrow." Then we left him alone—exactly what he'd been afraid of.

Brad was a stoic little soldier, never complaining, never crying. It would be years before I understood the toll that not crying would take on us both.

On the drive back home, my father said, "Your mother left you with me because she knew I'd always take care of my kidlings. It doesn't mean she doesn't love you."

I stared at the dark road ahead of us. If it didn't mean that, what did it mean?

"You have to understand. She needed a man with an income. Not an 'if-come' like your old daddy." He chuckled at his own joke, which he'd cracked before. He was trying to make like my mother's leaving wasn't my fault, but I knew better.

The next day, while I was at school, my father went to the hospital rather than to work. After a week of visiting Brad every day, he lost his job selling cable TV door-to-door.

"Daddy, what are we going to do now?" He'd given up his dreams of having his own business for a steady income. But if a job couldn't be relied on to be steady, what was the point of it?

"Don't worry, your old dad will figure something out."

Up until that moment, it seemed we'd already lost everything there was to lose. Now, with a shock, I realized there was plenty more that could disappear. Like a place for us to live. I didn't want to sound like my mother, but I wanted to tell my father to get another job.

When Brad came home from the hospital, he was thinner and more fragile, and he couldn't be without his inhaler. He clung even more tightly to our father's hand. No matter where we went, Brad had to hold on to him. Even getting into bed at night, he never wanted to let my father go.

One day, my father tried to unlock the car door with one hand while Brad squeezed the other. Suddenly, the car keys slipped from my father's fingers and landed right next to an open grate. Brad was still clinging tightly as my father tried to scoop them up.

"Bradley, let go of me, for Chrissake!"

Brad jerked his hand away.

"I'm sorry, son," my father said, looking stricken. "It's just that sometimes I need to be able to move my bloody arms."

After that, my father would have to force my brother to take his hand.

CHAPTER 6

MARRY IN HASTE

TORONTO, 1954

MY PARENTS STAYED MARRIED for fourteen years, a period my father would later refer to as "the fourteen miserable years I spent with your mother." He'd never say just "fourteen." It was always "the fourteen miserable years." But he said it without rancor, as if "miserable" were simply another measurement of time.

Their engagement he measured in weeks.

Three weeks?

I wanted children. I wanted you and Brad.

What had my mother wanted?

Looking for clues, I conjure up the night they met. They are in the Brass Rail Tavern in London, Ontario, two hours by car from the big city of Toronto, but only one hour by Greyhound bus from the small town my mother ran away from when she was a girl.

My mother is working the cashier's booth at the entrance to the Pump Room. Never one to call attention to herself (unlike my father or, for that matter, me), she waits until no one is looking to slip off her high-heeled shoes. She bends over to rub one aching foot, her auburn curls falling across her cat-eye glasses. At that moment, the air moves.

I like to think that when my father comes whizzing by, he is wearing a black dinner jacket with military epaulets and gold lamé braiding around the collar and cuffs. I have a photograph of him like that. In it, he is dark and dashing. His hair is untamed, but his mustache is pencil thin—an over-earnest shaving habit that would prove more durable than his marriage. That one picture of him has somehow survived a lifetime of our shedding those things most people hang on to, the way a snake sloughs off skin. But in fact, the photo is from another time and another bar. Still, I prefer to imagine him dressed like that as he passes my mother for the first time, a tray with two highballs, a martini, and a Carling beer balanced on the tips of his fingers.

She has been promoted from waitress to cashier; no tips, but it's easier on her feet, which are deformed by painful bunions. From her station, she can hear the music coming from the Pump Room, dark and smoky and exotic. It's the fifties: jazz musicians from south of the border have found an appreciative audience in Canada, except for my mother. A childhood bout of scarlet fever has left her hard of hearing. Besides, she favors classical music—which she plays well enough that she could get away from bar work if she dared.

The bluish smoke swallows my father with his drinks tray aloft. A waitress on break stops at my mother's cash booth and lights a cigarette. Her name is Lorrie, and I will be named for her. "I hear the new waiter's some kinda war hero," she says.

My father was, in fact, a war hero, decorated for the battle immortalized in *A Bridge Too Far*. But his superiors, he would later tell Brad and me, never forgave him for taking the initiative to save those British paratroopers. Naturally, he hadn't waited for their orders. Offended that a lowly soldier like him—a "sapper"—could possibly be awarded the Military Medal, they toasted his success but filled only their own glasses. It was something that stuck with him.

Sapper Harry Dacre Thicke, MM, Royal Canadian Engineers, 1943

Being decorated may not have earned him a drink with the officers, but that night it garners a recommendation from Lorrie. "Helen, you need someone like him." My mother's track record with men is not that great.

"He's not my type," she says, and if Art, who she will leave us for, is anything to go by, that is certainly true. She wants someone with a job; my father has one now, but it won't last. He's not employee material, really. To use his own words, he's a wheeler-dealer, a scrounger, a hustler.

Dad, please don't tell people you're a hustler.

Why not? I am a hustler. I hustle every day for you children.

Trust me. It doesn't sound nearly as good as you think it does.

As for how well the hustling has been working out for him up to this point, well, the war has been over for nine years, and here he is, working as a waiter. Despite all his dreams. That should tell my mother something. But everywhere you look in my family, there are misguided hopes. In this one way, at least, she isn't any different from the rest of us.

As for my father, he will soon move on to something else. He's the king of reinvention. Even his name is made up.

When I enlisted, the sergeant goes, "They're too many Harrys here. What's your middle name?" So, I told him. It was my mother's maiden name.

Actually, Dad, you spelled your own middle name wrong. For the record, it's D-a-c-r-e.

Well, whatever. From then on, I was Dacker. Dacker the Dasher.

That night in the Brass Rail, when my mother takes off her high heels, she's already been working on her feet for twelve years. She is twenty-six and a divorcée; all she'll ever say about her first marriage is that she'd been nineteen at the time and that he was a taxi driver.

Her childhood dream was to become a piano teacher, but waitressing work has always been easier to come by. When she meets my father, she is living in a boardinghouse for young women, with no piano to practice on. By that summer of 1954, her disappointments are already legion.

She grew up in Kincardine, on the shores of Lake Huron, in a meager house with no indoor plumbing. Each winter, strips of the tarpaper siding were torn off by the storms roaring off the Great Lake. Inside the house, *her* mother, Eliza, was as strict as the metronome she set on the piano. If, during lessons, my mother was distracted by the other children playing outside, Eliza would rap her knuckles with a ruler.

Tommy Thorburn, my mother's father, didn't believe in striking children. Slight and gentle, with a persistent cough, he worked his whole life in the Andrew Malcolm furniture factory, finishing wood shipped in from Manitoulin Island.

"Hard work never killed anybody," my mother will often say, as if to no one in particular.

"I'm not so sure about that," my father will respond, stretched out on the couch.

He will turn out to be right. In time, her beloved daddy, shot through with the kind of cancer you get from varnishing wood in an unventilated room, will prove that you can die from hard work.

Only now, as I write these words, do I realize that I've gotten something wrong about my parents' story. At the time my mother looks up and sees the Pump Room's newest waiter, she is pregnant. That's why she's not working the floor as a waitress. Her feet are swollen from the pregnancy. And with a figure as light as a whisper, she's showing heavily.

My mother is alone, having caught her fiancé in their bed with another woman. Sometime after meeting my father, she has her baby. She and my father are not really friends, but afterward, she searches him out, distraught. It was a mistake giving her daughter up for adoption, she says. Can he help her get her baby back?

"Don't worry, Helen." He really thinks he can do it. He's got the gift of believing.

But the war hero is no match for the nun. "You signed the papers," she says brusquely. From behind her station, she looks down on my mother as a fallen woman. It was the fifties, when people believed things like that.

This is where the original connection between my parents comes to an end. Back at work at the Brass Rail, my defeated mother begins hunching over slightly. She will never again walk with her shoulders straight. Then there is the business with the union, come to organize the restaurant workers. My father, fancying himself a tycoon in the making, hates the very idea of collective bargaining. But he hates dirty tricks even more. Discovering that his boss has blackmailed everyone, including my mother, into voting no, my father is so outraged that he votes yes. The wheeler-dealer becomes the sole union supporter.

That afternoon, he finds himself alone in the middle of the Pump Room, with a towel draped over his arm. My mother huddles against the bar with the other staff as their boss strides over to him.

"I suppose you're going to fire me now," my father says.

"Oh, I'm not going to fire you, Thicke." The manager holds out a stained toilet brush. "But you're going to quit."

For my father, latrine duty ended with the war. He throws down his towel. "You're damn right I'm going to quit. And you know where you can shove that toilet brush."

When he moves to Toronto, my parents have never had so much as a date. My mother likes her men rough around the edges and everywhere else. My father isn't her type.

In the big city, my father decides to return to what he did to make money in the war: wheel and deal. Growing up in Kirkland Lake, he learned that gold was everywhere: you just had to figure out how to get your hands on it. (This figuring out would always be done on a couch, in the middle of the day, with his eyes shut.)

One person who got his hands on more than his share of the town's gold was square-jawed Harry Oakes. Striding across the wooden boardwalk in a trilby hat and full-length mink coat, he was the embodiment of my father's adolescent dreams. An American prospector, Oakes landed in Kirkland Lake as a nobody, with two bucks in his pocket to show for fifteen years chasing gold rushes around the world. By the time my father was stealing his way to a reputation as the town's bad boy, Oakes controlled the largest mine in the Western Hemisphere. Along the way, he became *Sir* Harry Oakes, the knighthood purchased with donations to England's poor. (Helping the needy of Kirkland Lake, had he been inclined to do so, wouldn't have yielded such high dividends.) He built a chateau on the shores of the town's namesake lake, then displaced the pristine water with mine tailings left over after his gold was extracted. When the tailings solidified, turning the tree-lined northern lake into a slimy moonscape, he moved to the Bahamas—taking with him twenty million dollars of the town's gold.

For my father, it's a happy ending he can only aspire to. I would find out later what really happened to Sir Harry. In stark contrast to my father's idea of his success was one inconvenient detail: Oakes was bludgeoned to death in Nassau, his body covered in feathers and then burned. The murder weapon was a miner's pick. The crime, to this day, is unsolved: the investigation was botched by the island's governor—the ex-king Edward VIII himself, who'd once gone searching for profits in the silver fields of Cobalt.

A few months have now passed since my father literally threw in the towel at the restaurant where he and my mother worked. His old Nash car carried him across 120 miles of flat Southern Ontario landscape back to Toronto. Now, on Christmas Eve, the winter winds from Lake Ontario are blasting up the corridor formed by the tall buildings lining Yonge Street. As my father comes up on the corner of Dundas, the wheels of his car suddenly lock up on the ice. He is heading right into the path of a red-and-yellow streetcar. With ease, he twists the steering wheel to spin out of the way. In Europe, he'd had to avoid worse things: land mines and bombed-out bridges. He bumps across the shallow streetcar tracks and then comes to a stop just outside the Brown Derby Tavern. The night before Christmas, when most people are with their families, my father is all alone—and craving plum pudding.

My mother is on her own for the holidays as well and feeling lonely. Leaving London to avoid ever seeing her baby in someone else's pram, she is now working at the very same Toronto restaurant my father is about to enter. She has taken the Christmas Eve shift so that the other waitresses can stay home with their husbands and families. After all, holidays pay time and a half.

When my father walks into the Brown Derby, my mother is resting her hand on the counter, supporting herself as she slips one foot out of her high heel to rub the aching ball against the tip of the other shoe. They don't see each other.

He serves himself liberally from the buffet, layering roast turkey and mashed potatoes on top of coleslaw and brussels sprouts. Going back to his table, he slows down to take stock of the desserts for later. He spies apple and pumpkin pies under glass domes, but no plum pudding.

"How can you have a Christmas buffet without plum pudding?" he grouses. He may not be a great believer in rules, but where food is concerned, there is a right way and a wrong way.

With her head bent down, my mother's loose curls have picked up a golden tint from the lights above. She slips her shoe back on, looking up to see who is making such a fuss.

"Oh, I should have known it was you." Smiling at the sight of a familiar face, my mother goes back into the kitchen and emerges with plum pudding on a plate. It is practically floating in cream. My father's heart beats faster.

After he has given his dessert its reverential due, he goes back to my mother's station. "Helen, I'm done with restaurant work." He hands her a business card.

"Tombstones?" She lifts her fine brown eyebrows in surprise.

"Why not?" He could joke about making a killing, but for him, business is serious. What he says instead is a kind of non sequitur: "This is going to be the Year of Dacker."

It is a phrase he will repeat often. But she is hearing it for the first time, and it must give her a frisson of hope. My mother's dreams are so small and simple, they can nestle easily within his oversize ambitions.

"I wish I had a piano," she says, though what she really means is a house and a garden. That is all she wants, and years later, that will be all she'll ever want for me: to marry a man who will give me a nice home. No thought at all that I might be capable of doing that for myself.

"Can I drive you to your place?" my father asks. He has his own dreams— just not the same ones.

My mother shakes her head. She lives only a few blocks away, in a boardinghouse off Yonge Street.

The very next day, my father says they should get married. You have to wonder what my mother thought she was getting into when she said yes.

Three weeks later, it is the night before their wedding. An argument about dinner leaves them in bruised silence. Even though she doesn't particularly enjoy being in the kitchen, she feels it unseemly for a man to cook.

"Let's just forget it, Dacker," she says.

"Sure. We can go out if you like."

"No, the wedding. I don't want to marry you."

Another man might have seen peril there. Not my father. "It'll all work out," he says. "We'll be fine."

In a photograph taken the following day, my mother is wearing a white brocade skirt with a matching jacket and a crown of flowers in her hair. She has taken off her glasses. My father is wearing a tuxedo borrowed from a bartender he knows. The only witnesses are that bartender and my mother's best friend, Lika Bicaku, an exiled Albanian countess who waitressed with my mother. For better or worse, my parents marry.

My parents' wedding, Toronto, 1954, with Countess Lika Bicaku as witness

CHAPTER 7

WAKE ME WHEN IT'S OVER

TORONTO, 1958

THE NIGHT BEFORE I married your mother, she said she didn't love me. I told her not to worry, that the love would come.

Three years after their dash down the aisle, the love still hasn't come. Instead, what my mother is feeling is her labor pains kicking in. According to my father, his pains are starting, too. He's just remembered something he forgot: the car insurance.

"Dacker, I told you this would happen." As the next contraction rips through her belly, she stubs out her cigarette in the ashtray.

"Don't worry. I have time to get the insurance. I'll go now."

"No—take me to the hospital." My mother glares at him through her cat-eye glasses.

"Look, I'll get the license plates. Be home before you know it." My father pulls out a few bills from his pocket to show her. "I have the money right here."

"Dacker, just call me a goddamned taxi." A baby on the move isn't about to wait for my father to sort out his car insurance.

"It'll be fine, Helen."

A late snow has fallen during the night in Toronto. My parents are living in a basement apartment, next to the laundry room, while my father works on various schemes; the tombstone business went under when he got sued for placing a headstone upside down. The landlord is Old Man Maxwell; he lived on the same street in Kirkland Lake as my grandparents did during the gold rush.

My father tucks the expired insurance papers under his arm, then crunches through the snow to the curb. A car is coming down the street. He sticks his thumb out. The car shows no signs of slowing, so he steps into the road and waves. The driver swerves around him, skidding in the snow. He doesn't stop. My father has to walk the mile to the insurance office.

Down in their basement apartment, my mother's labor pains are intensifying.

Your mother never forgave me for that.

Come on, Dad, I'm sure there were other things.

Oh, there were.

When he makes it back home, my mother is sitting near the door with her overnight bag at her feet. Her winter parka is open where her stomach bulges.

"I told you it would all work out," he says.

She gives him her blackest look.

"I'll just get your bag." His words tiptoe around her as much as he does. She lets him help her up to the car. He tosses her bag in the back seat, then bundles her into the front.

Inside the car, it's colder than outside. The sound that comes from my mother's pursed lips condenses into a white cloud that hangs in the air between them.

"Helen, your knee." He gives her a tap. She jerks both her legs to the right as if his touch were ice, then stays pressed up against the passenger door. He reaches across her belly to open the glove compartment. Pulling out a flathead screwdriver, he notches it into the ignition, then turns the handle to start the engine.

"Hang on, Helen!"

She is already bracing herself, one hand on the dashboard and the other on her door.

Dr. Charleston is waiting for them at Toronto General. When they arrive, my father sails past the arrows to the parking lot, then swerves up the ambulance ramp. From the passenger seat, my mother is braking with both feet.

"Watch you don't wear those brakes out," he jokes.

My father parks in the tow-away zone, then jumps out to snag a wheelchair from the emergency department. He wheels my mother up to the first nurse to soft-sole by.

"I'll come find you," he calls, running back to move the car from the loading zone.

When my father finally locates my mother in the hospital, he has missed my birth entirely. So has my mother, as she is under general anesthetic.

"Congratulations, Mr. Thicke. You have a daughter."

My father is overjoyed.

You kids are the best thing that ever happened to me.

For my mother, it's more complicated.

My mother, Helen Elizabeth Thorburn Thicke, Toronto, 1958

CHAPTER 8

OUT OF CONTROL

TORONTO, 1968

THERE WAS A SHARP rap on our boarding room door. My father put his finger to his lips.

We were sitting on the floor of our turret room around containers of Chinese food. We'd had takeout so many times, to avoid the other boarders (and our landlady), that Brad could now pick up individual grains of rice with his chopsticks. We were using a bath towel for a tablecloth, but we were eating off real dishes, warmed up under the tap. For my father, there was never any excuse to eat off cold plates.

The rap became a banging. "I know you're in there. I can smell your food." It was our landlady. "Your rent was due Monday." Today was Friday.

"Don't worry," my father called through the keyhole. "I'm good for it." Then he turned to Brad and me and winked.

Sometimes his lack of worry reassured me: if he was still whistling, we were okay. But other times it frightened me: what if he was only pretending for our sake? The one solid thing in my life was my father. I needed to believe he had things in hand.

That was hard with our landlady reminding me how precarious our situation was. "We should have stayed in Kirkland Lake!" I yelled at him.

"Lori, keep your voice down."

"I don't care if she can hear me. I hate it here." I got up and kicked at my father's suitcase on the floor. "The old men look at me funny, and the bathroom always stinks."

Lying low, Brad concentrated on removing the peas from his fried rice, one by one. I knew I should stop for his sake, but I couldn't.

"This is all your daddy can afford right now."

I kept pushing, despite the anguish on his face. "You need to get a job!"

"What do you think I'm working on?"

Just then, I noticed Brad wheezing. My uncle Brian had said not to upset him.

"Daddy, quick! Brad's inhaler!"

When he finished taking care of my brother, my father went to his shaving kit and took out a pill bottle. Crushing half a tablet in a spoonful of sugar, he passed it to me, and I took it. This wasn't my first spoonful. Soon, I would feel pleasantly fuzzy and would forget my fears.

I don't remember why the doctor had prescribed tranquilizers for me, only that he'd said, "This is for when your daughter gets out of control."

But I wasn't out of control; my world was.

On Saturday, Brad and I were watching cartoons when my father carried our laundry in. He'd done the washing the day before, then pinned our things to the clothesline in the backyard. Now, holding a pillowcase full of our clean clothes, he wore an expression I couldn't read.

"What happened to your panties?" he asked me. "I put them on the line. Did you go get your things?"

I shook my head. I'd given him all the pairs that weren't balled up under our bed, white and pink cotton ones with flowers and kitty cats.

"Well, there were none on the line just now."

Had someone stolen my underwear? Mistaken mine for theirs? I was confused. There were no children here: all the other boarders were grown men.

From then on, my father washed my panties in the sink. And he took to insisting that I lock the door to our room, even if he was just going down the hall to take a bath.

The following week, Brad and I were waiting in front of our school long after all the other students had been picked up. It was the third time in a row our father hadn't been there when the bell rang.

"There he is!" Brad flagged him down as if he might not see us.

"Daddy, you're late," I reproached him.

He looked harried, as if he'd run there instead of driven. "I'm sorry, kids. I left my course early."

"What are these for?" Brad had climbed into the back seat and now was pointing to two mysterious suitcases, one flat, like a thick briefcase, the other bell-shaped, like my uncle Brian's doctor bag.

"I'll show you when we get home."

Back at the boardinghouse, we scurried into our room before the landlady could see us. My father had charmed her into waiting for the rent, but he didn't want to push his luck. He placed the flat suitcase on the bed. Inside was an electric device with dials and needles.

"Who wants to try out my audiometer?"

"Me!" said Brad, as enthusiastic as a game show contestant.

"Okay, son." My father placed the headphones over Brad's ears. "Just tell me when you hear something."

I went to the second suitcase, which folded open like a tackle box. Cubbyholes on both sides were filled with small, round batteries; ear molds; and crescent-shaped hearing aids spooning each other. It all reminded me of my mother. I could see her delicate fingers popping open the compartment to slip in a fresh battery, then flicking the little wheel backward and forward, tilting her head until she got the volume right.

"Okay, Lor. Your turn."

"No, thanks." Thinking about my mother made me feel bad, and feeling bad made me angry. "If you have to go sell those stupid hearing aids, who will take care of us?"

"School's out next week," he reminded me. "You kidlings can come with me."

"Oh joy."

After Field Day, a day of athletics that marked the end of the school year and the beginning of summer holidays, we were surprised to see our father on time—and leaning against a brand-new car.

"Is this ours?" Brad asked. It was a brown Buick with a cream top.

"Yep. Uncle Brian cosigned the lease."

"So, we can keep it?" my brother asked.

"If I sell enough hearing aids."

I looked to see if he was joking. The car seemed a lot more expensive than a hearing aid. I wondered how many it would take to pay for it.

My father opened the passenger door and waved us in like he was our chauffeur. Brad and I jostled each other for the front seat.

"What's that smell?" Stuck in the back again, Brad was wrinkling his nose in disgust.

It was the plastic, still on the seats. That could mean only one thing: my father wasn't sure we could keep the Buick.

The next day, we were heading out of Toronto to his first sales call.

"Now, kids, it's really important to stay in the car." My father pulled up in front of a white farmhouse. "The last thing I need is for you to kill the deal." I squirmed on the seat, which was sticky in the summer heat. "I'm serious," he said. "Do not come to the door. Not for any reason. You hear me?"

I watched him walk away from us carrying his two suitcases. I had a sudden urge to run after him. As the minutes ticked by, a thought wormed its way into my head. What if he didn't come back?

"Come on!" I said to Brad.

Inside the farmhouse kitchen, my father was fitting a hearing aid into an old man's bristly ear.

"Daddy!" I cried.

Startled, he lost his grip on the hearing aid. It clattered to the floor.

"What the heck are you kids doing here?" He picked up the device and shook it to see if any parts had come loose.

My panic faded, leaving me with the realization that I needed a good excuse for what I'd done. "We have to use the bathroom," I lied.

Brad looked up at my father as if to say, *I don't have to use the bathroom.*

The old man blinked like we'd broken a spell. "You know, this here hearing aid costs a lot of money. Why don't you come back another time, Dr. Thicke?"

On the ride home, I asked, "Why did he call you Dr. Thicke? Are you a doctor now?"

"No, darling. I said *Dacker*; he must have misheard me." He chuckled. "He *is* hard of hearing."

I was reassured that my father could find something to laugh about. But as the days went by without a sale, he stopped joking.

"I'll find the rent," my father kept repeating, as if it were lying around somewhere and he just had to locate it.

The following week, he had a lead in a town so far from Toronto, we had to rent a motel room. "And guess what?" My father's voice took on that tone he used to try to drum up our enthusiasm. "The room has a color television!"

"Real color?" I asked. "Or like that fake green-and-blue film you taped across our TV?"

I couldn't help the sarcasm. I was feeling too unsettled to give him a break about anything. Nothing was safe or solid anymore. Our life felt fragile, as if the slightest pressure could send everything crashing down.

"Real color, Miss Smarty-Pants."

True to my father's word, the motel room had a color television, and summer reruns were on. While we watched *Get Smart*, he got dressed in his gray suit and trilby hat.

"I'll be back in an hour."

"Where will you be?"

He pulled open the curtains to point to a house on the corner. Then he left.

When the commercials came on, I said to Brad, "Let's go."

"Daddy said to stay here." Brad's serious expression belonged on an adult.

"Oh, don't be such a baby." I took the room key from the top of the dresser and locked up.

This time, I didn't intend to follow my father; I just wanted to explore. But apart from the ice machine, good for cubes to put down each other's shirts, there was nothing to do, so we went back to watch our show. I put the key in the lock, but I couldn't get it to turn. I suppose I wasn't used to keys: doors in Kirkland Lake were never locked. I wiggled it, but it didn't budge. I tried again, using more force. Something snapped. I looked down. In my hand was half a room key.

"Oh, no. Daddy's going to kill us!"

"Why *us*?" Brad asked. "*I* didn't break the key."

I held my brother's hand as we crossed to the corner house. If I could just see my father, he'd say everything was all right.

The door was answered by a woman wearing the short hair-helmet ladies seemed to acquire as soon as they got married. She led us into the living room. I ran to my father and told him what had happened.

"That's okay," he said, while looking like things were anything but okay. He had been making an ear mold, and now the paste had gone hard. "Ma'am, you can throw this in the garbage."

That evening, we started our long drive back to the boardinghouse. "Don't worry, darling. It's only money."

This alarmed me more than a scolding would have. "Don't we *need* money?"

"Everything will work out."

Despite my father's words, I couldn't escape the feeling that things were getting out of hand. I wished we were back in the boardinghouse so I could have another spoonful of tranquilizer.

Brad, who I thought was asleep in the back, suddenly sat up. "What if Mommy is waiting for us in Kirkland Lake?"

By the headlights of a passing car, I could see that his freckled cheeks were flaming.

"You know she's with Art," my father said, sounding tired. "He's working in a mine in Red Lake."

"They have mines in Kirkland Lake, too," Brad said.

"Not anymore, son." He sighed. "The gold's all gone."

Brad began to sniffle. "But I don't like it here. We should go back. Then Mommy will come, too."

That night, after settling Brad and me into bed, my father tiptoed out of our room. When he didn't return, I felt a familiar sense of panic. I put on his big slippers and went out to find him. I followed his voice to the kitchen, where he was speaking into the landlady's phone.

"That's the thing, Mother," I heard him say. "Having the kids with me is making it hard to work."

I felt my blood turn to ice.

I crept back to our room and got under the covers. When he came in, I pretended to be asleep. But I lay awake long after I heard him snoring, my heart beating out of control. This was what I'd been afraid of all along. He was going to send us away.

CHAPTER 9

LIQUID GOLD

MILTON, 1959

UNTIL I OVERHEARD MY father talking to my grandmother, I'd never known him to voice a moment's doubt. Everything would work out. He'd find the rent. Not only that: he'd make us rich.

I believed him, even though every one of his businesses had failed. Like the time he booked a stand to hawk canaries at the Canadian National Exhibition, only to have a freak cold snap blow in from Lake Ontario and wipe out all the birds. Or the time he came back from a sales trip to find his partner had changed the office locks and hired employees who didn't know him. Or the time his car wash was stolen by a *different* partner, also a *rat bastard crooked son of a bitch.*

Each time, my father picked himself up and started looking for his next big thing.

"Helen, this time I've got it."

So many of his stories started that way. Even though I was only a year old when he went into the liquid gold business, I can imagine him now, reaching across the table for my mother's hands. Dressed in her terry cloth robe, her short hair tousled, she has a cup of Maxwell House in front of her and a cigarette on the go. He wraps both his hands around hers, the gold flecks in his hazel eyes shining.

"Liquid manure," he says, beaming.

"Liquid manure, Dacker?" She shakes one hand free to pluck her cigarette out of the ashtray. The end is tinged with her coral-colored lipstick. "Now you've really gone crazy."

"No. Hear me out. Think of an old lady with flowers on her balcony. Wouldn't she like some nice, rich horse manure to help her garden grow?"

My mother puts the cigarette to her lips, the tip blazing redder as she inhales.

"Of course she would," he continues. "There's no better fertilizer! But who wants a bag of horseshit in the city?" He jumps up excitedly. "That's why I'm going to bottle it. It will be like liquid gold."

"Liquid *gold*?"

"We'll sell thousands!"

"How the hell are you going to make liquid manure, Dacker? Do you see a horse around here?"

"I have a plan."

My father's plan will involve their new neighbor in Milton, a horse racer. It will be thoroughbred poop.

Red Holmes is just coming out of the stables when my father walks in through the gates. On the track in front of them, a sulky driver is flicking the whip lightly above the haunches of one of Red's champion harness racers. The air is sweet with the smell of fresh horse manure.

"How many city people buy your bags of manure, Red?" My father is looking at the steam rising from a heap of horse dung.

"I don't sell manure," Red grunts.

"Well, if you did, how many city people do you think would take a sack?" Red shrugs.

"Of course, no city person wants real horse manure," my father goes on, answering his own question. "So, here's my idea: I bottle the runoff from your pile and sell it. All I need to do is install a vat right there." Red's eyes follow his finger pointing to the base of the fragrant pile of horse plop.

"I don't sell manure," Red repeats. "It's not worth shit." (He's not trying to be funny.)

"But seriously, Red. If we make seventy-five cents for every bottle . . ."

"I got a race coming up in Greenwood. The purse is eighty Gs. What do I want with seventy-five cents?"

"Come on, Red. We'll sell thousands."

While he waits for the rain to fill up his forty-five-gallon drums with Red's manure runoff, my father finds a new use for the rent money that is due: he invests in crates of clear glass bottles with airtight stoppers. He has labels printed that he and my mother paste onto each one: DACK'S LIQUID GOLD.

True to its name, the liquid that starts collecting in the vats is a rich, golden brown. After every rain, my father fills more bottles. Then he loads them by the case into the back of his Chevrolet Brookwood station wagon. The bottles are capped so tightly that you would never get a whiff of what's inside.

The Brookwood, now sitting in their driveway full of their bottled future, is red with whitewall tires. It has been purchased, like everything else, on credit. Dodging bill collectors, my parents set out in the Brookwood to settle their debts by peddling pungent thoroughbred manure.

My father is in high spirits. As he always says, you feel like a winner with a new car—even one that isn't paid for. And his product is just what everyone needs—only, they don't know it yet. My mother sits pensive in the passenger seat. She is wearing her best dress: pale blue and white checks, a Peter Pan collar, and a full skirt cinched tightly around her waist. My father is wearing a wide-shouldered suit jacket and loose cuffed pants. Behind them, the manure bottles clink and jostle. The sun that streams in through the Brookwood's wraparound rear window splashes warm golden light across the inside of the car.

My father decides to start local, with a garden center not far from where we are living.

"You know you shouldn't shit where you eat," my mother warns him.

"They're going to love this." He pulls into the parking lot. "I'd like to see the manager," my father says to the cashier at the till.

She takes in my father's dress suit, my mother's Peter Pan collar, and closes her cash drawer to go get her boss.

As the manager comes from the nursery to greet them, a cloud of warm, wet air redolent of compost follows him out the door.

"How can I help you, sir, ma'am?" He wipes his hands on his overalls.

My parents are overdressed. My mother, who seemed so sure of herself while laying out their clothes, now looks hesitant. She steps into the background to let my father do the talking.

"Now, I want you to think of an old lady growing flowers on her balcony." My father helps himself to a patio chair from the garden furniture display, his pant cuffs riding up to show the herringbone pattern of his socks. "We're going to help that old lady," he says.

The manager leans forward.

In less than five minutes, they are speeding out of the parking lot, their whitewall tires churning up the gravel. My mother has a look of disbelief on her face. In front of her, she holds out a check.

"You see, Helen? I told you it would work." My father gives the steering wheel a victory smack.

They sell out the rest of their cases to the garden centers they visit that day. Loading up the Brookwood again and again, they distribute more stock to stores across Southern Ontario.

A couple of weeks later, they return to the garden center where they made their first sale. The manager has put in a standing order for their fertilizer.

"Would you look at that!" my father says, stopping before the shop window. Proof of his success is right there in front of him: bottles of Dack's Liquid Gold artistically arranged in tiers. He gives a low whistle, then puts his hand on the small of my mother's back. Inside the store, the sun shining through the liquid manure is gilding the floor tiles.

This window display, and all the others, will turn out to be a spectacularly bad idea. Inside the glass bottles, the sun is encouraging the methane to expand. It grows until it hits the stoppers. The airtight stoppers. There is no place for all that gas to go. All at once, on store shelves everywhere, the bottles explode.

Across the province of Ontario, shops are drenched in Dack's Liquid Gold.

In horseshit.

Then what happened, Dad?

Let's just say I didn't have to worry about the rent anymore. Your mother and I had to get the hell out of town.

CHAPTER 10

MOTHER LODE

KIRKLAND LAKE, 1968

ACROSS THE DEWY LAWN, the Toronto boardinghouse was dark. No one had come out to say goodbye, not even the landlady. Maybe she was mad about the rent.

With the new Buick back where it came from, we were once again in the yellow Valiant, with its homey smell and dashboard full of parking tickets.

"Why do we have to leave so early?" Brad groused, still wearing his pajamas so he could sleep in the back.

"We have a long drive to Kirkland Lake." My father turned the key in the ignition. "Now, who's excited to go to Gramma's house?"

"Gramma hates me," I said.

"Don't be silly. Your grandmother doesn't hate you. She's just English." He pressed the Drive button. "And you'll have my sister's family downstairs."

"Aunt Dixie hates me, too."

"Aunt Dixie doesn't hate you. What about Bev? Aren't you excited to see your cousin?"

"That's different," I said. "Bev doesn't hate me."

Eight hours later, we'd rolled through the exhausted silver fields of Cobalt and were coming up on the mother lode: Kirkland Lake. My father was steering with one hand now, so he wouldn't disturb Brad, who'd crawled into the front and fallen asleep again against his shoulder. Driving along the Mile o' Gold, we passed an abandoned wooden headframe. Two hundred feet tall, it towered over a mine shaft so deep that at one time, it was the closest any human had ever come to the center of the earth.

"Almost there," my father said as we passed the gelatinous Slimes, once the town's namesake lake, now choked with mine tailings.

We turned onto Prospect Avenue. Coming up on the IGA store, I felt for a moment like we were going home. I could almost believe that our mother was at the kitchen table, waiting for us. Then my father swung the Valiant left. He parked in front of Duncan Villa, the house he'd grown up in and where we would now be living.

Just then, I caught sight of a stunning mane of hair. It was my cousin Bev. Cascading down the back of her purple baseball jacket, her hair was the color of an Ontario autumn.

The Valiant's horn wasn't working, so my father leaned out the window to imitate one. "Ah-ooh-ga!"

Bev whipped around. "Uncle Dacker!"

My cousin—who, naturally, was made captain of any team she played on—pulled off her baseball mitt and tossed it into her yard. Then she came around to my side of the car.

"Hey, LoriLove," she said, touching my arm. "Welcome back. Are you guys really going to live in Gramma's den?"

I climbed out of the car and gave her a big hug. "Yup, and just upstairs from you!" With my cousin around, I wouldn't need my tranquilizers anymore.

Bev, who was four months younger than me, had my round face, but in most other ways, we were opposites. I wore thick, black-framed glasses while Bev had perfect vision. Her eyes were large-lidded and green while mine were on the small side and hazel. Her nose, before it would be broken by a baseball, was aquiline while mine was broad like a country road. Her forehead was sloping while mine was high and wide. We had the same build, although she had longer legs, and I had a narrower waist. But it was our hair that really set us apart. Mine was dark and fine, and although I had been growing it forever, it reached only midway down my back. Hers was a luscious golden red that fell beyond her waist.

The length of our hair was an old competition between us. As in most things, she would win.

Bev took my arm, and we walked up to her house. "Be careful not to wake my mom," she warned in a whisper. "She's on nights."

"Aunt Dixie's sleeping," I yelled back to my father. Bev shot me a look: I was so excited, I hadn't noticed that I was standing right below her parents' bedroom window.

During the gold rush, Duncan Villa, Bev's home, had been one of the finest houses in town. It was two stories high, with a stately front door opening onto a green lawn bordered by flower beds and an elegant fieldstone fence. The fence's rockwork was echoed in the magnificent three-tiered fountain in the center of the garden. But after the death of my grandfather Charles—or Chuck, as he was known—everything went to seed; even his perennials perished. Now the flower beds were filled with weeds, and the house was sagging. Only the stone fountain retained its former grandeur.

My father had used his war allowance to pay off the mortgage on Duncan Villa. Then he put it in my aunt Dixie's name so their parents would always have a roof over their heads. She moved Chuck and Dorothy to the small upstairs apartment and took over the main floor for her family. Now we would be living with our grandmother in the smallest part of the smallest part of the house: the upstairs den.

It should have been clear to us that we were a poor family living with a poor family. But that was not how my father saw it. Whether because he'd grown up in a house with a name and a three-tiered fountain or because Kirkland Lake was a town where dreams seemed more real than reality, he believed we were the crème de la crème. We just happened to be a little short of cash, that's all.

"Race you!" Bev called as she took off for the door. I ran after her and up the stairs to our grandmother's apartment.

My grandmother was wearing a flowered dress and shoes with a slight, stylish grandma heel. She was short and plump, with a bosom so large it had traveled down toward her waist, leaving the top part of her chest completely flat. Her white, wrinkled Yorkshire skin was set off by a head of improbably black hair.

"Oh, you're here, are you?"

I stood with my arms at my sides, longing for her to hug me.

She opened the fridge instead. "Do you children want some milk?" My grandmother took out one of the bottles that lined the top shelf. Bev's father was a foreman at Archer's Dairy, so milk was the one thing they were never short of in Duncan Villa.

My grandmother's British accent had long ago flattened into a Canadian one. I knew from a photo I'd seen that she had once been a flapper in Leeds. While healing from his shrapnel wounds during World War I, my Canadian grandfather must have spun quite a tale to get her to leave her cosmopolitan English city for this frozen wasteland. As soon as she discovered her mistake, she had wanted to leave.

Chuck, I can't take another day of forty below. Send me back to Leeds.

Chuck, the blackflies are eating the children alive.

Chuck, not moose meat again.

Finally, my grandfather, a gentle baker who preferred poetry to pastries, cracked. *If you hate Canada so much, then go back to England. Just leave me the children.*

My grandmother must have come to some uneasy truce with her life in the North, though she never showed any warmth to my grandfather, who had dragged her there, or to the four children who kept her rooted. There would be no warmth for me, either, I realized as I stood there wishing for her affection. Without a mother to mother me, I was aching for my grandmother to grandmother me.

My aunt Dixie came up the stairs while my grandmother was pouring the milk. She was groggy and annoyed: I had woken her up. Her eyebrows were not yet penciled on, giving her a frightening look. She had her mother's dark hair, though hers was cut short and razored at the back. She also had her mother's big bosom, which she refused to confine in a bra unless she was going to work at the hospital.

My aunt looked at me with pursed lips. "Helen never should have left you kids," she said. "What am I supposed to do with you?"

"But we're staying up here at Gramma's, not with you," I protested.

"You're still in my house."

My father came up the stairs then, carrying a load from the car.

"Hello, son," my grandmother said, then pointed to the den, where he could put our things. I ran ahead to pull aside the curtain.

My father let out a whistle. "I didn't remember it being this small."

Our new room had a sloping ceiling so low that even Brad couldn't stand up under it. There was a single bed on the right, and a slightly larger one on the left, which Brad and my father would share. At the end of the room, one small window looked out over the laneway. The floor and walls were unvarnished plywood.

"Well, Lor, we'd better give this room a paint job. You choose the color."

"Me?"

"Yes, go ahead. This is your home, too. You choose."

"Any color?"

"Any color."

"Okay, turquoise."

"Turquoise? That'll make the room seem even smaller. How about white?"

"You said I could choose the color!"

"Okay," he said, sighing. "Mother," he called over his shoulder, "we're going to paint your room turquoise."

"Are you out of your ever-loving mind?"

With the wisdom of a ten-year-old, I thought turquoise would be cheerful. But the next day, when my father had finished painting, the room seemed twice as small, just as he'd said. From that moment on, every time I ducked my head to enter the den, I felt guilty.

Despite our close quarters in the turquoise den, I hoped my grandmother would warm to me. I yearned for her to put her arms around me, to show me she cared. But the only scraps of affection came through warnings:

You'll catch your death of cold.

You'll ruin your eyes.

You'll get people talking.

The other way my grandmother showed affection was by cooking. If anyone wanted a hot meal in that house, it came either from my grandmother or my father. My uncle rose so early for the dairy that he was back home and snoring in his chair by three in the afternoon, and my aunt always seemed to be on night shift. She knew when someone else was cooking, though. If my father happened to fry steak, the smell would rouse her from the deepest slumber, and she'd be there with a plate, her eyes alight like a kid's at Christmas.

Are you going to finish that?

No one cooked downstairs, but there were always dishes everywhere because the dishwasher was rarely unloaded. The dining room table was unusable because of the piles of fabric and patterns and notions and bric-a-brac that littered its surface. (*Hoarding* wasn't a word we used back then: we just knew that my aunt Dixie liked to shop and that she fished the credit card bills out of the mailbox before her husband discovered what was keeping their two-income family poor.) Between the cluttered dining room and the cluttered kitchen was a ledge that housed my aunt's extensive stash of prescription drugs. They would turn out to be far too accessible to a troubled young girl like me.

The disorder that my aunt could tolerate in her living quarters she couldn't tolerate in her own appearance. Or in mine, as I was to find out. One day, while Bev and I were playing a silent game of Crazy Eights on a spot we'd cleared on the dining room table, Aunt Dixie came out of her bedroom dressed in her nurse's uniform. She walked past us, adjusting the cap on her head so that it covered her cropped black hair.

Suddenly, she stopped and pointed at me. "When was the last time you brushed that hair?"

My hand went to my head.

"If you don't brush that mop, young lady, I'll cut it off." She looked at me as if she thought my hair slatternly. And maybe, compared to her surgically trimmed head, it was. But I could pull my long hair around to hide my broad nose and thick glasses. It was my security blanket.

When her mother had gone out the back door to the laneway, where she parked her car in the summer, Bev gave me a worried look. "My mom cut my hair once when I was a little girl," she said. "My dad almost killed her." She picked up a card from the pile. "You should really brush your hair."

"Okay."

She laid down her card. "Pick up two."

But my aunt's warning passed over me like all things she told us.

Don't touch my tarot cards.

Empty the dishwasher.

The Ouija board is not for you kids.

Not listening to her was the biggest mistake I could have made.

One day toward the end of summer, while my father was away selling hearing aids, I went into the garden to wait for Bev while she tried to find her bathing suit in the mound of dirty laundry. The hot air was filled with the low buzz of insects. Suddenly, I felt a presence behind me. I whirled around. It was Aunt Dixie. Holding a pair of garden shears.

My aunt stepped forward. "I told you I'd cut your hair if you didn't brush it."

"I'll brush my hair, Aunt Dixie, I promise. I'll go brush it now."

She grabbed my hair and pulled my head backward until it hurt. "I warned you."

My heart was pounding. The shears were close to my head, and the blades made a metallic sound as she pulled them apart.

"No, please." I couldn't move, couldn't breathe. She couldn't mean it, not my hair.

Snip went the shears. I put my hand back and felt the bare nape of my neck.

"No. No."

"Move your hand or I'll cut it off, too."

She was an adult. How could I fight her? With a pain so profound I can feel it still, I let her hack away until my beautiful long hair lay on the grass.

I was still sobbing when my grandmother sat me at her kitchen table. Brad peeked around the corner of the doorway at me. No one seemed to have noticed that his hair, longer than mine was now, was also unkempt.

"Stop your sniffling," my grandmother said, wrapping a towel around my shoulders. "Or you'll get a nick from the scissors." A woman visiting her was trimming what was left of my hair into a pixie cut.

I was crushed by the grief of losing my hair. I couldn't imagine anything worse happening. And I'd been powerless to stop it.

I heard footsteps coming up the stairs; then Bev appeared.

"LoriLove?"

I wiped my nose on the back of my hand.

Bev took one look at me and squeezed my shoulder. "Don't worry. It'll grow back." But we both knew it would take an eternity.

When he came home that evening and saw what my aunt had done, my father blazed downstairs to confront her. Our grandmother was in the living room watching television, so Bev and I crept into her bedroom. After opening the flap of her heating grate, we could hear everything the adults were saying.

"Dixie, you had no right to cut my daughter's hair."

"I told her what would happen if she didn't brush it."

"That was a horrible thing to do. She had lovely hair."

"Someone had to tame that girl. She looked like she'd been raised by wolves."

"What gives you the right to cut my daughter's hair?"

"You should thank me. She looks much better now."

"No, she doesn't."

I jumped back from the grate. Bev looked at me with pity. I would never be lovable: I was too ugly.

CHAPTER 11

THE FACTS OF LIFE

KIRKLAND LAKE, 1969

I'M A MOTHER AND a father to my children.

When he said that, which he did all the time, my father wasn't complaining. He was bragging.

In a way, he was right. He was the only mother we had now. My grandmother's child-rearing was limited to telling us not to watch TV in the dark. As for Aunt Dixie, since she'd cut off my hair, we'd taken to avoiding each other. Comparing my aunt and my grandmother with my father, my grandfather, and even my great-grandfather, I could reach only one conclusion: in our family, the mothering was done by the men.

But I needed a real mother. My family was quick to tell me what was wrong with me. *You come on like a storm. You're just like your father. Try to be more feminine.* Even Bev, a tomboy who beat the boys at every sport she played, was better at being a girl than I was. With her long, shimmering hair and easy laugh—neither of which I possessed—she drew people to her, including the boys she'd just out-batted or out-skied or out-skated. I drove them away. I thought if someone just showed me how to be a proper girl, I'd be lovable.

One day at school, I went into the washroom while a couple of girls from my class, rinsing their hands in the circular sink, were discussing the facts of life.

"Which facts of life?" I asked.

The girls immediately started tittering.

"'Which facts of life?'" The taller girl, whose father had been a mine boss, repeated my question mockingly. "The ones your mother tells you, of course."

"Oh, those." I was trying to sound like I knew, but I was puzzled. There had to be many facts of life: how could she be sure that all mothers told their daughters the same ones?

Not long afterward, with Aunt Dixie safely at work, I had gone downstairs to see Bev when our neighbor Paulette burst through the side door. "Quick, I need a pad."

Paulette, who had lived her whole life across the street, was used to running in and out of Bev's house. At fourteen, she was miles older than Bev and me, but for some reason, she liked to hang out with us. Still in her boots and fur parka, she unzipped her blue jeans.

"I hope to fuck your mother has a Kotex," she said to Bev.

Bev ran ahead of her to the bathroom with an urgency I didn't grasp. "Here!" she called.

I followed them in. Bev was holding a cardboard box I'd never noticed before; it was decorated with flowers. I was still confused. "A Kotex?"

"Yeah, I'm bleeding like a stuck pig." Wiggling the jeans off her skinny hips, Paulette sat down on the toilet.

"You're bleeding?" I was shocked she was taking it so calmly. "Do you need a Band-Aid?"

"Wait, nobody told you about periods?"

We both looked at Bev, who shrugged.

"No," I said. "What's a period?"

"It's when you bleed, stupid. Once a month. It goes on for bloody days."

"What do you mean 'bleed'?"

"All girls do it, you know. From there." She wiped herself between her legs and then examined the piece of toilet paper. On it was a bright red smear.

"Lor, you okay?"

I must have gone pale, because Bev searched my face while Paulette attached the pad to a belt around her waist.

"I'm going upstairs." Rare was the time when my grandmother's company was preferable to Bev's, but what I'd just discovered had made me feel sick.

My cousin gave me that familiar look of pity. "Sorry, Lor. I thought you knew."

Girls bleeding out of their vaginas every month: what else did mothers tell their daughters?

That evening, I was writing one of my stories in bed when the phone rang. Next to me, Brad stirred but didn't wake up. I heard my grandmother turn down the television and pad to the kitchen in her slippers.

"Oh, hullo, Helen."

I sat up in bed so fast, my head hit the low ceiling. I hadn't spoken to my mother in almost a year.

"Yes, they're all here," my grandmother said, and I realized that my mother must have known all along where we were. "Let me get Dacker."

With my heart banging in my chest, I crept out of the den just as my father took the phone.

"How are you, Helen?" His voice held no bitterness; he believed he'd walked away from the divorce with the better deal.

I got you kids. That's all I ever wanted.

He caught sight of me. "Hold on a minute." He pressed the receiver to his chest. "Come talk to your mother."

He spoke so loudly, I was afraid she'd hear. I shook my head. *Please don't make me.* My reaction confused me. I'd been looking for a mother in every adult woman I knew, but now that my real mother was on the other end of the line, I didn't want to talk to her.

"Lori's gone to bed," my father lied. I felt a burst of gratitude that he'd done it to protect me.

"You can't avoid your mother forever," he said after hanging up. "She misses you and Brad."

My mother had moved a thousand miles away; that's how much she missed me. She'd followed Art across Ontario to Red Lake, another mining town. My father told us he had easily won full custody because the judge knew that he would never give up his kidlings. But I'd never heard of a judge giving the children to a man, and slowly the real reason dawned on me: our mother hadn't put up a fight. She didn't want us.

The next morning at breakfast, my father announced that our mother was coming back to Kirkland Lake.

Brad looked like he was going to fly off his chair. "Forever?"

"No, son, for the weekend."

Brad seemed excited about our mother's visit, but I felt torn. Why was she coming anyway—and why had it taken her so long?

Before my mother was due to arrive, Bev's older sister, Shelley, returned from art college down in Toronto. I hadn't seen her for a long time, so it took me a moment to recognize the beautiful woman who walked into Bev's house. She had large eyes like Bev and cheekbones that were high and round and, at the moment, so red with the cold that they looked like little apples. Each of her fingers had its own ring: a flower, chunky stones, a gold serpent. Under her coat, Shelley wore a peasant blouse and a billowy skirt over high lace-up boots.

While my grandmother went upstairs and boiled the kettle for tea, I pushed myself back against the wall, out of the way. I was ashamed of my hacked-off hair. I looked like a boy, while my older cousin had grown into a stunning woman. Finally, Shelley saw me there and came over to hug me. She smelled like perfume and oil paint. I burrowed into her. I couldn't remember the last time a woman had put her arms around me.

I followed Shelley upstairs, bringing my chair right next to hers as she read my grandmother's tea leaves.

"Lori!" my grandmother scolded. "Stop being so clingy."

The next morning, I came out of our den to see Shelley in front of the full-length mirror in the hall. She was stroking some blush onto her high, round cheekbones.

"Come here," she called. "Do you want to try some of my makeup?"

"Sure!"

"Let's put a little eye shadow on you." She clicked open the case to reveal a palette of colors. "How about some green to bring out your hazel eyes?"

I took my glasses off so she could brush some on my eyelids.

Just then, my father walked out of the bathroom in his baggy underwear. He gave me an amused look.

"My mom's coming next weekend," I blurted out to my cousin.

"Aunt Helen! I've always loved her. I'm sorry I won't be here to see her."

"You won't?"

"I have to go back to art college tomorrow."

I was crushed. I wanted to be with her. To *be* her. Now she was leaving.

After Shelley boarded the Greyhound bus for Toronto, I went downtown. I knew what I needed to do.

Kirkland Lake's main drag consisted of one long road with a movie theater on either end and plenty of bars in between. The closing of the mines had thrown so many people out of work that the town had become known as the drinking capital of Canada. My destination was the Kresge across from the old Gold Range Hotel, one of the original saloons.

I could have asked my father. Regardless of our situation, he never would have refused me the money; he never refused me anything. But I remembered his amused look when Shelley had made me up. He wouldn't understand what a girl needed.

There must have been a senior special that day, because the lunch counter was full. I surveyed the store from the big front windows all the way to the back, where dishes were clattering. I found the makeup section and selected an eyeshadow kit from a display. I looked around. No one was watching, so I slipped the kit into my pocket.

Stealing was easier than I'd expected. I secreted a tortoiseshell blush compact in my palm, then slid it into my coat. I did the same with the darkest foundation I could find. The bottle clinked against the compact, and I froze. But no one even glanced in my direction. To be safe, I put the mascara into a different pocket. The only thing missing was lipstick, but that seemed a little too mature for an eleven-year-old.

I checked around me, dropped my arms to my sides. My hands hid my bulky pockets. I tried to look casual as I made my way to the exit, but my heart was beating wildly. I pushed on the handle to open the door. The blast of cold air as I escaped outside filled me with a rush of exhilaration.

Back at Duncan Villa with my treasures, I went into my grandmother's bathroom and hooked the door shut. On the toilet seat, which Shelley had decorated with a flower power decal, I laid out my new makeup. Trying to remember how my cousin had done it, I applied the foundation, blush, eye shadow, and mascara. I made sure to put the foundation on nice and thick. Then I went out to see if anyone would notice. My grandmother was the only one there. She immediately creaked up from her television chair with her usual *pffffft* of gas.

"Young lady," she said, peering at me, "did you put that makeup on with a trowel?"

I grinned. I couldn't have been happier. My grandmother had called me a lady.

A week passed. Then, on a crisp winter night, my mother's Greyhound crunched to a stop in the snow outside the terminal. Condensation from the tailpipe enveloped the bus in a cloud. There was a whoosh as she stepped out through the white brume. She was wearing her camel coat with the fur collar, and as she walked through the snow toward us, the hem of it swirled around her ankles.

My mother seemed like someone I'd known well a long time ago but who was a stranger now. I clutched my father tighter.

Brad ran past us, into her arms.

"Bradley!" she said, lifting him up. "You're such a big boy now." Then she looked at me, expectantly. My father gave me a push. My mother tried to embrace me, but my arms were frozen at my sides.

After an awkward moment, my father asked which of the bags the driver had deposited on the sidewalk was hers, then we were all in the Valiant, Brad in the back with our mother, me in the front with our father. Our usual configuration.

"How are you, Helen?" My father looked at her in the rearview mirror.

"Fine, Dacker. You?"

"We're all fine."

My mother was silent.

"Good trip?" my father asked after a few seconds.

"Long."

"How's Art keeping?"

"He's working underground. You know what that's like."

"Yep. Miserable job."

There was silence again.

"Mind if I smoke, Dacker?"

"Go ahead."

My mother rolled down her window and held the cigarette outside. I felt the draft on the back of my neck. I couldn't believe my parents were talking like nothing had happened. I'd only been able to nod in response to my mother's questions. I didn't know how to react. Was I supposed to be happy to see her, as Brad was? I couldn't be. I was angry. I was angry she'd left and angry she hadn't come back until now. Most of all, I was angry that she hadn't said how sorry she was, that she'd made a huge mistake leaving us, that not a day went by when she didn't miss us.

I didn't realize I was asking too much; my father and I were the expressive ones.

"It's late," my father said. "Do you want me to drop you at Verna's now?"

"No. I'll walk over later. I want to be with the kids a bit."

Instead of going up the stairs to my grandmother's apartment, we went into Aunt Dixie's, perhaps because my father didn't want to reveal the tiny den we three shared. No one was home: Bev's family had made themselves scarce. My mother placed her boots next to the fireplace, where two deer heads were mounted, a doe and a buck shot by my uncle. My mother walked in her stocking feet across the carpet, my brother beside her. With Brad suddenly talkative and me silent, it was like our two personalities were reversed.

She sat on the couch, with Brad on one side of her, me on the other. My parents waited for me to say something, but I had no words for what I was feeling, so I lay my head on my mother's lap and pretended to fall asleep.

Her smell seemed unfamiliar to me. Even when we'd lived together as a family, I didn't remember being this physically close to her. Now, as she stroked my head, I took in the mix of cigarettes and Chanel No. 5 that emanated from her pores. I found the sweet, peaty smell slightly off-putting. If my father had any odor, it was indiscernible from my own.

"She's just tired, Helen," my father was saying now. I wondered if I had fooled him or if he was covering up for me again.

"What happened to Lori's hair?" My mother was whispering so as not to wake me.

"Dixie cut it," my father said. "While I was away."

"What gave her the right?"

"She said she couldn't get Lori to brush it."

"Lori always was a bit wild. But your sister shouldn't have done it."

"I told her. But you know Dixie. She says we're in *her* house."

"Didn't you pay your parents' mortgage?"

My father grunted. "That was a long time ago."

"You always *were* a sucker, Dacker."

"How's Red Lake?" he asked, changing the subject.

"Just another depressing mining town."

"I always said you'd be miserable in heaven."

"Have *you* ever been to Red Lake?"

There was another silence. Then my father asked, "You working, Helen?"

"I used to sell Avon." I felt her sigh through her abdomen. "But seeing mothers with their children made me think of Lori and Brad. I cried every time. I had to stop." Her voice held so much sadness, it puzzled me. If she missed us, why hadn't she called? "So, now I work as a night janitor with nothing to remind me of what I did."

"Don't worry about the kids, Helen. They're fine. I'm a mother and father to them now."

"That's what you always wanted." Her voice was bitter.

When I woke the next morning, my mother was at my grandmother's kitchen table playing cards with Brad.

"Do you want to join us, Lor?"

"I have homework to do."

"Snap." My brother smacked his hand on the table. "Mom, you weren't even looking!"

For the whole weekend, Brad left our mother's side only when it was time to go to bed. Soon, he would start spending his school holidays with her— that is, as often as Art would allow. I didn't know what I wanted. Being with her was hard, so I ignored the hurt look on her face as I found excuses not to spend time with her. I still wanted a mother. I just didn't want her.

Then, thankfully, she was leaving again.

The four of us were back in the yellow Valiant, driving my mother to the Greyhound terminal. The snow had melted, and the whine of the Valiant's tires cutting through the slush filled in the space of our silence. Parking directly behind the bus, my father left the motor running while he grabbed my mother's blue suitcase out of the trunk. She swung her feet to the curb, holding up the hem of her coat to protect it as she stepped out. Brad grabbed her hand, and I followed at some distance.

My father slid the blue suitcase into the luggage compartment of the bus, then took off his buckskin mitts to shake my mother's delicately gloved hand.

"Good luck, Helen." He nudged me. "Lori, give your mother a hug."

My mother stood stiffly in front of me, the wet snow already making semi-circles on the toes of her boots. She reached down to give me a squeeze. I gave her a half hug in return, my body angled off to the side. When I stepped back, Brad wrapped his arms around her waist. It sounded like he was crying.

"You be a good boy," she said and wiped her eyes.

Back in the car, where it was still warm, I put my head on my father's shoulder. He kissed my hair, then ruffled Brad's. "I love you kids more than a whole herd of Shetland ponies."

I sighed. "Dad, we've heard that a zillion times." I was glad he'd said it, but I needed more than a father's love. Why, then, couldn't I accept my mother's?

A couple of days later, my father asked about her visit. "Did she have 'the talk' with you? You know, the one mothers have with their daughters?"

"Yeah, we talked."

"So, you know all about sex now, right?"

"Yeah, sure. Everything." I knew nothing, but if my shock discovery of periods was anything to go by, this was not a conversation I wanted to be having with my father.

Yet I convinced him so thoroughly that he offered to take Bev and me to see a restricted movie that had just come out, *M*A*S*H*.

"Lori, don't you ever tell my parents we went to see that movie," Bev whispered as we were getting ready. Then she took the eye shadow out of my hand and put a splash of blue on her eyelids so we'd both look older.

We parked in the loading zone in front of the Strand Theatre. At the ticket window, my father fished a ten-dollar bill out of his wallet and passed it to the white-haired lady in the booth.

"Three tickets, please."

"I'm sorry, sir. This movie is restricted. Eighteen and over."

"Restricted?" My father snorted. "Let me tell you, ma'am, these two girls know more about sex than you and I do."

I felt my cheeks burn.

"Uncle Dacker!" Bev turned red to the roots of her hair.

The ticket seller shrugged, then handed him three tickets.

My father was not as good a mother as he believed himself to be, but thanks to him, and that movie, I learned what the facts of life were about.

CHAPTER 12

THE PONY

KIRKLAND LAKE, 1933

I LOVE YOU KIDS more than a whole herd of Shetland ponies.

I thought that was something every parent said. Like, *I love you to the moon,* or *You're the best thing that ever happened to me.* Over time, I realized my father was the only person who used ponies as a measure of love. The story he told Brad and me about Old Bill helped me understand why.

I'll never forgive that sonofabitch.

Daddy, don't swear.

It's 1933. Gold has brought more than prosperity to Kirkland Lake; it has brought dreamers. Elsewhere, the Great Depression is raging mercilessly. But while unemployment settles like prairie dust over the rest of the continent, Kirkland Lake is booming. In boardinghouses, one bed is rented out to three miners, each working a different shift. Twice a month, men line up for blocks to get their wages. Afterward, the brothels are packed, the bar patrons spill out into the streets, and Saturday night is always all right for fighting.

Old Bill is a prospector. After the Klondike Gold Rush, he landed in

Kirkland Lake. The town is so rich in minerals that a road-building crew, having mistaken ore for waste rock, literally paved the streets with gold.

Bill may have a nose for gold, but he's no Sir Harry Oakes. I see Bill now, grizzled, maybe a bit smelly from all that time staking claims in the bush. Coming into Kirkland Lake for supplies, he stops to warm himself by the potbellied stove at my grandparents' bakery.

Chuck, my grandfather, learned baking from his parents, S.E. and Belle, but in truth, he prefers to pen poetry. In his poems, he writes about hunting and fishing, about gold and about the Queen—sometimes all in the same verse.

De 24 of May is de Queen's birtday
De mine she no work so I take offa day
Maybe I go to de lake for a fish
If my Marie don't make me help wid de dish

"Close the door, Bill," I can hear my grandmother Dorothy say. With the bobbed hair and headband of a flapper, she looks like she belongs in Europe, not in this rough-and-tumble frontier town. As Bill comes in wearing his battered old hat, a trail of yellowed poplar leaves swirls around his hobnail boots.

Dorothy is filling the cooling racks with the loaves her husband, Chuck, has just baked. She's so small that she has crowded all the bread onto the lower shelves, and now Chuck scoops up a few loaves, placing them on a higher rack, where the air can circulate. Bill sniffs the fresh-baked bread appreciatively and then, rubbing his hands, goes over to the stove in the center of the room.

The door opens again, and a band of schoolchildren comes in clutching their coins. Smiling, Chuck lifts a heavy glass jar off the counter and holds it down low so they can pick their sweets. Like his father, Chuck will always be remembered for his kindness to children—and his penny candy.

Just then, my own father, all of nine years old, reaches into the jar.

"Harry!" Dorothy scolds him. My father, who has not yet reinvented himself as Dacker, runs to where Bill is warming his palms over the stove.

"Hello, young man," the prospector greets him. "A little birdie says your birthday is coming up. What do you want Old Bill to give you?"

My father doesn't hesitate. "A pony! That's what I want more than anything."

"A pony, eh?" The prospector takes the loaf of bread my grandmother is holding out to him as a hint that others want to warm themselves by the stove, too. "Just leaving, Dorothy," he says.

"Close the door after you, Bill." She will never like unkempt men, or drafts.

Bill winks at Harry, dropping his voice low. "You just wait. I'm going to get you that pony!"

The next time Bill shuffles into the bakery, looking a little worse for wear, my father is alone at the counter. He wears a white shirt with light blue stripes that his mother ironed for him that morning. She threatened to wallop him if he got it dirty, and he has. His shirt, pants, even his hair, all are dusted with flour.

"Have you picked out my pony yet, Bill?" He can already imagine himself brushing its shaggy coat.

"Oh sure." The prospector sits down on Dorothy's chair. "But Harry, where are you going to keep your pony?"

"I'll keep my pony in the laneway and feed him grass every day."

"But you know, ponies like to eat oats, too. How're you going to pay for them oats?"

"I make my own money." He juts out his chest. "After school, I sell sawdust to the butchers."

Bill whistles. "How do you carry them heavy sacks of sawdust, little man?"

"I use my brother's wagon."

Just as Bill is about to go, my father tugs on his sleeve. "Is my pony a boy pony or a girl pony?"

"A boy pony, of course. You'll have a boy pony for your birthday."

"Stop filling that child's head," says my grandmother, who is just coming in from the back. "He's enough of a dreamer as it is."

The night before his birthday, my father is so excited, he can barely sleep. In the morning, he is the first one up. He runs to the window to look outside for his pony. He's not out front. My father figures he must be in the laneway, so he runs through to the back door just as his mother is getting up.

"When is Bill coming?" he asks her.

She gives him a curious look. "Old Bill? Why would Old Bill be coming to our house?"

"Because he's bringing my pony!" He's frustrated that she has forgotten. "I'm going to go look outside," he tells her. But when he comes back in, he is crushed. There are no hoofprints in the snow, nor any sign of a pony.

"Chuck," Dorothy calls. "Come talk to your son." Then she says to my father, "Don't tell me you believed that old drunk."

My father never got over that broken promise. Now, when I think back to him saying he loved us more than a whole herd of Shetland ponies, I understand just how much love that was.

CHAPTER 13

HORSES IN THE HOUSE

KIRKLAND LAKE, 1969

I HEARD A WOMAN'S laugh coming from my grandmother's kitchen and hurried out to see who it was.

"Sugar?" My grandmother was pouring a cup of tea for Sue, who had been delivering her newspapers for years.

"Lovely," said Sue, in a warm, low voice. She had dark, gently curling hair, and I guessed she was in her late twenties, a few years older than my cousin Shelley. Sue worked as a papergirl for *The Northern Daily News*. For over half a century, my family had been subscribers, even after the newspaper stopped publishing my grandfather's poems and broke his heart.

My grandmother handed Sue her cup of tea. "Just swirl the leaves as you drink, dear. Then I'll read them for you." My grandmother liked adults more than children; she never called us "dear."

With fingertips darkened by newsprint, Sue pulled off the newspaper bag that had been slung crosswise over her chest and swept a curl off her forehead with her wrist. A fine gold chain dangled between the pearly buttons of her blue jean shirt.

"Well, don't just stand there gawking at us," my grandmother scolded me. "Sit down."

She began to examine the bottom of Sue's teacup, turning it clockwise as Shelley had taught her. "Well, this is something."

"What's that?" asked Sue.

"See where the leaves are all gathered here? That's the near future." My grandmother put the china cup down. "It looks like you're in for some big life changes."

We heard the toilet flush, and my father lumbered into the kitchen. He'd put on my grandmother's flowered robe, and now he was scanning our faces for a reaction. His pretend-innocent expression made him look younger than forty-five.

"Hello, Dacker," Sue said, ignoring the robe.

He looked deflated.

"Sue's brought my paper," my grandmother said. She peered at Sue as if trying to figure out what my father was looking at. "You're a little pink, dear," she said.

"I guess I am." Sue gave another low laugh. "I was out in the sun yesterday, horseback riding."

"Horseback riding, eh?" My father sat down at the kitchen table. "When I was a kid, I was promised a Shetland pony, but I never got it."

Brad ambled into the room rubbing the sleep out of his eyes with his fists just as I was thinking, *Not this story again.*

"Good morning, son," my father said. "What say I get you a little pony?"

"A pony?"

We all looked at my father, thinking this was another joke, like wearing my grandmother's robe.

"Yes, a pony," he said in earnest. "Why not?"

Brad surveyed my grandmother's tiny apartment, most of which he could see from where he was standing. "But where would the pony live?"

Everyone laughed, except my father.

"We'll see."

Later, after Sue had gone to deliver the rest of her papers, I asked, "Daddy, why did you say you'd get Brad a pony? What about me? And Bev?"

"You and Bev are too big for ponies."

"That's not fair!"

"You'd need horses."

"For the love of God, what would you do with horses?" my grandmother asked, returning from the roof, where she'd been hanging the washing out on the line. The ice-cream bucket for the clothespins was still looped around her arm.

"I'll figure it out, Mother."

"Where in hell's name would you keep them? In the laneway?"

My father gave her a sharp look. Then he opened the newspaper Sue had delivered and, taking out his stub of a pencil, circled one of the livestock ads.

The next day, Bev, Brad, and I were racing one another down the stairs when the screen door opened from the other side. It was Sue again, with her newspapers.

"Where are you kids off to in such a hurry?" She removed her oversize sunglasses to see us better in the dark stairwell. It looked like she had a black eye. She quickly put her glasses back on.

"We're going to buy some horses!" Brad danced from one foot to the other with excitement.

"I love horses!" she exclaimed. "You're so lucky. But where'll you keep them?"

"We don't know," I admitted.

"Your father will figure something out, I'm sure."

I walked out to the car beside Sue, breathing in her light perfume.

"How's it, Dacker? I hear you're getting some horses." Her laugh was warm, and she didn't blink at my father's decision.

"We're going to look at a couple now," he said. "You're welcome to come along."

She patted her bag. "I still have papers to deliver."

"Okay, then, let's go, kids." He opened the door, and we all piled in.

As we drove out of town, my father turned on the wipers to get rid of the bugs splattered on our windshield, but that only made things worse. I was left peering through a greenish streak as we passed swamps, beaver ponds, rivers, and lakes. Finally, we turned into a long driveway. My father parked next to a paddock.

"I know you're excited, but you kids stay in the car," he said. "The last thing I want is you driving up the price."

"Sure, Uncle Dacker. We'll wait." Bev gave me a meaningful look; she wasn't as easy to fool as my father was, and she knew I had a hard time following orders.

Sure enough, the minute he'd gone, my hand was on the door.

"Lori," Brad warned.

"I just want to see."

As I walked toward the paddock, where a few horses were grazing, the smallest one nickered and came toward me. He was bigger than a Shetland pony but smaller than a horse. His coat was salt and pepper, like my father's hair. The pony looked at me with intelligent eyes, like inside him the lights were switched on.

Just then, a woman with a weathered face came up beside me.

"Shadow's one smart little pony," she said, putting her foot on the lowest rail of the fence. "He never met a gate he couldn't open."

Suddenly, my father's voice traveled down the driveway. "Seventy-five smackers!"

I went up to where he was speaking with an old, bowlegged farmer dressed in a pair of crusty jeans. The farmer was stroking the back of a fine-boned horse. She was a deep blood red with a black mane and tail.

The old man ran his hand down her right foreleg to the tuft of hair at the bottom. "C'mon, lift yer foot," he said and gave her fetlock a tug.

My father and the old man bent over to examine her hoof.

"Pretty clean, eh?" the farmer said.

My father nodded as if he knew what he was looking at. "What happened here?" He ran his hand from her withers to her rump, where she had a black,

T-shaped scar. I knew my father thought this was like a scratch on a car: something he could use to drive the price down.

"Bear got her when she was a filly," said the farmer. "She's fine now. Long as she don't smell bear."

As I came closer, the horse flicked her ears forward and extended her muzzle to me. I stretched out my hand, revealing a clump of grass. She picked it up delicately with her lips. "Oh Daddy, she's beautiful." I ignored the dirty look he was giving me. "Can we get her, please? Please, Daddy?"

My father ended up buying Doll for the full asking price because I'd ruined his negotiation. Agreeing to pay in monthly installments, he also bought the intelligent-eyed Welsh pony Shadow, who'd never met a gate he couldn't open.

"What happened?" Bev asked as we got into the car, where she and Brad had been waiting, per my father's instructions.

"I got Lori a horse," my father said, then turned to Brad. "Son, you see that pony over there?" He pointed through the window at Shadow. "He's going to be yours."

Brad looked at our father in astonishment. "Mine?"

"Yes, there's one for each of you."

"That's great, Brad, LoriLove," Bev said. I was attuned to every nuance in her voice, and I could hear her hiding her disappointment.

"Don't worry, Bev. We can share."

"Hey, did you think we were done?" my father chided.

Bev perked up. "We're not?"

At our next stop, my father bought a long-legged Appaloosa–Tennessee Walking Horse for Bev and a large buckskin for himself. We had four horses and no stable, but that didn't faze my father one little bit.

The very next day, he took us to the outskirts of Kirkland Lake—where you moved if you were so stone broke you couldn't afford to live in town— and pulled up in front of the shabbiest, most-falling-down house we'd ever seen. The windows were broken, and where the painted wooden planks had been pulled off, the siding had gaps like rotted teeth.

Brad gasped as we peered inside. The walls were covered in graffiti. The floor was strewn with cigarette butts and empty bottles of rotgut. "Daddy, are we going to live here?"

"Hell, no, son. This house is for the horses."

Over the next few days, my father used the money he'd gotten from selling hearing aids to buy wood to build stalls inside the house. He sprinkled sawdust on the linoleum so the horses wouldn't slip on their pee and covered that with a layer of straw to catch their manure. He hauled the bathtub out to the backyard for them to drink from. Afterward, he invited Sue to see what he'd done and seemed excessively pleased by her praise.

When the horses were delivered, the house soon filled with their warm, loamy smell: manure mixed with sweat. Bev was a good sport about grooming the horses and mucking out their stalls, but I was a princess, preferring to leave my share of the dirty work to the horse-crazy young girls who started coming from town and who would do any amount of work just to be there. The boys never came, just that gaggle of town girls, all of us drunk on the power of controlling those muscled beasts with our skinny little arms and legs.

Over the summer, the horses taught us to approach their front ends with caution—and to avoid their back ends altogether. They taught us to watch out for the baring of their teeth or the flattening of their ears, the signal that they were about to let fly with a kick. We learned how to hold their halters without getting close enough for a nip, how to slip our little thumbs into the gap at the back of their mouths to nudge the bit in, how to take back control if they got the bit in their teeth and tried to run away with us on their backs.

We also learned that all horses were different, with personalities as distinct as people's. Shadow, true to his reputation, was a master gate-opener, forcing us more than once to intercept him and the other escapees on their way into town. Bucky, the buckskin who carried my father effortlessly on his broad back, was part Belgian workhorse, with a steady, dogged personality to match. Apple, Bev's lanky gray Appaloosa, carried himself like a Tennessee gentleman. My horse, Doll, had an innate ability to sense how I was feeling.

Every day when I came to the "stable," I would bring Doll a carrot. She would see me coming up the road and nicker. I knew it was because of the carrot, but it still made my heart swell when she did that. Then one day, after a fight with my grandmother (me: *You're not my mother*; Gramma: *Thank heaven for that!*) I stomped out of the house without grabbing a carrot from the fridge. As usual, when Doll saw me coming down the road on my bike, she trotted right over. Putting her head over the fence, she reached toward me.

"I'm sorry, I don't have anything for you," I said as she brushed her whiskery lips across my empty palm. I'd disappointed Doll, just as I had everyone else.

Arguments like the one with my grandmother always made me feel worse, yet I couldn't stop myself from provoking them. I was too much—noisy, rebellious, headstrong, unmanageable. Too much but also not enough. *Why can't you be more like Bev?* But what if I had gone too far this time, and my grandmother kicked us out? Now that the horses had their own home, I wished we had one, too.

Suddenly, I felt a pressure against my chest. Doll was rubbing her head on me in a way that comforted me. My flaws didn't matter to her; her affection was unconditional. For Doll, I was enough.

Maybe horses weren't like people after all.

About that time, Sue became more than our papergirl. She showed up almost every day after her route to help with grooming and mucking out the stalls, and she stayed to ride whichever horse was free.

One day, I noticed my father staring at her. I followed his gaze to where she had four little bruises on the soft part of her arm, like fingerprints. When Sue caught us looking, she tried to pull her sleeve down over the bruises.

"Have you got your makeup on you?" she asked me, and I nodded.

"Let's go inside."

I would have followed her anywhere she asked. She seemed to accept me as readily as Doll did.

Sue pulled me into the bathroom, where a shard of mirror was still attached to the wall. "You first. I'll show you a trick with your foundation. We don't want it too thick." She pointed to the demarcation line along my jaw, between my white skin and the dark makeup. "See that? You shouldn't be able to tell the difference with your natural color. You need to blend it in."

I handed her my foundation and closed my eyes. Smoothing the line of makeup over my cheeks and along my jaw, she stroked my face with a mother's gentle touch. After helping me, she dabbed foundation on her bruises to cover them up.

Outside, my father was leading his horse to the bathtub for a drink. With Bucky's muzzle still dripping, my father slid the bit into his mouth.

Sue, who'd been watching beside me, gave me a squeeze. "Can I take Doll and go out with your dad?"

"Sure."

Sue went over to my father, looked up at him with her big brown eyes, and said something I couldn't hear. When she came back, I handed her the reins. I watched my father swaying comfortably on Bucky's back as they set off, followed by Sue on my horse, who was high-stepping delicately. Just as they were about to enter the forest trail together, Sue turned back.

"We won't be long," she called to me with a warmth that made me feel cherished. She sounded so loving, I thought that someone who needed a mother would be lucky to have her.

Someone like me.

Riding with my brother, Kirkland Lake, 1969

CHAPTER 14

BEDTIME STORIES

KIRKLAND LAKE, 1969

"YOU'LL NEVER LEAVE US, will you, Sue?"

I was sitting up in bed, my library book *The Black Stallion* splayed on the floor. Sue had just tucked in my brother, pink and fresh from his bath. Our single beds were set in an alcove on one side of our new living room. On the other side there was a bedroom, and that was where my father and Sue slept.

We had moved out of my grandmother's den months before so that Sue could come live with us.

My father had rented us a basement apartment just up the street from Duncan Villa, past a chip stand. Our entrance was at the rear, reached by a wooden walkway that wound along the side of the small white house and then down a flight of stairs to the backyard. We came in through the kitchen—the kitchen where Sue cooked and hummed and told us we shouldn't even think of tracking our dirty riding boots inside.

I was so happy. I had the family I'd always dreamed of. From the moment Sue moved in, she was like our mother—only better. She was warmer, hugged us more, and wasn't disappointed by my father. She laughed a lot, loved to hold us and stroke our heads, and was patient about spilled milk and unmade beds. She was perfect.

She would wrap her arms around me when I came in from school and buy me fries from the chip stand, and she never said, like my father sometimes did, "Just for once would you give me a goddamned break?"

Sometimes my father said things to Sue I didn't understand—*Sue, you're telling stories again. Sue, you wouldn't know the truth if it bit you.* Still, I knew she was perfect for him, too. I could tell by his whistling.

My father stopped whistling for a whole year after our mother left. But ever since we moved to this basement apartment with Sue, he whistled all the time.

"We're ready for our story," Brad called out to Sue from under his covers; she had gone back to the living room and was now sitting with her legs across my father's lap.

"You can't have a story yet, silly," I told him. "Daddy didn't give us our back scratches."

Sue gave a low chuckle. "Dack, you're up."

My father bustled into our alcove and sat down on the edge of Brad's bed.

"I'll keep your spot warm," Sue called after him.

Brad roused himself and lay on his stomach, pulling up his pajama top. My father scratched Brad's back, getting all the good spots. Then it was my turn.

"Harder," I instructed him. "No, not that hard."

"There you go, that's enough," he said, finishing off my back scratch with a little rub.

"Daddy!" I shrieked. "You ruined the back scratch with your rub. Now you have to start over."

He went through the process again; then it was Sue's turn. Coming into our alcove, she sat so lightly on the bed beside me that she barely made a dent in my mattress. I curled as much of myself as I could into her lap. As she stroked my hair, I shut my eyes to enjoy the feeling of being loved by a woman, which was softer than being loved by my father.

"Once upon a time, there was a magical pony named Brad," Sue began.

The stories were for my brother, but I always put down whatever I was reading—a book about horses or a Nancy Drew adventure—to listen to her.

"*Brad!*" scoffed my six-year-old brother. "That's a silly name for a pony." His eyes fluttered closed again, long lashes brushing his freckled cheeks.

Sue finished her bedtime story, then tucked us both under the covers. She was tiptoeing out of our room when, once again, that terrifying thought came into my mind.

"You'll never leave us, will you, Sue?"

She came back to kiss my forehead. "Of course I'll never leave you."

I'd driven everyone else away—my mother, my aunt, my grandmother. Even my father found me too much sometimes. But for Sue, I was just right. Yet the happier we were, the more I became afraid of losing her. Like the back scratch and the bedtime stories, asking for reassurance became part of our nightly ritual. *You'll never leave us, will you, Sue?*

One morning, my father announced that he was off to sell some hearing aids in Timmins and wouldn't be back until the evening. At lunchtime, while Brad was at school eating with the younger kids, I came home looking forward to having Sue all to myself. When she wasn't waiting in the kitchen, I called out, "Sue, I'm home!"

In my ears, the emptiness of our apartment was as loud as thunder. It was a sound I already knew.

With a hollow feeling in my chest, I went into the bedroom. She wasn't there. The closet doors were thrown open. The hangers were all tangled, as if Sue had yanked her clothes off them. I went into the bathroom. The laundry basket had been turned upside down, and the medicine cabinet was emptied out. All that was left were two bottles of NyQuil.

Shaking, I ran to get the phone book. I flipped to the section for Kirkland Lake and found Sue's mother's name. I dialed the number. Sue answered.

"When are you coming home?" I demanded.

"I'm not coming back, Lori." Gone was the warmth. Her voice was like a splinter of glass.

"You said you'd never leave us."

"I have to go now."

Long after she hung up, I cradled the receiver. The hurt of being abandoned by two mothers in a row was too big for my little heart.

The receiver in my hand started making a beeping sound, so I put it back on the hook.

I went into the bathroom and leaned against the cold sink. My father's steel razor was on the edge, dribbling his stubble down the basin. I picked it up. The blade was loose. Usually that made me uneasy. This time, I deliberately turned the ring at the bottom of the handle. The flaps snapped open. Inside was a new Wilkinson Sword razor blade.

Looking at the sharp edge, I saw myself crumpled on the bathroom floor, blood pouring from my veins. Sue would be kneeling by my side, crying over the terrible mistake she'd made.

I picked up the blade and drew it across the blue veins of my wrist, etching a faint red line on my skin. I tried to go deeper, but I was afraid of the pain. I'd have to find another way to get Sue to come home. Tugging open the bathroom cabinet, I grabbed the two medicine bottles. I gagged on my first swallow of the NyQuil. I let the nausea subside, then took another swig. Retching with every gulp, I managed to force both bottles down. I would have to move quickly now.

I hurried down the street to my aunt Dixie's place because I knew Bev would already be back at school. As I tiptoed past the fireplace, the glassy eyes of the deer heads followed me. I hurried across the brown carpet, so thin the floorboards creaked under my feet. In the kitchen, I poured myself a glass of water. On the ledge next to the kitchen was my aunt Dixie's drug stash. Unscrewing the tops of her prescription medicines, I swallowed pills from each one. I chewed through the whole bottle of baby aspirins like they were candy.

To get back home, I had to pass the chip stand. The greasy smell of fat mixing with the treacly sweetness of the NyQuil made me want to throw up. I rounded the corner of our house, then quickened my pace, thinking that Sue might have come back. I opened the door and listened for the sound of her humming.

The kitchen was empty, the living room dim. Aching, I dialed the phone.

This time Sue's mother answered. She put her hand over the mouthpiece. "It's Dacker's daughter again." In the background, I heard a little boy singing.

Sue has another family, you know, my aunt Dixie had once said. I thought she was just being mean.

Sue took the phone, her voice guarded. "What?"

"I don't feel good. I swallowed a lot of pills from Aunt Dixie's."

"You did what?"

Her coldness made my desperation worse. "Please come get me. I don't want to die."

"Stay there," she ordered.

I wiped my eyes and started to plan how she should find me. I positioned myself on one of our wingback chairs with my head thrown back and my legs flung over the arm. It was the perfect way for her to discover me. I closed my eyes and waited to float into darkness. It never occurred to me that I could really die. I thought the pills and the NyQuil would only put me to sleep so that Sue would rescue me.

A minute went by, two minutes. I was still awake. I changed position again and waited to pass out.

Suddenly, the door scraped open, and Sue was standing there, the light streaming through the kitchen making it hard for me to see her face. Rather than bend down to sweep me into her arms, as I'd imagined, she grabbed my hand and hauled me to my feet.

"You're coming with me," she said. "I can't leave you alone."

If not for the nausea and a sort of fogginess in my head, I would have been happy when she led me to her car. Everything was going to be okay. I closed my eyes as she put the car in gear and drove away. Soon, we were stopping. It was a house I didn't know surrounded by a chain-link fence.

"Where are we?"

"My aunt will take care of you."

"I don't know your aunt. I want to be with you."

"Look, you have to stay here until your father gets back from Timmins."

"What about Brad?" I asked. "I have to wait at home for him."

"I'll get your brother after school."

Her voice was as hard as it had been on the phone. She unhooked the metal gate and took me inside the house.

I was feeling unsteady and put my hand on the wall. A woman got up from the kitchen table, holding a cigarette. To the right was a small living room with a slipcovered couch. I felt dizzy.

"Can I lie down?"

"Sure, go on. Turn on the TV."

As I dropped down onto the couch, I was only dimly aware of Sue talking to her aunt. Suddenly, I woke up to the feeling of my feet being swept to the floor.

"Shoes off the furniture." Sue's aunt glowered at me.

"Where's Sue?" I managed to ask.

"Gone to get your brother."

I sat up, but my head was spinning. I must have made a retching noise, because all of a sudden, Sue's aunt was dragging me down the hall to the bathroom. On the back of the toilet was a doll with a hoop skirt crocheted in white and orange. Sue's aunt reached underneath the skirt and handed me some toilet paper just as I felt the vomit building. The medicine was bitter coming back up; it burned my throat.

"I took some pills," I said, wiping my mouth with the toilet paper.

"You've probably thrown everything up."

I went back to the couch and blacked out. The next thing I knew, Brad was standing beside me with a worried look.

"Tell that lady you want to call Gramma," I whispered. "Ask if we can go there."

Feeling vomit rise into my throat, I ran to the bathroom again. After flushing the toilet, I rested my cheek on the cool porcelain.

"Lor, are you okay?" Brad was standing there watching me.

"What did Gramma say?"

"She says we can't go there."

"We can't go to Gramma's? Why not?"

"She says you're too much to handle."

"Help me up," I said to Brad. "We have to get out of here."

Sue's aunt stepped into the doorway, her arms crossed. "You ain't going nowhere. You just wait here till your father gets back."

I wanted to fight her. I wanted to run. I wanted to yell, *You can't keep us here!* But I was eleven and afraid. Maybe we could sneak away. "Can Brad and I play in the backyard?"

"Just stay where I can see you."

Sue's aunt watched us through the kitchen window, smoking. Feeling wobbly on my feet, I slowly traced the perimeter of the fence. One corner was sagging. When Sue's aunt disappeared from the window, I tugged on Brad's hand.

"Let's go." The fence was low enough for us to get over. "You first," I said. "Quick!"

Brad scrambled over the fence. Landing on the other side, he put his hand out for me. I wedged my foot into one of the links. The fence started to cave in. I grabbed the post to keep from falling.

Brad called out just as I felt a hand on my shoulder. Sue's aunt yanked me back into the yard. On the other side of the fence, Brad watched, helpless.

"You get back in here, too."

Obedient, he climbed back into the yard.

Suddenly my legs were buckling. "I'm sleepy."

"Then go lie down." Sue's aunt frog-marched me inside the house. Brad followed.

Back in our prison, I curled into a ball on the couch. At some point, I became aware that the TV was on and that Brad was sitting on the floor with his back against the cushions. Then my eyes closed again. I began to slip beneath the surface of a calm, black lake. I didn't want to die; I just wanted to keep floating down and down until Sue was back home and we were a family again.

The next thing I knew, I was being hoisted into the air. My father had heaved me up in his strong arms and was carrying me to the doorway. He was yelling something, but it was like I was underwater. I couldn't hear his words, but I felt the vibrations of his voice through his chest. Sue's aunt said something; then there were more vibrations. They all seemed far away. I felt someone clutch my fingers, and I opened my eyes. Brad was holding my hand as my father carried me to the car. It was night.

The next time I woke up, I was in the hospital. I tried to ask my father if Sue was coming back, but I didn't know if I said the words out loud or just thought them. I'd gone deaf.

But I could still hear Sue's voice. It was the same every time I asked the question.

Of course I'll never leave you.

CHAPTER 15

FREAKS

KIRKLAND LAKE, 1970

AFTER SUE, THERE WOULD be no more girlfriends, no more mothers.

My stomach was pumped; my hearing came back. We moved out of that basement apartment, and then we moved again. In the two years since my mother had left, we'd been unable to settle in any one place, like our old dog Daisy, who turned around and around to find the right position. But one day, my father discovered that having spent five years overseas, he was eligible for a war veteran's loan. He bought us a farm seven bush miles out of Kirkland Lake. It would be the only home we'd ever own.

Our new farmhouse, at the end of a looping country road, was small and square, with red bricks made of tarpaper. Between the living room and the bathroom was a bedroom just right for a princess bed. Upstairs there was an attic with space under the peaked ceiling for two mattresses on the floor for my father and brother. There was also a barn for our horses and, across the corral, an old prospector's cabin for chickens and goats. Looming over the back of our property was a rocky ridge covered with boreal scrub pines. Hunkered down close to the earth, not even their branches reached for the sky: the short growing season had stunted the trees—like everything else in the North.

We had a home at last, but I was still unsettled. Living with two males made me realize I had to work out femininity on my own. It's not that I felt like a boy. But I didn't feel like a girl, either. That was how I ended up on the main floor of Green's Department Store, studying the rack of fifteen-cent comic books. I was looking for a character I could try on like new clothes.

What kind of girl could I be? I swiveled the rack to the *Archie* comics. I would have liked to model myself after Betty, except no one thought I was sweet. As for Veronica—my aunt said I was spoiled, but I wasn't rich. I spun the rack again. Maybe I was the bad girl from *True Confessions*? I *was* turning into an Olympian shoplifter. Yet I also studied and did well in school. Where was the role model for a good bad girl?

I gave the rack one last spin and landed on the love comics: *Young Love, First Love, Girls' Love.* To judge by their covers, being a girl involved shedding a lot of tears over boys.

Then I saw a glossy cover with a different kind of girl. She had a tear, too, but it was a small one. A guitar was slung across her back, and she had her thumb out. She seemed strong and independent as she hitchhiked away from anyone who could hurt her.

I was too young to hitchhike, and I couldn't play the guitar, but I wanted to be *that* girl.

I took a casual look around. A mother was pulling a boy away from a toy display; a couple of clerks were chatting by the stationery; a man in the white shirt and black pants of a manager was walking in the opposite direction. With my heart banging in my chest, I shoved the comic book up my shirt.

The hitchhiker offered me one kind of role model. My father inadvertently offered me a different one: delinquent.

Not long after I shoplifted the comic book, the three of us were driving back to the farm in our black Volkswagen Beetle, the replacement for our old Valiant. That day, I'd gotten into trouble at school for talking back to a teacher.

"You're a chip off the old block." My father was beaming with pride.

"When I was your age, I was known as the bad boy of Kirkland Lake." He was boasting.

"Dad, not that story again."

"*I* want to hear," said Brad from the back, as he tried to get a baby goat settled on his lap.

Yes, a baby goat.

"The cops brought me home so many times, my poor parents didn't know what to do with me." My father let go of the wheel, steering with his knee so he could use his fingers to count his crimes. "Tipping over outhouses, stealing pies off windowsills, skiing down the street by latching onto buses, peeking at the Finnish girls in the steam baths, stealing cars—"

My brother looked aghast. It was hard to reconcile the hooligan our dad was describing with the father we knew. He was so honest that if he found a dollar on the ground, he'd go looking for the owner.

"—sneaking into movies, being a lookout for the Dutch Schultz gang, mobsters, you know. Oh, and I cut the buttons off a movie usher's long underwear. That's what I got caught for."

Struggling with the goat, Brad asked, "Daddy, did you go to jail?"

"Not adult jail. They sent me to the Bowmanville Reformatory for Boys. It wasn't so bad. At least I finished grade eight. I had to—if I didn't study, the guards would beat me."

I was quiet. His crime spree was hitting too close to home.

Suddenly, my father sniffed the air and swiveled his head toward the back seat. "What's that smell?"

"The goat?" I suggested.

"It's hot here behind my seat," said Brad, pointing to where the VW's engine was located. "I think the motor's on fire."

"Christ." My father pulled to the side of the road, jumped out of the car, then hauled out my brother, who was still holding the goat. I climbed out the other side.

"Well, that's it," my father said. "Come on kids. We're going to have to hitchhike." Behind him, the Beetle was smoldering. "Brad, give me the goat."

I was stunned. "You act like this is nothing. Our car is on fire!"

"Stop being so dramatic." He adjusted the goat on his hip, making it bleat. "It's only smoking."

"You're always getting us in trouble," I shrieked. "I'm never going to be like you."

Of course, I was afraid it might already be too late, that I was becoming the bad *girl* of Kirkland Lake. Despite having promised myself I'd give up shoplifting, I went back to Green's. It was the first Saturday with no ice on the lakes, so the summer fishing season was beginning, and the store was nearly empty. I secreted the newest love comic up my sleeve, excited to find out where my guitar-playing hitchhiker would be going to next. Then I spotted a magazine cover. I didn't usually pay attention to adult magazines, but this one jumped out at me. Its cover featured the faces of joyous, long-haired young people.

We didn't have hippies in Kirkland Lake; trends took much longer to make their way north. Instead of shaggy-haired boys, we had greasers like my older cousin Don, with his black leather jacket and slick pompadour. But here, on the cover, were real hippies—hippies for Jesus.

They called themselves Jesus Freaks, and I was instantly drawn to them. From what I knew, the whole point of Christianity was to love everyone, even if, like me, they were unlovable. As freaks themselves, these people would know what it felt like to be different.

In that moment, I decided to join the Jesus Freaks, despite having never been religious. The only problem was that I'd have to get to Dallas, where the rally for Jesus was. I tucked the magazine under my arm and glanced around, trying to act nonchalant. When no one was looking, I released the comic book I'd stashed up my sleeve, and replaced it on the rack. Then I reached into my purse for two quarters and took the magazine to the till.

I forgot about the Jesus Freaks as soon as Brad and I walked into the house.

Every surface in our living room had been taken over by Styrofoam heads. They were arranged along the back of the couch and on the television set, in our two wingback chairs and on both end tables. Each head sported a woman's wig of a different color and a different hairstyle.

"Wha-a-t?" My brother dropped his schoolbooks onto the floor.

My father came out of the bathroom wiping his hands on his pants. "Can you believe this? I wrote a company in China for some samples, and look what they sent me. For free!"

"What are you going to do with all these wigs?" I asked.

"Sell 'em."

"Oh, goody. We need the money."

On top of trying to figure out what kind of girl I was, I was still trying to understand what kind of poor we were. We seemed different from the other poor families. My father didn't think of us as poor at all, only temporarily strapped for cash. In his mind, that didn't stop us from being one of the best families in town. It was only a matter of catching our big break. A decade would pass before it would dawn on me that we weren't an upper-class family who only happened to be broke.

My father threw a wig at me. "Here. Try it on."

I wouldn't give him the satisfaction. The week before, he'd embarrassed me by saying, *Hey, are you getting a shape?* Only later did I hide a few wigs under my arm to see what a new me could look like.

I'd selected three wigs with long hair like I used to have before my aunt took her shears to me. Now, in front of the bathroom mirror, I slipped on a glamorous blond wig. I'd hoped for a transformation, but behind my dark-framed glasses I looked the same bookish girl. The brunette wig made me look even more so, while the red one would have worked for Halloween. I replaced the wigs and crept back to my room, not one inch closer to finding out who I was.

The next morning, I was drawn out of my bed by the sweet, fat smell of sizzling bacon. Brad was sitting at the table. My father was at the stove wearing a mischievous smile—and a Lady Godiva wig. I pretended not to notice. Disappointment flashed across his face, as if amusing me would have made his day.

"Dad thinks he's hilarious," I said to Brad, rolling my eyes as I sat down beside him. I opened my magazine at the table to read the article again. "I'm going to Dallas," I announced. The day before, I'd had to ask the school bus driver where it was. "Dallas, Texas," I clarified now, in case there was another one.

"Say again?" My father set plates of bacon and eggs in front of us, sunny-side up for me and over easy for Brad.

"I'm going to join the Jesus Freaks."

Grabbing his own plate from where it had been warming on top of the woodstove, my father sat down on the bench across from us. He raised his eyebrows. "You're what?"

Ignoring his long, blond wig, I plunged into my defense. "I'm going to become a Jesus Freak. That's what they're called because they're freaks for Jesus. And Dad, they're so full of love."

"Oh, my naïve daughter. You see good everywhere, but the world isn't like that."

"Yes, it is."

"So, is this a religious thing? Like a cult?"

"It's not a cult!" I was indignant, though I wasn't sure what a cult was. "They're just Christians who happen to be hippies. And their rally is like Woodstock, without any drugs." I was making up the part about the drugs: I had no idea.

"You know that every night of my life I pray to God for you and Brad—"

"Yes, you've told us like a million times."

"I just don't believe in organized religion."

I thought of the pictures from the Jesus rally. "They're not that organized."

"You know what I mean," he continued. "But I'm not going to tell you what to believe."

"Groovy."

My father picked up a slice of bacon in his fingers and dipped it into the egg yolk. "I just wouldn't get your heart set on going to Texas."

The thought never entered my twelve-year-old brain that I couldn't go to Texas if I wanted to. Only that I would have to earn enough money for the ticket. And that I needed a job. I was too young to find work in a store, so instead I went to a part of town that was slightly less poor than the other parts. I knocked on the first door I came to.

"Do you have any odd jobs I could do?"

I heard no at door after door, sometimes with the chain still on. Or *non*, because Northern Ontario was full of French speakers. But finally, a woman who hadn't brushed her hair in a long time said she'd be very happy for help with the ironing.

"In fact, you can start right now," she said and led me to a room off the kitchen where a laundry basket overflowed onto the floor.

When I'd told her I lived with my father and brother, she must have thought I had stepped into the space in our household vacated by my mother. Little did she know that my father ironed all our clothes. But I made like I had held an iron before, and soon she left me alone to try to work out how to use the steam so that it wouldn't drench her husband's shirts. By the end of the day, half the shirts had water marks. I got paid, but she didn't ask me back.

Collecting empty bottles at Crystal Beach for the return money turned out to be a more reliable source of income.

One day, my father came to pick me up in town, where I'd been cashing in another load of bottles. After the Beetle caught fire, he'd managed to get us a blue-and-white Volkswagen van. Now the back of the van was filled with the wigs and mannequin heads.

"What're you doing with all this?"

"I've got a buyer, a beauty parlor up in Timmins. As they say, 'Take your first loss and get out.'"

"What loss? I thought you got them for free."

"Yeah, well, I spent a bit on advertising."

After seeing my father's businesses fail time and again, I realized that maybe I wasn't a chip off the old block after all. For one thing, I had more money than he did.

CHAPTER 16

CRACK THE WHIP

KIRKLAND LAKE, 1971

TO EARN MONEY TO join the Jesus Freaks, I started guiding people on trail rides. We were up to thirteen horses now, plus Shadow, the canny little pony. We called ourselves the Rocky T Ranch, and we rented out our horses at two dollars and fifty cents an hour to groups of people from Kirkland Lake. Bev and I alternated taking riders out; in addition to guiding, we had to make sure they didn't gallop the horses too much.

I preferred to ride alone. In fact, more and more, I liked being alone. Saddling up Doll, I'd take her along the hidden trail that ran up the back of our rocky ridge. We'd climb through a forest of dappled poplar and birch leaves until the trail flattened out and we were entering the pines. With a carpet of needles muffling Doll's steps, the world would suddenly become as silent as a book.

One day, we emerged from our ride on the precipice of the ridge. I tied Doll's reins to a tree so she could graze and then inched over to the edge. Laid out below was our little farm: the house with a curl of woodsmoke from breakfast, the corral where the other horses were gathered eating hay, and, beyond that, the fields, the forests, the low hills.

I felt a kind of euphoria. Up on that ridge, I could see for miles. The expansiveness of the view gave me a new perspective. I was a freak without a mother, a freak who didn't know how to be a girl. Yet there was this flame growing inside me. If I could just get out of Kirkland Lake, maybe I could go to university one day, travel the world, make my mark. Maybe I could even be a writer.

But while I was up on the ridge dreaming of glory, my father was down below dreaming of me following in his footsteps.

"How about I set you up in a business this Christmas?"

"Sure, whatever." The leaves were turning the color of Bev's hair, and December seemed a long way away.

That winter, as I sat in the cashier's booth of a closed-down gas station, I regretted my words. The cashier's booth, the same temperature inside as outside (minus forty degrees) was surrounded by fir trees leaning against one another in evergreen tepees. My father had chopped them down for me—presumably from our property and not the federal land next door—and we would split the profit on each one.

I spied my first customer—one of my teachers from Central Public School, located just down the hill behind the gas station. As I opened the sliding door, I could hear laughter coming up from the skating rink, a flooded oval in our schoolyard surrounded by wooden boards. Everyone from my school would be down there. I tugged my parka tightly around me and went to where my teacher was inspecting the Christmas trees.

"I'll buy that one"—she pointed to the tallest tree—"*if* you can bring it to my house. I live down on Spruce."

"Sure." One of the business lessons my father tried to drill into me was never to say no. It was a word I'd always have trouble with.

By dinnertime that evening, I had sold five trees. That was more than I expected, considering that anyone could go into the bush and cut down their own. Locking up the cashier's booth, I heard more laughter. This time, I stole down the hill to take a look.

Across the floodlit rink, I saw my cousin Bev in the middle of a group of skaters. Wearing her brother's hockey skates, she was, as usual, racing the boys and beating them. Her hair streamed behind her like a flame. The skaters began to form themselves into a chain, linking hands for a game of crack the whip. In no time, they were whipping across the rink, their blades making scissoring sounds on the ice as they gathered speed. They had just gotten to maximum velocity when Bev, the leader of the chain, made a sudden U-turn. The boy on the far end of the "whip" went flying into the rink boards with a thud.

While the skater picked himself up, Bev caught sight of me and waved me over. I shook my head. Even without the tree to deliver, I wouldn't have joined. I wasn't good at sports like Bev; usually it was me at the end of the whip.

I trudged back up to the gas station lot, my boots crunching across the snow. Flipping my teacher's tree on its side, I grabbed the trunk where my father's ax had felled it. Sap sticking to my mitts, I began to slide the tree behind me. The laughter from the rink dropped away. I was alone. The only sound now in the still, dark night was of the branches swooshing along on the snow.

A few days later, I sold the last Christmas tree. My father couldn't have been happier. "You're going to be a great businesswoman!" he said. "Just like your old daddy."

"First of all," I said, "you're not a businesswoman. And second, I'm going to be a writer."

"You'll see." His smugness was infuriating.

I'd saved enough money for my trip to the Jesus Freaks the next summer. Now Bev had a plan for how we'd spend the rest.

The next afternoon, the two of us ventured across town to a building that hadn't seen paint for decades.

"You sure you know where we're going?" I asked. The building's stairwell was dark and reeked of tobacco and urine.

"This way," Bev said, and led me up to the second floor and down a corridor. The bulbs were gone from the fixtures, but several doors were open, laying oblongs of light down at our feet. Emaciated, grizzled men looked up as we passed. Some lay on single beds and smoked their rollies, staring up at the ceiling. In one shabby room, an old guy snapped his head up like he wanted to talk to us.

"Keep walking." Bev grabbed my arm. "The one we want is at the end."

The last door was answered by another old man. Unshaven, his face seemed to cave in below his cheekbones. The suspenders he wore kept his pants from falling to his ankles.

He looked the two of us up and down. "What d'you want?"

"A bottle of Baby Duck." Bev handed him the money.

"Stay here," he said, motioning to his saggy bed.

"That's okay. We can wait on the street."

He pulled on a dark oilskin jacket. "I don't want nobody to see you, is all."

We waited for our bootlegger inside the dark entry. When, finally, he returned from the government liquor store, he handed us a brown paper bag that I hid in my purse.

We crossed town to the French Rocks, behind the Catholic church. Bev unscrewed the top, took a swallow, then handed the bottle to me.

The wine was sickly sweet, but I glugged some and handed the bottle back to her.

Big snowflakes had begun floating down. I watched them alight on Bev's face and hair. By the time we finished the bottle, the fresh snowfall at our feet was soft and new like down.

I felt a warm glow. "Bev, I want to sleep here."

"Let's go, LoriLove. It's cold."

I didn't know what she was talking about. I was as toasty as if I were sitting against my grandmother's heating vent. The fluffy snow was like a bed of cotton puffs.

Bev was pulling on my arm. "You have to get up."

I wanted to snuggle into the snow. It was like not wanting to get out of bed in the morning, before my father lit the woodstove.

I don't remember how we got back to Bev's place, where my family was sleeping to conserve our dwindling supply of furnace oil. Before we went out, Bev had left her window open a crack so we could sneak back in. Now I found myself standing in front of that window as she cried, "Oh no. I can't get back in."

I roused myself. "What?"

"My bedroom window is locked. My father must know about me sneaking out."

"Bev, I don't feel well."

"We have to go inside." She leaned her face so close to mine, she went out of focus. "But if anyone's up, we just pretend we're normal and we go to bed, okay?"

"Okay."

Downstairs, all was quiet. A table lamp had been left on, and it shot jagged shadows behind the antlers of the buck mounted above the fireplace.

I stumbled, and Bev whipped around, a finger to her lips.

Suddenly, Bev's father, six feet and furious, stomped out of his bedroom. "Beverley, I'm so disappointed in you."

Bev put her head down. Her father's disapproval would always hurt her more than any punishment.

It felt like my brain was being pulled out through the back of my head. Suddenly, I heard my own father's voice. "What the hell were you girls up to?"

I opened my eyes. My father wore an amused expression.

"Daddy, I feel sick."

Later, as he cleaned up after me, he said, "You shouldn't drag your cousin into things like this."

I interpreted that to mean that he wasn't concerned about me. *You're in charge of your own real estate,* he'd started saying, as if I alone had responsibility for myself. Getting drunk, coming home late: I was just doing the kinds of things he had done, and he had turned out fine.

It never occurred to either one of us that he should have worried more.

A few weeks later, I found myself on the main floor of Green's being watched by a store clerk. I pretended to study the rack of comic books, although I'd already spotted the new one with the bold hitchhiking girl on its cover. Turning the rack nonchalantly, I never lost sight of that comic book's placement. On three sides, there were boys' comics. The fourth side had *Archie* and my love comics. I was calculating the right moment to slide the issue with the hitchhiker up my sleeve when I remembered the clerk. She was still observing me. I stopped fingering the comic I wanted and feigned interest in an issue of *The Incredible Hulk*.

When a customer approached the clerk, I whipped the rack around, grabbed the comic, and shoved it up my sleeve. By the time she turned back to me, I was innocently spinning the rack.

The comic was lodged up near my armpit. I clamped my arm tight so it wouldn't slide down and headed for the exit. I felt the urge to run, but I forced myself to linger by some Love's Baby Soft perfume; I'd come back for that later.

Behind me, the clerk was still at her station. Ahead of me was the exit. I pushed on the door. Suddenly I felt a hand tap my shoulder. I jerked away. The hidden comic book fell to the ground.

The man retrieved the comic from the floor. "Come with me."

His face was a blur, but I can still see the white shirt and the tag reading ASSISTANT MANAGER. He led me into the store office. In it was a curtained-off area, like a fitting room. Would he strip-search me behind the curtain like they did with the kids who took drugs? Would he call the police?

The man pulled a chair off a stack of them. "Sit down."

I began to shake. I could hear my own teeth chatter.

He took out a yellow pad. "What's your name?"

I stammered out my real name: I was a better thief than liar.

"Teck?" he asked.

We lived in Teck Township. "Yes."

He wrote down the name he thought I had given him, misspelling my first name. I was caught between the fear that he'd discover my lie and the hope that "Laurie Teck" would get away with this.

"I don't want to *ever* see you in this store again." He tapped the pad of paper with his pen. "You're just lucky I'm not calling your parents."

I got up, terrified he'd change his mind about letting me go. I passed the clerk, who scowled and crossed her arms over her chest. If it had been up to her, the cops would've already had me in cuffs.

That day, realizing how easily I could end up in reform school like my father, I gave up shoplifting. But for a teenage girl in the seventies, there were other ways to get into trouble.

It wasn't long before I found one of those ways, in a party in someone's basement. When Bev and I entered, the air was already blue with smoke and incense. "Paranoid," by Black Sabbath, was playing on the turntable.

"Isn't this far out?" Kracky, a scrawny guy in his twenties, handed me the record jacket. "I got it in Toronto, at Sam the Record Man." He reeked of musky patchouli.

I looked around to see where Bev was. Through the party's haze, I located her on the other side of the room, under a psychedelic black-light poster. She was drinking rye and Coke with some girls from her softball team. She raised her plastic glass to me with a questioning look. I shook my head. That was my mother's favorite drink, and the smell of it made me feel sick.

"Toke?" Kracky was trying to hold his breath, which made it sound like he was swallowing the word.

"I don't smoke cigarettes," I said, and immediately thought I sounded prim. But given that my mother smoked, I had sworn never to put a cigarette to my lips.

"No tobacco here." Kracky's voice sounded as raspy as a miner's. "Pure weed, man." He held out the joint to me.

Suddenly, Bev's laughter rang out from across the room, rising above the hum of voices. Then she caught sight of me with the joint in my hand.

I could see she was afraid I would go too far. But I thought she was wrong. I didn't know that I was too young and too damaged to be entrusted with the care of myself. My father's love, unconditional but also careless, felt like permission to do anything.

I took a hit from Kracky's joint. It was erasing the feeling I usually had, that I was worth nothing.

The next few years would be like crack the whip. I would be on the wrong end again, accelerating out of control, and Bev wouldn't be around to stop me from smashing into the boards. While any physical threat, like skating too fast, scared me to death, I would become fearless about doing things that were much more dangerous.

Bev Thicke Wilson, Kirkland Lake, 1971

CHAPTER 17

PEACE

KIRKLAND LAKE, 1972

IF YOU'RE SO SMART, why ain't we rich?

It was something my mother had often said, jokey at first, bitter toward the end. I didn't have the same doubts about my father, even when the heating oil ran out. I just bustled my brother in the door and told him we were going to bed in our coats, mitts, and toques.

"Oh, come on, you kids," my father said. "You're not wearing that getup to bed. It's not *that* cold."

"We're freezing," I insisted. Brad gave me a look that said *he* wasn't freezing and that this had all been my idea. His bedroom was in the attic, directly above the kitchen, and the kindling my father had set in our cookstove was now crackling away. But that did nothing to keep the winter out of the rest of our poorly insulated farmhouse.

"Are you just trying to make your daddy feel bad?"

My father wasn't entirely wrong. I planned to sleep in my full winter gear so that when he woke me for school, he would see it and feel guilty.

At breakfast the next morning, I brought my most reproachful look to the table. "Dad, you have to get serious: we need money." I poured out enough pure maple syrup to make my french toast float.

"Hey, save some for me." Brad grabbed the bottle from my hand.

"Yes, darling. I know we need money," my father said. He was looking out the picture window. In the snowy corral, the horses were gathered around their bright blue salt lick, which was deeply grooved by their tongues. Soon my father would have to put his mukluks on and give them their morning meal of oats. I wondered when we would run out of those, too.

"You could sell the horses," Brad said. At eight, he was more interested in driving than riding.

"I don't mind," I said. "Beats freezing." In truth, I hardly ever rode Doll anymore. I was always sleeping over at Bev's, because town was where the parties were, and parties had drugs. My cousin had the sense not to go, but I went to every single one, even if I spent most of the time in a corner tongue-tied by the pot I'd smoked.

My father agreed to sell the animals. His dream had always been to have his own pony, but the horses, chickens, and goats had become a burden.

In the end, I was sadder than I expected to see them go. Even Shadow, whose parting gift was a houseful of manure after he managed to open our back door, letting all the horses inside. And now they were nickering to one another as they were being loaded onto horse trailers and taken away. Doll was the last one we sold. As my father led her into the trailer, she looked back at me and whinnied. I felt as if I'd betrayed her.

I went to more parties; I smoked more drugs. At thirteen going on fourteen, I had no built-in brakes: I would try anything.

One night, I got myself drunk on vodka out in the back lane. It was past midnight, and Bev was sleeping, along with everyone else in the house. I crept upstairs to my grandmother's apartment and turned her radio on low to our local station.

"The CJKL request line is open," the evening deejay said. His voice was as smooth as polished gravel. "Call us at seven-two-five-five-five."

I called the number. "Could you play 'In-a-Gadda-da-Vida'?" Last year, in grade seven, I'd written a story about grooving to all seventeen minutes of it at a street dance.

"Whoa, that track goes on forever. I can't play it on AM radio."

"Oh, that's too bad. I really like that song."

"You have a nice voice. Do you sing?"

I was starting to feel warm. "No. My brother says my voice is terrible."

"I'm about to get off work," the deejay said. "If you really want to hear that record, I can play it for you at my place."

He must have heard the slurring of my words, must have heard the youth in my voice. But he gave me his address. I was elated: a famous person on the radio wanted to meet *me*.

My head was spinning because of the vodka, but I somehow made it to the street he'd named. When an older guy opened the door, I was taken aback. On the radio, he'd sounded younger, and taller.

"Come in." He held a bottle in the hand he used to usher me inside. "Want a beer?"

I was starting to sober up fast. "Just some water."

I knew I had to get out of there, but I didn't want to be rude. I sat down on his couch, on the far end. He put a record on and then came over to sit beside me. I pulled my knees up close to my chest.

The record wasn't "In-a-Gadda-da-Vida." It sounded like "Carolina in the Morning," but the words were different: "Nothing could be finer than eating her vagina in the morning."

"Would you like that?"

I didn't know what he was talking about.

"I'll bet you're pretty without your glasses." He came closer to take them off me. I shrank from him and felt the hard wooden arm of the couch against my back.

"I should go."

"No, stay."

"I have to. My dad is waiting outside," I lied. "He drove me here."

When I got back to Bev's, I managed to slip into her bed without waking her. I would never tell her—or my father—what happened. I blamed myself. I was too bold, and too grateful for the smallest attention. I deserved whatever I got.

Trembling in bed at the thought of what had almost happened, I remembered the Jesus Freaks. Maybe I needed God to protect me—from myself.

The next day, aching from a hangover and the creepy memories of the night before, I walked up Duncan Avenue to Trinity United. It was my grandparents' church, but I'd never been inside.

Trinity was set like a triangle on the street with a smaller triangle in front for the entrance. The door was unlocked. Inside, it was quiet, with the light slanting through the arched windows illuminating the dust motes in the air. From somewhere behind the altar, a boy in his twenties emerged carrying a guitar case. He was tall with curly brown hair. I knew who he was. In a little town where everyone knew everyone, he was even more noticeable because of his malformed arm. A child's arm. When he caught sight of me, I could see the surprise on his face: I guess he knew who I was, too.

"Hey," he said, "what brings you into our church?"

"*Your* church?"

"I run a youth group here." He put the guitar case down.

"I'm a Jesus Freak." I'd never met a real Jesus Freak, but I was trying to impress him. "I've been saving up to join them in Dallas."

"Dallas, Texas?"

"Yep." I still didn't know if there was another Dallas.

"Why so far?"

"That's where they are."

"You know, don't you, that there's a congregation in Toronto?"

"Really?" It had never occurred to me that they could be in Canada. I asked again, just in case I hadn't heard him right. "There are Jesus Freaks in *Toronto*?"

"Of course. Once school's out our youth group is organizing a bus tour to one of their services."

"You are?" My voice dropped to a whisper, the way it did when I wanted something so badly, I could barely trust myself to speak. "Can I come?"

He put his good hand on my arm. "You're welcome to."

The kindness in his voice felt like it would split my needy heart in two.

"How much does it cost to go?"

"The bus and meals work out to forty dollars a person—if you can afford it. Otherwise, I'm sure the church will sponsor you."

"No, it's okay. I earned some money selling Christmas trees."

"It's settled, then."

That evening, I walked into our farmhouse kitchen to the smell of my father's fresh-baked bread. He had just pulled a loaf out of the oven and was using his left hand as a plate for the slice he was buttering.

"Dad, you won't believe it! There are Jesus Freaks in Toronto! They have this service on Thursdays called the Catacombs, and I'm going to go with a group from Gramma's church."

I could tell by my father's expression that he was relieved I wasn't still talking about Dallas.

"But, Toronto—where would you kids sleep?"

"In a church basement. I have to take my sleeping bag."

"You're not going to come back a Holy Roller, are you?"

"Would you grow up?"

"Sheesh." He sighed, folded the buttered slice in two, and shoved it into his mouth, then pulled his wallet out of his baggy pants. "Okay, how much do you need for the trip?"

"Nothing. I've got it," I said.

"Even better." He put his wallet away and glanced toward a pile of papers at the end of the kitchen table. "I guess I should send that damn insurance company a check. Remind me to pay that, won't you, Lor?"

He often said things like that, as if I were the adult in the room. *Remind me to do this. Don't let me forget to do that.*

He put the loaf back in the woodstove to keep it warm.

I forgot to remind him.

The next day, my father was putting a moose roast into the oven while Brad and I played Crazy Eights at the table.

"Did I ever tell you kids what happened when I got out of reform school?"

"Not another story!"

"When I got back to Kirkland Lake, they were desperate for laborers," he started, ignoring me. "So, even though I was only fifteen, I got a job working construction on the Park Lane Hotel. One day, there I am, shoveling sand into the cement mixer, when an old teacher of mine walks by with her class. I'm just a boy, working alongside the men, so I show off a little, taking bigger shovelfuls of sand, thinking my old classmates are admiring me. Then my teacher turns to her students—I can still hear her to this day—and says, 'See, children? That's what happens if you leave school. You end up like that Thicke boy.'"

He wiped his hand across his eyes. "Look at me crying. Gets me every time. I thought I was doing well because I had a job, but for her, I was a failure at fifteen. That's when I understood that if I was ever going to be a Somebody, I had to beat it the hell out of Kirkland Lake."

"Yeah, tell me about it."

My father gave me a sharp look.

Even though I complained about them, his stories were important to me. As I struggled to find some value in myself, it comforted me that my father wasn't like other fathers. If he was special, maybe I could be, too. Looking back now, I see that the petty crimes, the war adventures, the businesses that failed so spectacularly—they were my affirmations.

As the day for my trip to Toronto got closer, my father announced that he wanted to drive me there himself. "I'm going to check things out down south. You can't make a buck in this goddamned town. Toronto's where the money is, you know."

At the time, I didn't notice that he was talking about giving up the one stable home we'd had since my mother left. All I heard was that he wanted to ruin my trip.

"Dad, you're just stealing my idea to go to Toronto. And it's a youth group trip, not a family trip. There's no way in hell I'm going with my father and brother."

"Don't swear."

"*You* just did."

"Anyway, it's a free country," he said. "You can't stop me and Brad from going."

"Yeah, but where would you stay?" I had an image of him snoring next to the kids in their sleeping bags.

"We'll visit your uncle Brian."

"Fine, do what you like, but I'm not seeing you there. And when I get back, you'll pick me up at the bus station, right?"

"Of course."

"And don't you dare show up at the Catacombs."

"I wouldn't dream of it."

"Dad . . ." I said in a warning voice.

"What?" he said, all innocence.

A couple of weeks later, I waved goodbye to my father and brother. They were setting off in our blue-and-white Volkswagen van down the same highway south, but I would be traveling with the youth group.

Ten hours after I boarded the charter bus, we pulled up in front of the biggest church I'd ever seen. It had a grand facade and high stained-glass windows. Solid stone steps led up to three wooden doors set into deep archways. I went in through the middle one, feeling nervous.

It was like stepping into a warm, beating heart. The church was filled with long-haired boys and long-haired girls twirling and swaying, singing and dancing. At the altar in front, musicians were playing guitars and shaking tambourines. People raised their hands: *Praise the Lord.* Around me, everything was alive and flowing and electric. I left the youth group behind and began to dance by myself.

The following days, we visited other churches, but there was nothing like the energy and the love I'd experienced at the Catacombs. I felt so changed inside that I was surprised when no one commented on how different I was.

Sunday evening, we all set out in the bus for the long drive back to Kirkland Lake. I sat alone. At the front, the youth leader, unencumbered by his diminutive arm, took his guitar out of its case and began to play "Amazing Grace." One by one, the others started to sing along, making a softly elegiac sound. I rested my cheek on the bus window. I felt deeply, quietly at peace.

CHAPTER 18

FREEDOM'S JUST ANOTHER WORD

KIRKLAND LAKE, 1972

I WOKE WITH A start as the bus bumped over the curb. We were pulling into Kirkland Lake, and my father and brother were waiting for me next to our Volkswagen van. Brad had his head down, kicking at something by his feet. My father was scanning the bus windows with one hand up to shield his eyes from the sun. He didn't seem to see me inside waving madly. Behind them the van hiccuped; I wondered why the motor was still running.

The driver opened the doors, and we filed out. I'd been gone less than a week, yet I felt like I was already closer to being the person I wanted to be. I went to get my sleeping bag and suitcase from under the bus just as my father came around the side. The case was heavy. Later, I would be glad I'd overpacked; I'd even grabbed my jewelry box with my father's war medals inside.

I was still holding the suitcase when my father crushed me in his arms.

Hugging wasn't something we did, and it made me uncomfortable. I squirmed away.

"Dad, the Jesus Freaks were so groovy—"

"Lor," he interrupted.

I took in his expression for the first time. "Everything okay?"

"I have something to tell you. But I don't want you to panic." He made a calming gesture with the flat of his hand. "Everything works out for the best. Remember that."

"You're scaring me."

"There was a fire. Our house burned down."

"You're joking, right?" I looked for the telltale grin, anticipating his punch line. When he didn't smile, I turned to my brother. "There was a fire at the farm?"

"Aunt Dixie told us." Brad kicked at another stone. "But I don't think it's true."

So that's why the van was idling: they were in a hurry to get to the farm.

"Let's go," my father said. "Maybe there's something we can salvage."

My father and Brad had driven all night to get here, and now we had another seven miles to go. Past Swastika, we sped to the turnoff at Culver Park and spat gravel the rest of the way down the road where we lived.

At the end of our driveway, we parked. I climbed down from the van and stood in shock. My father put his arms around us. Our home, along with everything in it, was gone. It had been wiped from the landscape so completely that now I could see clear up to the ridge, where I'd go to dream of a bigger life. It had never occurred to me that our farm would have to burn down for that to happen.

We would soon remember the expired fire insurance. And my father would raise his arms to the sky to tell us we were free. But we weren't free. If we were, it was the freedom of careening down an icy slope toward a precipice. Before, we had had our house to keep us from going over the edge. Now we had nothing.

"Come on, kids, let's get going." Despite what he had said earlier about being free, he looked concerned. Shoulders slumped, he walked to the vehicle that held everything we had left in the world. His demeanor scared me. I depended on his being able to see a rainbow above a pile of soot. If he did, I could, too. Now he was staring straight ahead with his arms resting on the steering wheel.

Brad got into the van without a word. I was silent, too. Not even the ignition made a sound as my father turned the key.

The starter was dead.

With our history of balky vehicles, my father always parked on a hill, facing downward—just in case. Now he loosened the emergency brake, opened his door, and stuck his leg out. Pushing against the ground with his left foot, he moved us forward. We gathered speed on the downhill. Stalks of wheat flicked in and out of the hole rusted through the Volkswagen's floorboard. When the driveway flattened out, my father popped the clutch. The engine caught and roared to life.

As we passed the fork in the road that separated our property from the *real* farms, the van came up over a slight rise. Usually that was where my father would accelerate, catching a little air and giving Brad and me butterflies in our stomachs. This time he took the rise slowly.

He stopped where our country road met the highway. Left would take us south. Right would take us into Kirkland Lake.

"Where are we going?" I asked. The jagged rock cuts where the highway had been blasted through were streaked with yellow. It was fool's gold.

"You know," he said slowly, "there's nothing keeping us here."

"We can't leave!" Brad's voice was rising with panic. Landlocked between us, he looked from me to our father. "What about Mom?"

I was shocked he still thought she would come back.

"Son—"

We were close enough to Kirkland Lake for CJKL to suddenly crackle to life. I reached across my brother to fiddle with the dial.

"Heyyyy," said Brad. I ignored him and turned the music up. My father was still idling the van at the crossroads.

"Me and Bobby McGee" was playing on the radio. Like any AM hit, it was on rotation, but I'd never noticed the words before. "Busted flat" was something I could relate to now. Then I felt shivers. Did I just hear that right?

Was that freedom—having nothing left to lose?

"Dad, that's our song!"

My father tilted his head to hear the lyrics, but he didn't get the connection until the chorus came around again. Then his face seemed to lighten.

We didn't have much left to lose, that was for sure. Did that mean we were free to go anywhere, like my father said?

Humming, he turned right toward Kirkland Lake. I knew what was going to happen now. We'd stop off at my aunt Dixie's house, help ourselves to whatever we could find in the fridge—bologna and white bread, probably, with French's mustard. If no one had emptied the dishwasher, we'd stack our dishes on top with all the others. I'd say goodbye to my beloved cousin Bev; Brad might go up the street to tell his best friend, Billy; and then we'd set out.

My father was whistling along with the music, tapping his fingers on the dashboard. We didn't know what the future would bring or where these wheels would take us. But for that moment at least, we were free.

We came upon another rise in the road.

"Hold on, kids!"

Brad and I grabbed the dashboard. As we drove up over the hill, my father accelerated just enough for the wheels to lift.

CHAPTER 19

JESUS LOVES YOU

BRAMPTON, 1972

THE BELL RANG. Up and down the hall, doors were flung open. Students poured from their classrooms, filling the corridor with the swell of voices and the clatter of lockers. Unnoticed, I slipped past high schoolers eddying around the popular kids.

I moved to the bottom of the staircase and felt the cool of the wall ride down my back. I was wearing the jeans I'd bought at a hippie place in Toronto. They were the right amount of faded, with the right number of holes. But they'd been a mistake: Centennial was a preppy school. As the kids streamed by, their upturned collars flopped over like dogs' ears.

We had started again, just as my father promised. I was in a new school, in a new town. My hair was long enough now to part in the middle, and I'd traded my black frames for silver Janis Joplin glasses. But despite my new look, I hadn't made any friends yet. School in Brampton was feeling a lot like my old life back in the North. Just no Bev in it.

The other students laughed and jostled one another. I hugged my mother's white Bible to my chest, one of the many things she'd left behind. Then, just as a group drew beside me, I called out, "Jesus loves you!"

The students looked up and snickered. I was happy: at least they'd noticed me.

After we lost our farm, I'd wanted to move to Toronto, where the Jesus Freaks were. Instead, we'd come here, to Brampton, almost an hour away, because my uncle Brian had found us a house. It belonged to one of his nursing home patients, so it came with everything we needed, even sheets and towels. "Beggars can't be choosers," my grandmother had warned us, but now we were beggars in a grand two-story brick house. There was a leafy chestnut out front, a large green lawn, and a white porch supported by pillars. We'd hit the jackpot.

Our new front door was inset with beveled glass. Inside, a red-carpeted staircase on the right led to four upstairs bedrooms. To the left was a paneled living room with two couches and a television. Between the living room and the kitchen was the dining room. That was where my father and brother would sleep. I had my own room, leaving the three other bedrooms for the three boarders my father found through a newspaper ad.

Nancy and Kate were in their twenties. From the moment they moved in, they barely registered my presence. I thought maybe the third boarder, Candy, and I would become friends, because at sixteen, she was just two years older. She had been placed in our home by the government.

"Dad, why would they take Candy away from her parents?" I couldn't imagine anything worse than being ripped from your home.

"There's usually a reason."

"But she'll never see them again?" What would parents have to do to lose their daughter? Or was she the bad one? If she was, maybe I could help her find God.

A few days later, after witnessing for Jesus again in the halls of my high school, I walked into the house to find my father waiting for me with a triumphant look on his face.

"See," he said. "I told you it would all work out." He pulled a handful of bills from his pocket, then started to fan himself like a southern belle. The boarders must have just paid their rent. "Your old man always provides."

"You're not the Lord, Dad."

My father sighed and put the bills back into his wallet. "A man is never a prophet in his own land."

"You're not a prophet, either. But I'm glad you've got some money."

In our family, we talked about money all the time. How much we did or didn't have, where to find more. Yet, for someone who was always trying to make a buck, my father was surprisingly unmaterialistic. He barely noticed the beautiful home we were living in. He didn't desire luxury items like a good watch, fancy furniture, or nice clothes. It didn't bother him that rust had rotted through our Volkswagen van. He didn't care where he lived, what he drove, or how he looked—just as long as we were never too poor for the occasional Oysters Rockefeller.

I was starting to see that as far as earthly possessions went, my father and Jesus were on the same page.

That Thursday night, as usual, my father drove me the twenty-five miles to Toronto to where the Jesus Freaks had their service. Brad came along for the ride.

"Don't come into the church," I begged as we pulled up outside. "You and Brad will embarrass me."

"How do you know *you* won't embarrass *us*?"

"Very funny."

"Okay, Brad," my father said. "Let's go get dessert somewhere. Your sister's going to join the hippie Holy Rollers."

I slammed the door shut.

Recently, the cover of *Life* magazine had showed a gathering of Jesus Freaks with transcendent faces. Now I was one of them. When I walked into the church that evening, I felt the joy in the air. It was electric. My father had gotten me there a bit late, so the young people were already holding hands as they listened to the minister in his striped poncho strumming his guitar. Later, as we danced to the beat of tambourines and bongo drums, I felt the love.

Two weekends later, I was wading into the cold, dark water of Lake Ontario. My jeans felt like a weight dragging me down. My teeth were chattering, but I plodded deeper.

Two men took my arms. One wore a T-shirt and jeans. The other, bearded, had on a brown robe that was floating up around him in a semicircle.

"Sister," the bearded lay minister said to me, "I see a Jesus-size hole in your heart."

I nodded mutely, grateful for the attention. Looking back, I think that hole was the exact size and shape of my mother, but at the time, I thought he was right and that it was Jesus I needed. He put his hand flat on my forehead, then tipped me back into the frigid baptismal water. I was born again into the Jesus Freaks.

When I got home, my clothes and hair were still wet. As I tiptoed up the stairs, my father came out of the kitchen wiping his hands.

"Dare I ask?" he said, eying me.

"Dad, I told you I was getting baptized today."

"I imagined a sprinkling of water."

"Yeah, well, that's not the way the Jesus Freaks do it."

"You sure they're not a bunch of nuts?"

I let out an industrial-strength sigh. There was a time when I saw my father as a hero. But lately, he just seemed clueless.

The next evening, I came home from school to find a massive pool table taking up most of our dining room. A man was leaning over the green-felt edge while my brother, Nancy, Kate, and Candy looked on.

"Lori, meet my new business partner, uh"—not surprisingly, my father had forgotten his name—"the world junior snooker champion."

"Angelo," the man said, glancing up. His hair was boyishly cut, but he had crow's-feet around his eyes. *Oh, Dad*, I thought. He was betting our future on an aging pool shark.

Our three boarders seemed to be taken in by Angelo as well and were competing for his attention. Kate curled up like a kitten on the ottoman. Candy made some brash joke I didn't understand. Nancy, a tall beautician, leaned her hip bone against the table as Angelo pulled his stick back. The soft pop of cue on ball was followed by a crack like thunder as the rest of the balls broke. Nancy jumped back to where the others were, all of them spellbound now as, one by one, Angelo dispatched the balls into their pockets, calling each shot. Even Brad seemed hypnotized.

I gathered that my father and Angelo were supposed to be discussing their new pool table business, but that evening, Angelo seemed intent on eliciting more admiration from our boarders.

Doesn't he have a wife? I wondered. *He looks old enough.*

After Angelo finally left, Brad called out to my father from his bed, which had been pushed against the wall to make room for the pool table. "Daddy, my feet are itchy."

My father turned on the dining room light. He held up one of Brad's narrow feet so we could examine it. The soles were red and scaly, with deep crevices slashed across his tender skin.

"They've gotten worse." My father touched one of the cracks, and Brad winced, pulling his foot away. "Why didn't you tell me?"

"I don't know." Brad sounded afraid he would be in trouble—which was weird, because we were literally never punished.

"We'd better put on some more of that cream your uncle Brian gave us."

The next morning when I came down for breakfast, Nancy was at the table looking at her coffee cup as if trying to remember why she'd picked it up. She displayed her trade on her face: even in her housecoat, she was wearing full makeup and a pair of thick eyelashes.

"Dack, I'll get another job," she said in her froggy morning voice. "Don't worry."

My father clearly wasn't worried about Nancy's rent money. In our family, worrying was *my* job.

Brad sat down to eat his cereal, so small at nine years old that the tabletop was even with his chest. He wore plastic bags on his feet to keep his psoriasis medication from rubbing off.

Kate came padding into the kitchen in her furry slippers. "I'll take a coffee, too, Dacker." She tightened her robe around her tiny waist. "Do you mind if my brother stays over this weekend?" She touched Nancy's arm. "You're going to love Roddy. And you can get rid of that effing Bennie."

"Who's Bennie?" Candy asked, grabbing a cup from the drying rack on her way to the table.

"You remember Bennie!" Nancy pushed aside her bangs with the flat of her palm, protecting her long nails. "He's the one with the crooked thingy." All three laughed.

I didn't understand the joke, but I wasn't meant to. With my father paying attention only to whether Brad and I had food and the girls had coffee, I was starting to feel like I did at school: invisible.

I wasn't any more visible at the Catacombs. I loved everything about those evangelical services—from the dancing in the aisles to the leaders, Merv and Merla, who were like ideal, guitar-strumming parents—but I arrived alone and left alone. If I still had time before my father came to get me, I'd hang out in the rectory, where Merv and Merla, in their matching striped ponchos, would greet the people they knew. I would lean against the wall, shyer than I normally was, longing for someone to see something interesting in me.

When our van ended up in the backyard of my father's mechanic, I didn't mind missing the Catacombs. My cousin Joanne had told me that the minister at the local church was from Kirkland Lake. I took this coincidence as a sign that I could find the Spirit closer to home.

Sunday, I walked up the stone steps of St. Paul's, anticipating the moment when the Spirit would fill me. I took a place near the back and waited. But there was no guitar music, no dancing, no electricity. The air felt lifeless. When the congregation stood to sing, the hymns were as wooden as the pews. This place needed a guitar and a few Jesus Freaks.

The only person who seemed to have the Spirit was the minister. He was effervescent. After the service, he chatted with the parishioners on the church steps. With longish hair brushing the top of his collar, he could have been a closet Jesus Freak. He must have noticed me staring at him, because he smiled. His eyes crinkled up, and his cheeks dimpled. I fell a little in love with the reverend.

When it was my turn to meet him, I stammered out my name.

"Ah, yes, I know your family well." His smile deepened. "My father was a boxer in a club your grandfather started. He met my mother while she was working for your grandmother. Your family is the reason I'm here."

"I can't wait to tell my father I met you, Reverend Williams."

"Call me Rev," he said. "Everyone does." Then he leaned close and whispered, "This service isn't your bag, is it?"

I shook my head. "There's this other one I go to, with the Jesus Freaks, but it's in Toronto. And my dad's van is broken."

"The Catacombs," he said approvingly. "Good place. But we have a coffeehouse right here in the church. On Saturdays. Teenagers more your age. How about giving us a hand?"

"What kind of coffeehouse?"

"It's part of our outreach to the street kids. Sometimes we convert them; sometimes we just give them something to eat."

"I'd love to help out." I was sure to make some friends at the coffeehouse.

As I turned to go, I took a closer look at Gage Park, a hangout directly across from the church. A group of teenagers was sitting on top of the picnic tables with their feet on the benches. I thought they might be the street kids I was going to help save.

Over the next few weeks, I went to the bus depot every day after class. Because Christians were supposed to spread the Word, I thought it would be a better place for witnessing than my high school, where carrying a Bible around wasn't making me as popular as I'd hoped.

One evening, I was home earlier than usual, having run into both Hare Krishnas and the Children of God, scarily aggressive if they caught you competing for converts. Arriving home, I dropped my schoolbooks onto the stairs with a thump.

"Dixie!" my father shouted. I knew he was going to start cycling through a litany of names before getting to mine. "I mean Helen," he said. "Daisy. Lori."

"Thanks, Dad, for finally getting my name right."

"You know I'm lousy with names. It doesn't mean I don't love you."

"Daisy was a dog."

"Well, anyway, don't leave your books on the stairs. Someone's going to trip on them."

As usual, I ignored him. "How's it going with Angelo?"

"We sold a pool table today."

"Praise the Lord!"

The front door opened, and Candy started up the stairs, sending my schoolbooks tumbling.

"I told you someone would trip on them," my father said. "Doesn't your religion tell you to respect your elders?"

Before I could answer with my usual sarcasm, I heard Candy upstairs. She was turning on the squeaky bath taps. I hoped an evening bath didn't mean her boyfriend was coming over. Although the government had taken her from her family, it didn't mean she had to follow any rules in our house. If she wanted to have her boyfriend over, it wasn't up to us to stop her. But I didn't like it.

After dinner and a couple of TV shows, I said good night. Brad was already tucked into his bed on the other side of the pool table, but the sliding doors were open because he didn't like being left in the dining room alone. I knew he'd be listening to the TV as he lay there with plastic bags on his feet. My uncle Brian said Brad's psoriasis could be from the stress of being separated from our mother, though Brad went to visit her more than I did. (*I* certainly wasn't going to waste my school holidays on her.) The crevices in his soles had become so deep that he cried when my father put the cream on. I didn't know how the little guy was able to walk.

I was up in my bedroom doing my math homework when I heard the front door open, then giggling, then footsteps on the stairs. It wasn't long before noises began coming from Candy's room. They started slowly, but soon she was crying out in time with the bounce of her old bedsprings.

It's one thing listening to people having sex when you're an adult, but as a fourteen-year-old virgin, I was mortified. And what if my father and brother were also hearing this?

I started to sing hymns as loud as I could. My favorite, "Maranatha," called upon the Lord to come soon. I didn't know enough about sex to get the irony—I just knew I had to drown out Candy's moans. And I could keep belting out songs all night long.

The next morning, as I sat down at the table beside Brad, no mention was made of my hymn singing. When Nancy came into the kitchen, I remembered what had happened the day before, when the menacing Children of God chased me away from the bus depot. "Nancy, I saw your boyfriend Bennie get on the Greyhound for New Brunswick."

"Tell Kate," Nancy snapped. "I don't give a shit." Her false eyelashes were akilter, as if she'd slept in them.

Kate came into the kitchen, ignoring Nancy as she went straight for the coffee. She turned to my father.

"So, Dack, I guess that bastard Angelo's not coming around here anymore."

"Let's hope not," Nancy said darkly.

After both had stomped back to their respective rooms, I asked my father what was going on. Brad had taken his cereal box of Lucky Charms into the living room to watch his Saturday-morning cartoons, walking gingerly in his plastic bags. "Why are Nancy and Kate mad at each other?"

"I guess you're old enough to hear this. The girls have been passing VD around."

"VD?" I knew you got venereal disease from sex, though the mechanics of that escaped me. "What do you mean 'passing it around'?"

"Apparently, Bennie gave it first to Nancy and then to Kate. Nancy gave it to Kate's brother Roddy, then to her fiancé."

"Whose fiancé?"

"Nancy's."

I had forgotten that Nancy had a boyfriend *and* a fiancé.

"Then Roddy gave it to his girlfriend Thérèse," my father continued. He moved his finger-counting to the other hand. "Then Kate gave it to her ex-husband. Either Kate or Nancy gave it to Angelo. Angelo gave it to his wife."

"What about Candy?" I would always have a soft spot for her because she had been taken away from her family, and I found that too sad for words.

"Candy says she wasn't involved in those shenanigans," my father said. "As for Angelo, I'm done working with that crumb bum."

"Who's a crumb bum?" Brad called from the other room.

"No one, son. Go back to your cartoons."

It didn't occur to me that this kind of household was not the ideal environment for two young children. Neither would it have occurred to my father: to him, this was real life, and you shouldn't shy away from it. But it had occurred to *someone*. Although we didn't know it at the time, someone had reported my father to the authorities.

One day, I came home from school to see my father at the kitchen table staring at a letter. It was stamped with the logo of child protective services.

"Is that Candy's check from the government?" I asked, wondering why he was looking so serious.

"No, it's a letter for me." He passed it across the table. "You might as well read this."

With a shock, I realized the letter was referring to Brad and me. "Dad," I said, looking up at him, "what's this?"

"Someone has made a complaint about us. They say I'm not providing you with a proper home." He looked baffled, like there was no world where that made sense.

"You mean they could take us away from you?" I was horrified. I could end up like Candy. My father would be left all alone, while Brad and I would be shipped off to live with strangers.

"It'll all work out," my father said. "Look." He pointed to the paragraph at the end. "It just says they're investigating us. Don't worry. I'll never let them take you."

"Candy's parents probably said that, too." I realized he couldn't promise that nothing bad would happen, and I felt sick.

"Hey," my father said, his face brightening. "What if you get your Reverend Williams to write us a letter of recommendation?"

"You want me to ask Rev to help us?"

My father nodded.

He couldn't fix this. He was depending on me to do it.

CHAPTER 20

THE FIRST CUT

BRAMPTON, 1973

THE DOOR TO REV'S office was ajar. Framed by St. Paul's leaded-glass windows, he leaned back in his chair, twirling a pen in his fingers. I knocked on the doorframe.

"Well, hello," Rev said. "What can I do for you today?"

"They're going to take us away!" I blurted.

His brow folded like an accordion. "Who is?"

I told him about the letter.

"I've known your dad since I was a kid. He's a little . . ." He looked for the right word. "Different, let's say. But his heart is in the right place."

"Could you put something like that in a letter?" I asked. "But without the 'different' part?"

Despite my father's relentless belief that nothing bad would happen to us, I didn't have the same faith in him that I used to. I prayed every night that Rev's letter would convince the government that my father was fit to raise Brad and me. But my father was already taking steps in case it didn't.

Whereas someone else would have simply given the boarders notice, he scoured the classified ads and called people up until he had found new homes for Nancy, Kate, and Candy. Now we had only one boarder, Diane, a quiet nurse with slightly crooked front teeth who had just moved in. Brad and my father were used to sleeping next to each other in the dining room, so even with two empty bedrooms, their beds stayed downstairs.

"It'll all work out. Don't worry," my father said. Because the alternative was unimaginable, I had to believe him.

I began 1973 with a new diary. On the inside cover, I wrote, "Highly personal and none of anyone's business. In the event of my death this book is to be read only by my cousin Bev." Below that, I signed my name, dotting my i's with three flower petals.

Six weeks later, I wrote, "Dear Diary, My mom and Art got married today." That was it, one line. Earlier that week, I had given three lines to the Diana Ross movie I'd seen with my father and brother. Even in my own journal, I pretended not to care.

My mother was still more than a thousand miles away. I'd visited her two months before. Deep in his La-Z-Boy, Art came between us again, just when I wanted some time with her.

"It's not nice for us to leave Art all alone."

"But Mom, he's watching *Hockey Night in Canada*. He hasn't even noticed we're in the bedroom."

"Well, you know, it's just not polite to leave him."

"But this is the first chance we've had to talk!"

"All right, but we shouldn't stay long. What do you want to talk about?"

"Nothing."

My mother didn't leave me just once. She left me dozens of times.

When she didn't invite me to her wedding, I wondered what it said about her feelings for me. I didn't know if she'd gotten married in a church or at the Red Lake town hall (if there was one), nor if afterward there was a reception or a dinner with friends. Maybe it was just her and Art at the kitchen table with a bottle of Canadian Club. Her wedding was another reminder of how little I seemed to matter to her.

It was all too raw. I should have stayed home that evening, but it was a Saturday night, and I decided at last to take Rev up on his offer. Brampton was still a lonely place for me, and it had gotten worse without Nancy, Kate, and Candy. In my high school, I had no friends: *I* was also "different." I didn't go to the Catacombs anymore: it was a long way to travel only to feel that as the youngest Jesus Freak, I would never fit in. So, the evening of my mother's wedding, I descended the stairs to the coffeehouse in the church basement, hoping to make some friends.

The humid heat of bodies rose from the basement. Inside, there were about a dozen card tables set up around the room, most of them occupied by the street kids we were there to save. At the far end, a guy walked over to a microphone. Introducing himself as Joe, he picked up a guitar and began to play. At the open kitchen off to one side, older ladies were arranging slices of cake and pie on paper plates.

It was easy to spot the Christian kids. The boys had short hair, and their jeans had creases ironed into them. They wore pristine white tennis shoes that looked like they'd come out of their boxes that very day. The girls wore dresses. These were kids who didn't live in boardinghouses where sexually transmitted diseases were passed around like a Nerf ball. Kids whose dining rooms weren't for sleeping in, but for lively conversations around the table. Kids who didn't have the government threatening to take them away.

Standing alone, the murmur of voices eddying around me, I felt the excruciating sense of something lacking in me. It was how I felt with my cousin Joanne, even when her mother didn't ask me to polish their silverware. I could never measure up to my rich cousin with her perfect post-orthodontic teeth, her two closets full of designer clothes, her football star boyfriend. I'd never had a boyfriend, and as for my clothes, I wore whatever was cheap. According to my father, I also swore like a trooper, while Joanne's worst swear word was *cripes*. Next to my cousin, and now to these kids, I felt like a big fat nothing.

I glanced over at the lost souls from the park. *Please, God, don't let me be like them.* But I was afraid it was too late.

Down in that coffeehouse, the street kids seemed feral. They were wired and wary, likely to grab a scrap of food and then disappear back into the wild. I knew from Rev that the youth group was to pick up plates from the kitchen ladies and deliver them to the tables. So much for witnessing: the few Christians who dared approach the street kids laid the plates down in front of them and then quickly retreated to the kitchen to stand in a clutch.

On my own outside the Christian group, I was feeling more awkward with each passing minute. My father always said, *When you feel out of place, do something,* so I grabbed two plates off the counter.

"Hold on."

I felt an unfriendly grip on my arm. I turned to see one of the clean-cut church kids.

"You don't serve yourself here," he said severely. "Just sit down, and we'll bring you something to eat."

"I . . . What? Okay."

I was too stunned to tell him I was one of them. In that moment, I saw myself as he must have seen me—scraggly and homeless. It never occurred to him that I could be one of the Christians, that I could be like *him.* How could I have been so stupid as to think I belonged with the "good" kids?

The suffocating air of the basement weighed on my chest. It was too sticky to breathe. Putting the plates down, I fled to the bathroom. In the refuge of a stall, I felt myself starting to come apart. I had to get out of St. Paul's before anyone saw me crying.

After splashing cold water on my face, I emerged from the bathroom and into the dim light of the coffeehouse. The red letters of the Exit sign were just ahead. I was making my way to the stairs when Rev stepped in front of me.

"Do you mind taking a couple of plates over to those two?" he asked.

He indicated a table where a boy and girl sat, clearly inhabiting separate worlds. She was grooving to the music while he was tapping his fingers on the table—not in time, more like to expend nervous energy. The glow from the kitchen caught the girl's face, her skin so white it was as if she never saw the sun. The boy, tawny-skinned, wore a black T-shirt. His muscles bulged under the short sleeves.

"Sure, I'll take the plates over," I said, planning my escape right afterward. "But who is that?"

"Roy?"

I shook my head.

"No, who's that girl?"

"That's Suzee. New here."

Outside of a magazine, I'd never seen anyone like her. Long, straight black hair, black eyes, red lips. She was wearing a plaid shirt knotted up under her bra, her bare midriff so lean it barely creased as she sat. She got up to listen to the musician, the only one paying him any attention. Her jeans fit like a coat of paint. I wished I could be so body confident. Turning back, she caught me looking at her and smiled.

I was still watching her as I laid the plates on the table, surprising the tawny-skinned boy. He looked tough, but also, I thought, vulnerable. The hole in his black T-shirt made me feel hopeful for the first time that evening. I'd learned to sew in Home Economics class, and that hole was something I could fix.

When you're fourteen, there is no end to the number of ways you can fool yourself.

I walked back to Rev, who had taken his jacket off. Despite the weather, the coffeehouse was steaming. But the tawny-skinned boy was the only one of the street people with bare arms.

"Why are they all wearing their thick shirts?" I whispered. "They must be boiling."

Rev looked at me in surprise. "None of the others told you? Junkies always hide their needle tracks."

I'd rolled my sleeves all the way up to stay cool. And still, I'd been taken for a user.

"What about her?" I asked.

"Her? No, Suzee's not a junkie. She's a speed freak."

I didn't know the difference.

The following Saturday, I was back at the coffeehouse. Rather than serving, I took a seat at one of the card tables, telling myself I was going to help the street people from the inside. Suzee wasn't there, but Roy was at the next table, sitting on his own. By then, I knew from Rev that Roy had been in and out of jail; he was seventeen now and living with one of the church elders while he turned his life around. Rather than scare me off, this revelation filled me with purpose. I gave him a smile, still too young to know its power of invitation.

Roy looked surprised, then leaned forward. "Do you want to join me or what?"

My heart fluttered. I joined him.

It seemed only minutes later that the kitchen ladies started covering the leftovers with Saran wrap, and Joe the singer packed up his guitar. I didn't want the night to end.

"Let's get out of here." Roy stood up, as if he knew I would follow. He was the same height as me. "There's a place we can go."

My watch said ten p.m. My father had never given me a curfew, so I thought that if ever there was a moment to take advantage of my freedom, this was it.

Roy and I went to the Satellite, an all-night restaurant where he knew the manager. He led me to the back, to the narrow part near the washrooms, so we could be alone. A small jukebox sat on our table, push buttons along the sides. Roy, whose fingers never stopped moving, paged through the songs while we talked. Suddenly, he reached his hand across the table to me.

There's no word I know of for the first time a boy, one with smooth brown skin and a black leather jacket, a boy who's a bit older, a bit edgy, reaches across a table to take the hand of a young girl who has never been touched like that before.

"You're my girl now."

Wordless, liquid, I nodded.

At two a.m., Roy walked me home. I had just slipped in through the front door when my father came barreling out of the dining room.

"Where the hell have you been?"

"I thought I was in charge of my own real estate."

"Don't be smart."

"I'm just telling you what you said."

"In that case, sis, you'd better manage your real estate wisely."

My father had taken to calling me "sis" lately, as if we were peers—which, in retrospect, was how I was beginning to act.

"Whatever. I'm going to bed." I left him at the bottom of the stairs.

"You'd better straighten up and fly right, sis," he called after me.

That night, I knelt by my bed to pray for God to save Roy, in Jesus's name, amen.

By the next afternoon, I thought I would expire from wanting. I'd never had this feeling before, of wishing for a boy to *please, please call me*. Suddenly, the doorbell rang. I flew out of my bedroom.

I wasn't fast enough. My father was standing in front of the half-opened door as if his hand were glued to the knob. He was staring at Roy's stringy black hair and leather jacket.

I wrested the door from my father's death grip. "Dad, this is Roy." Seeing the horror on his face, I decided to be nice and reassure him. "I met him at church."

My father eyed the tattoos on Roy's fingers, which I think now might have been jailhouse ink.

"We're going up to my room," I said to my father.

Use your real estate wisely, his look said.

For the next three weeks, Roy came over every evening after dinner, which was exactly when I was supposed to be studying.

"He'd better not be here late, sis," my father said every time. But Roy always was.

Lately, an anger had been building inside me—about the government threatening to take us away, about the many times we'd had to move, about the expired fire insurance and our never having enough money. I used to think my father was a special kind of dad, but now I could see all the ways he'd fucked up.

"I don't care what the old boy thinks," I later wrote in my journal. I'd lost respect for him.

The evening before my big science exam, Roy took my books from me. I'd spread them out on the bed with the intention of studying.

"Don't let me stop you," he said with a smirk, hiding the books behind him. As I tried to reach them, he pulled me close, trying to tickle me. I wriggled away. Then he caught me by the hand, and my whole body flushed.

"I wanna get a tattoo of your name," he said, looking into my eyes.

On his upper arm, through the crisscross scars of a razor blade, I could still make out four letters: NORA.

"No way," I said. Secretly, though, I was thrilled.

After he left—late for a school night—I put my head down on my pillow. It seemed that only a minute passed before my father was hollering at me to get up. He drove me to school so I wouldn't be late, but just as we were pulling up, the bell rang.

I'd been a straight-A student, but I failed my science exam that day, and math soon after that. I was in charge of more than my own real estate: both Brad and I were in charge of our own schooling. So, my father didn't notice that my marks were plummeting.

When I stopped caring about school *and* about being a Jesus Freak— both at once, strangely—Rev noticed. One day, when I'd forgotten to avoid the church side of the street, he hurried down the stone steps toward me in his black coat and backward white collar.

"We haven't seen you at church for a while," he said. His hair and sideburns had grown longer since I'd last seen him—probably too long for his conservative congregation.

"Um, no, I—sorry, Rev." My feelings were a mix of guilt and regret. I missed the times his eyes used to crinkle with a smile for me. Now his brow was creased with concern.

"And we've missed you at our outreach."

I thought of the coffeehouse and the girl with the black hair. "Does Suzee still go?"

"Suzee?" He peered at me so intently, it was like he was looking through my skin. "No, I haven't seen her in a while." He put a firm hand on my arm as if to pull me back to his side. "I'm taking our youth group to the Catacombs on Thursday. Can you come?"

"I'll try," I said, but I didn't mean it. I would never go to the Catacombs again.

Just as I was about to cross the street, he called me back one last time. "Did that letter I sent help your dad?"

"We haven't heard anything," I said. "It must be good news, right?"

The day I turned fifteen, my father bought me two T-bone steaks for a fancy dinner I planned to make for Roy. Then he and Brad set up the trays to eat their TV dinners in front of the television. When the doorbell rang, I shut them inside the living room.

Seeing Roy there, with his long black hair and round, dark eyes, I felt my heart throb fiercely. The fact that he kept coming around, week after week, after I'd repeatedly pushed away his wandering hands, seemed like a declaration of love. Roy's affection had given me a confidence I'd never known. So, when he seemed distant that evening, I put it out of my head at first.

I didn't realize at the time that there were two competing stories going on in my head—one forged by my mother's leaving, the other by my father's staying. One said I wasn't worth much; the other said I was worth everything. Having a boyfriend like Roy was making me believe my father's version of me: lovable after all.

But that night, something was wrong. I thought it would go away, but I could feel a tautness in the air between Roy and me. Roy pulled out a chair for himself, but instead of sitting where he could watch me at the stove, he kept his back to me. As I laid out the steaks in a pan hot with butter, the way my father had instructed me, he drummed his fingers on the table.

"Are you mad at me?" I was so scared, I could only whisper.

"I don't want to say anything, because it's your birthday."

"Tell me, please, what is it?"

"We can talk tomorrow."

"Did I do something wrong?"

Roy stopped drumming. "Here's the thing," he said. "Nora wants me back."

His words cut right into me.

"Are you okay?" he said.

"I'm fine." I turned to the stove. I had to keep from crying in front of him. "I just need to cook the steaks."

"I should go," Roy said.

I didn't trust myself to answer. He left. Turning the burner off, I hurtled myself into the living room. Brad and my father looked up in surprise.

"Is your dinner over already?"

I sank to my knees. The two of them stared at me, stricken.

"That sonofabitch." My father pounded his fist into his palm. "Who does he think he is, hurting my daughter?"

Brad stroked my hair as I sobbed. "Lor, it's okay."

"He's not worth your little finger," said my father.

If only I'd been able to hear those words.

What does a young girl learn the first time her heart is ripped in two? That the first cut hurts the most? That a boy you cry about today may surprise you on your doorstep tomorrow? (As Roy would three years later, earning extra jail time for breaking parole to hitchhike across five provinces to see me.)

That you need to leave them before they leave you?

In time, I would learn all those things. But at that moment, I felt like my father's love had tricked me into thinking I was worth loving. And now Roy had shown me I wasn't.

CHAPTER 21

LOSING MY RELIGION

BRAMPTON, 1973

"THIS STUFF IS A DRUG," my father said, pointing to the piles of packages on the counter.

"Oh, there's a great sales pitch."

"People get addicted to it, you know."

"Tell that to your customers," I said. My father's customers were restaurants, to which he was selling what, back in 1973, passed for specialty coffee.

"I wouldn't thank you for a cup of that. I haven't touched a drop since the war."

"I know, Dad. You told us."

"I thought I was afraid to go into battle. But it was only the goddamned coffee."

"Yeah, the coffee and not the guns shooting at you."

"The minute I gave it up, I stopped being nervous."

"Great. Let's tell the army we've got the secret to braver soldiers."

"Anyway, who the hell needs something you can get addicted to?"

In my father's worldview, my mother was a double addict: coffee *and* cigarettes. *You really need that, don't you, Helen?* he used to say while handing her an ashtray and her second morning cup.

Judging by his poor coffee sales, my father didn't have the right attitude for the java business. "What are we going to do for money now?" I asked him.

"Swimming pools!"

"In Brampton, where it's winter nine months of the year?" I rolled my eyes. "That's it. I'm getting a job."

We hadn't heard back from child protective services since Rev wrote his letter, but when we did, I figured it would look good for me to be bringing in some money. By lying about my age, I managed to get hired on as an after-school cashier at Kmart. In my father's eyes, it was a huge step down. He'd dreamed of me at the helm of my own international business, so he thought this job was beneath me. But he was happy when I stopped asking for my allowance.

One evening, I was getting ready to close out my cash desk when I saw Suzee weaving through the aisles. She was as arresting as the night I'd seen her in the coffeehouse.

"Hey, man. I remember you," she said a few minutes later, laying down a pack of tampons on my conveyor belt. (It didn't occur to me until I knew her better that she'd probably shoplifted something else of far greater value.) "Wanna go for a drink after your shift?"

I almost looked around to see who she was talking to. Unless they were my cousins, people as cool as Suzee generally didn't strike up conversations with me.

After work, we walked back through Kmart to the mall entrance. Just outside the dressing rooms, I caught sight of the two of us in a mirror. Her reflection was dramatic: white skin, red lips, black hair, black eyes. Then there was me: dark, medium-long hair parted in the middle; wire-framed glasses; a loose shirt to hide my tummy. I had no place being in the same mirror as her.

We went to a bar where they didn't check ID. I looked older than fifteen, and Suzee, at seventeen, was nearly legal anyway. She ordered a Tom Collins for each of us. Sweet and lemony, it went down like pop and made me feel warm and fuzzy.

"You ever go back to the coffeehouse?" I asked her.

"I'm not welcome there, man." Suzee fixed me with her black eyes. "Rev converted some witches—and now, like, he's getting death threats from the rest of the coven. He thinks I'm one of them."

"Are you?"

"Yeah, man." She chuckled. "But I didn't write the letters."

"You're a witch? So is my aunt Dixie."

"Is she a black witch or a white witch?"

I thought of my aunt's tarot cards and seances and sightings of dead people. "She says she's a white witch."

Suzee scoffed. "I'm a black witch."

When the bill came, Suzee paid, as she always would. With the exception of my clothes, which she would liberally help herself to, she would ask little of me, leaving me to wonder, *What does she really want?*

A week later, Suzee and I were hitchhiking to the mall when a couple of hippies stopped for us in their souped-up Beetle.

"You wanna do some weed?" The guy in the passenger seat turned to look at Suzee and me, squeezed into the back.

I shook my head. "I don't do drugs."

Suzee elbowed me hard. "Yeah, man. Lay it on us." As I would discover, where drugs were concerned, Suzee didn't fool around.

The boys pulled into a parking lot off Queen Street and lit up.

"Gimme a hit," Suzee said. She reached for the joint, inhaled, then passed it to me.

It seemed like a small thing. Besides, God wouldn't mind: He'd made it. I put the joint to my lips.

That night, I wrote in my diary, "Wow man, far out, I'm ripped out of my head. I acted straight, so I don't think the old man noticed."

After that, I started skipping classes to smoke pot.

One afternoon, Suzee showed up at the front door unannounced. "I have a present for you." She opened her hand. Inside was a little baggie of white powder.

I grabbed her arm. My father was right there in the kitchen! I pulled her upstairs and closed my bedroom door behind us.

"What is it?"

"A dime bag," she said. "Brampton's so dry, man. It's harder to get weed right now than it is to get this speed."

"I'm not going to do speed!"

"Trust me. If you like weed, you're gonna love this." She must have seen the fear on my face. "It's no big deal. You'll just feel full of energy and have a really good time." She laughed. "It's perfectly safe. Except for the speed rapping. You might talk your head off." She dropped the baggie on the bed beside me.

I jumped up. It scared me to even have it there when my father could just walk in.

"Then *I'll* do it." She snatched the baggie back and tucked it into her purse.

"Are you mad at me?"

"Just forget it." She grabbed a sweater from my closet and left.

Thursday morning, after a night spent fearing I'd lost Suzee, she phoned to invite me to her apartment for the next evening. I had just put the receiver back on its hook when I got a call from my supervisor, who wanted me to work an hour later on Friday evening. To my surprise, I said no. In a short time, Suzee had become more important to me than God, than school—and now even more than work.

Back in my room, my *Jesus Christ Superstar* posters seemed to belong to a different person. I took them down one by one, then put away my Christian books. I thought it was temporary: I didn't admit even to myself that I was leaving the church. But I had finally found a place where I fit in—with the druggies. And Suzee was always there to make the introductions.

The next morning, my father brought me breakfast in bed. Lately, his trick to rouse me for school was to put the plate or bowl into my hands so I'd have to wake up or get food all over myself.

He raised his eyebrows as he registered the stark look of my room without my books and posters. "Doing some redecorating, are we?"

"Now that I'm not on that religious 'kick,' as you call it, you should be happy."

He looked anything but happy.

After my shift that night, I went out to the highway that runs from the Shoppers World mall right into Brampton. It was dark. When I was a Jesus Freak, I wouldn't have given a second thought to hitchhiking alone at night. Now that I no longer believed in God, there was no one to protect me. I moved to stand by the light of the gas station: I needed to see who was picking me up before I got into the car.

I wouldn't always be so lucky, but that night, my ride took me straight to my destination.

Suzee buzzed me in. Her mother was at work. She worked a lot, Suzee told me. I couldn't help comparing her apartment to the grand brick house I lived in. Her place was small and surprisingly ordinary. I'd expected something exotic, like her.

"You're gonna love this," she said, leading me into the bathroom.

I perched on the edge of the bathtub. She wet white powder in the bowl of a bent spoon and stirred it. She held up a length of rubber tubing. "You can't trust anyone but me to shoot you up." She wrapped the tourniquet around my arm and tied it. "I'm not great at tying off, but don't worry, I'm the best hitter around." She picked up a needle, stuck the point into the bowl of the spoon, and pulled the plunger back. Then she held the barrel up and flicked it with her index finger. "That's good. No bubbles. They could kill you."

I was scared, but the speed was already in the needle. *Please don't do this. Please still be my friend.*

She examined the soft inside of my arm, then tightened the tourniquet until it hurt. "I've got to get your veins to pop." She tapped my skin with two fingers. After a moment, she said, "Your arms are too fat. I can't get the main line. But I can get this other vein."

What do you think when you're fifteen, when someone sinks a needle full of drugs into your arm? You see her black eyes blazing, and you wonder what the hell you're doing and why she looks so excited. Then the drug escapes from the tip of the needle into your vein. You are flooded with warmth, a tidal wave of fire. You are safe, you are loved, and no one will hurt you. You are flying.

From my warm cloud, I became aware of her jabbing at her own arm. The needle seemed to bounce off her skin. "Fucking calluses." Again, she tried to jam the point through. "Fuuuuck," Suzee screamed. "Fuckfuckfuck! I have to find another place." She grabbed her kit and went somewhere else. When she came back, she'd stopped swearing and had a spot of blood on her neck.

I put my hands on the cold sink to check myself out in the mirror. My pupils were huge and my skin blotchy. My pulse was racing. I felt alive, awake, clear. Suddenly, Suzee was pulling on me.

"You have to go, man. My mom's coming home."

"What? What should I do?"

"Don't worry, man. You just have to go, that's all."

I had to get my head together. I had to find the door. I thought she would help me, but she put on some headphones and started to dance. I let myself out.

It was just a few blocks to our house on Mill Street, but I was too jittery. A car passed, a white BMW. Paranoid, I thought it was my cousin Joanne, and I jumped into the bushes. When I finally got home, I slipped inside the door jangling like a set of keys. I grabbed my sweater from the front hall to cover myself up. My arms were scratched from the bushes and bleeding from the needle.

My father was in the kitchen. "Hungry? I kept your dinner."

Act straight, act straight, I told myself. "No, not hungry, couldn't eat a thing, Dad, can't even think about food." I meant to be low-key, but I just couldn't stop talking. "What did you make? What is that—liver and onions? I hate liver and onions. Don't you remember? Brad does, too. Hates it. You can't make a nine-year-old eat that stuff. I don't even understand why you made it."

My father sighed. "Where is the daughter who used to look up to her old daddy? Now it seems the older *you* get, the dumber *I* get."

"I don't know what you mean, old man."

"*That's* what I mean. You don't respect me anymore."

Later that night, the drugs began to evacuate my system. Why hadn't Suzee told me about coming down? It was the worst sensation I had ever experienced. My body felt like a jagged, empty cavern. There was a yowling inside me. I had to do something. My father was sleeping, so I slipped my clothes back on. I was sure to find someone in the park to give me some drugs, any kind of drugs. I just needed something to take the place of the ones that were leaving me. Only later would I learn to pillage Valium from my uncle Brian's prescription samples.

The next day, my father received a letter saying that the government was sending a social worker to our house.

"This is your fault," I said to him, and raged up the stairs to write in my diary.

I'd given my diary a name: Sam. Writing to Sam made me feel like I had someone to confide in, especially when the troubles at school began.

May 10. Oh Sam, what am I going to do? I skipped school again today. I can't make myself go! I bummed around Shoppers, got a fast motorcycle ride, went to Bramalea City Centre. I did a downer (30 cents) with my Tom Collins & was it ever a good stone.

May 14. Sam, help me please! I skipped school today, at about 7 I went into Obies & saw 2 guys sitting there. I sat down & got a Tom Collins, took a downer, & got stoned.

May 15. Hi Sam! Had a talk with Costigan, the guidance counselor & dad & everything's cool. I have to keep going to school, but that's all right.

I'll have to work hard. I mean really hard. We can do it, Sam! Today I bought Brad a gerbil for his birthday. Went to the show with Dad & Brad.

May 16. Hi Sam. Skipped only 2 classes today. I'm buckling down.

May 18. Hi Sam. Costigan called me up to the office & did I ever get shit for skipping again. He was furious! Swearing, banging his fist on the desk . . . I cried almost all 1st period.

May 23. Hi Sam. Today I missed school, and Costigan gave Dad shit. Big fight between Dad & Uncle Brian.

I didn't think about the repercussions of putting all this down in black and white until I came home to voices in the kitchen. I peeked in. A young woman with fine blond hair was holding a clipboard against her chest. I thought of Candy. What if the social worker discovered my diary? What if she spoke to my school? What if she saw the needle tracks on my arm?

I walked into the kitchen determined to show her I was a normal teenager living in a normal home. Just then, I heard my father say to her, "Do you find being so beautiful an asset or a handicap?"

I wanted to kill him. He was using his old chat line at the worst possible time. She'd see through it and know he was trying to win her over.

Amazingly, the social worker looked pleased. She put her hand up to cover her mouth as she laughed.

My father shot me a triumphant look. "Lori, this is Miss . . ."

He'd forgotten her name. *Oh God.* We were sunk.

"Miss Clark." She inserted her pen into the spring of the clipboard. "Thank you for your time," she said to my father. "The letter from Reverend Williams was supportive of you continuing to care for your children. This visit was more of a formality. Everything seems in order."

A short time later, Suzee came over to the house with her mascara running. "Man, I really want to quit speed." She threw herself down on my bed. "I just don't know how. I've tried everything."

"I thought you said we couldn't get addicted."

"Well, we can't. But it's tooooooo good to give up."

I hadn't thought about stopping. But I had begun to question whether the high compensated for the shards of glass you felt in your bloodstream when you were crashing. There had to be better drugs.

"We'll quit together," I said.

That wasn't the answer she was looking for.

"Oh, forget it. I gotta split." Grabbing one of my shirts off a hanger, she ran down the stairs and out the front door.

Two nights later, Suzee hit me up again, then hit herself between her toes.

My own speed high was on the wane when I walked into the house. I had some of my uncle's Valium upstairs in my room. If I took enough, I'd be able to sleep tonight. I went into the kitchen for a glass of orange juice, which was supposed to help you come down. I could tell my father had just mixed it up from the Minute Maid can, because it still had ice crystals in it.

"Did you have a good time?" he called from the living room. He would always ask that, as if my happiness were all that counted.

I went to where he was lying on the couch watching TV, which he did every night. He had no friends, no girlfriend. He was living for Brad and me. Since the episode with Sue, he was always around when we got home.

"Yeah, I had a good time."

"Sweet dreams, then." His voice was sleepy. "And don't ever forget that you're special. There's no one like you in the whole world."

"Thanks, Dad. There's no one like you, either."

"I'm going to bed," he said, getting up from the couch with a little grunt from the effort. In that moment, I felt an unbearable tenderness for him.

CHAPTER 22

REBEL, REBEL

BRAMPTON, 1973

QUITTING SPEED TURNED OUT to be easy. I simply replaced it with other drugs: LSD, MDA, mescaline, weed, magic mushrooms. In the early seventies, there was so much for a fifteen-year-old girl to choose from.

I would never know if Suzee managed to kick the habit. I was coming to suspect that the only thing she liked about me was seeing the reflection of herself in my eyes. The next time she called me to get stoned, I told her I was trying not to flunk my school year. I would meet her only once more, months later, when she was downtown dealing acid.

Late one evening, I was sneaking in, trying not to wake anyone, when my father came out of the dining room in his underwear. I wasn't too high to see how worried he looked.

"I realize now I've lost control of you." He gave a slow, sad shake of his head.

I didn't know what to say. I'd lost control of me, too.

My daughter has nothing to rebel against, I'd often heard him boast. *I put her in charge of her own real estate.*

But if I wasn't rebelling against my father, who was I trying to hurt?

We both believed there was a limit to how far I would let myself go. After all, I'd stopped short of getting addicted to speed. And now, despite the other drugs and the drinking, I had managed to pass most of my grade-nine subjects.

After school let out, Brad left to spend the summer in Red Lake with our mother and Art. I'd refused to go. Our boarder had moved out, so it was just me and my father. We knocked around our brick-solid home angry and disappointed with each other in ways we didn't know how to articulate.

August promised a reprieve from the tension: Bev's parents were letting her visit for the month. She arrived in Toronto on one of those muggy summer evenings. It was the first time she'd traveled alone. I'd missed her so much. In her honor, I'd organized an acid party.

My father had laid out potato chips and Cokes on the front porch as if this were a kid's birthday. Bev and I and a few of the druggies from the park—Rusty, Pelican, Dave, Trudy, Angel—sat on the porch railing in the wafting summer heat. No one touched the food: the others were already too stoned on hard stuff, and Bev and I were too keyed up.

My father opened the door to the porch wearing his pajama bottoms and a graying Fruit of the Loom undershirt. He surveyed the park kids with dismay. "I'm going to bed now. You all be good." He fixed me with his eyes. "Lor, you keep a lid on things. I'm trusting you."

Everyone knew that was the last thing he should be doing.

My father shut the door, leaving us outside on our own. I turned to Rusty. A heroin addict with rotting teeth, he gave a smoker's rattle of a chuckle. I put my hand out. Rusty laid a pill in my palm. I broke it in two with my nail and offered half to Bev.

"I don't know, Lor."

"Come on. You'll love it." I spoke the way my father would when trying to drum up enthusiasm from Brad and me. "It'll be a trip."

"That's what I'm afraid of."

Bev swallowed her doubts along with the acid.

"You'll see. This is good shit," said Trudy, a plain seventeen-year-old whose eyes were all pupil, like Suzee's had been. She smelled like weed and cherry lip gloss.

Bev went off to sit by herself on the steps. She was wearing bell-bottoms and a new halter top that she'd bought for the trip. Her hair was freshly washed. Even when you're planning to get wasted, you want to look good. Or, at least, I did. Bev was just following along, easygoing to the end.

I didn't know how much time had passed when Bev was suddenly at my side, clutching my arm. "Lori, look! The walls are melting."

I'd noticed that, too. Luckily, Bev hadn't seen the chestnut tree, dropping its leaves in a continuous shower of green.

"I don't like this, LoriLove," Bev said. "Can you make it stop?"

"It's okay, Bev." I decided not to tell her that her face was melting, too.

My cousin didn't have as much experience with drugs as I did. It should have occurred to me that she was in trouble. It should have occurred to me to help her. My life would have turned out differently if I had.

Sometime later, I thought I saw Bev down on her hands and knees, going into the house. I would find out the next day that she had crawled into the dining room, where my father was sleeping, whispering into the darkness, "Uncle Dacker, I think I'm having a bad trip."

The morning after the acid party, I crept downstairs, leaving Bev asleep in the next room. I hoped I could get something to eat without running into my father, but he was sitting at the kitchen table fully dressed.

"I finally got your cousin settled down," he said. "Now, you'd better get packing."

I whipped around to face him. "What are you talking about?"

"We're moving to your uncle Don's." His voice was so calm, it scared me.

"This is a joke, right?"

"Oh no. I heard about your little LSD party. I am getting you the hell away from Brampton. You're in with some bad elements."

"No way! I'm not going to move in with Uncle Don." My father's older brother lived in a shack two hours southwest. "I'm not going anywhere."

"Yes, you are."

He couldn't be serious. Leave our home? Again? "We can't just go. My school is here. And my job at Kmart."

"For your information, they have schools in London. We'll stay with my brother until we find somewhere to live."

Unlike London, England, there was nothing cool about London, Ontario. And my family there was poor. "Even Uncle Don says his place is a dump. And you want to move there just because I tried a little acid with my friends?"

"Yes, that was delightful, seeing my darling daughter with those dregs of humanity." He crossed his arms over his chest.

"Give me another chance." I pointed at his tattoos, sloppily drawn in red and black. "You did stupid things when you were young."

"Bev's going home tomorrow, so you'd better pack your things, missy. We're moving on Friday, when Brad gets back from your mother's."

"We're moving on *Friday*? Are you insane?"

I couldn't believe this was happening to me. We were living in the best house we'd ever called home. The boarders were gone, the government wasn't going to take Brad and me away, and I was finally making friends.

"Friday," my father said, and got up from the table. I had never seen him so firm. I'd never seen him firm at all.

I followed him into the dining room. On the floor was an apple crate with some of my little brother's clothes inside.

I pulled on my father's sleeve. "Please don't make us move again. I promise I won't see those people anymore."

"Oh, don't worry. You won't be seeing them. Not when we're living somewhere else."

I let go of him. "You're crazy if you think this is going to stop me from doing drugs."

He shook his head. "I don't know what the hell else to do with you." Then he picked up a pair of Brad's gym shorts and threw them into the crate. "You'd better get your stuff together."

"I hate you!"

I ran up the stairs to my bedroom and slammed the door. Throwing myself on my bed, I prayed through my tears, *Please, God, please, God.* I slid to my knees on the floor. *Don't make me leave.*

But if there was a God, I'd burned that bridge.

I took out my diary, my one remaining confidant. "Fuck fuck fuck," I wrote. "I just found out I have to move to London. And live in a fucking shack!"

A lifetime had passed since I'd inscribed the first page of my diary with flower petals dotting my i's. I was a child then, just eight months earlier.

My father promised he would never read my diary, but what about now, when he knew I'd had an acid party? I didn't want him to see all those entries I'd written since I'd crossed the street from the church to hang out in the park. For months, my diary had been filled with a hopped-up scrawl, my writing fueled by more drugs than my father could have imagined. I would put an *S* beside days when I was stoned and a *D* for days when I was drunk. "Fuuuuuuuck, I'm sooooooo ripped!" For the last few months, most of my entries started with either an *S* or a *D*, sometimes both. It had taken my father a long time to notice, but I *had* fallen in with a bad crowd.

I hid my journal between my mattress and box spring. The next day, we took Bev to Union Station to catch her train. I felt sad to see her slipping away from me.

"I'm sorry, LoriLove," she said, but the hug she gave me was cool. Then she added, "You just shouldn't do some of the things you do. You're going to get yourself in trouble."

I winced at her disapproval. Unlike everyone else in my life, she'd never criticized me before. I didn't know what to say. And then she walked away from me. I watched her move down the platform, her hands in the pockets of her softball jacket. She didn't turn back.

By Friday morning, I'd erased every sign of myself from my bedroom. Gone were my clothes, my books, my makeup. The old lady's furniture was put back the way it was when we first rented the house. I pulled my diary out from under the mattress and tucked it into my purse. I whispered goodbye to our house: the solid red bricks, the white front porch, the chestnut tree whose leaves tickled the second-floor bedroom windows.

When it was time to go, I couldn't stand to get into the front seat next to my father, so I climbed into the back and slammed the van's sliding door loud enough to express my feelings. My father and I drove in angry silence down Mill Street to Queen. On our right was my old church, St. Paul's. I thought about Rev, with his dimpled cheeks and eyes that creased when he smiled. Although I hadn't seen him since the social worker's visit, I realized now how much I would miss him. Across from St. Paul's was Gage Park, my home after I left Rev's church. I imagined I saw Suzee, though she would never have been out in daylight.

Our first stop was Toronto airport. Brad was coming back from Red Lake, where I'd refused to go because I hated my mother's husband. Art smoked, he opened beer bottles with his teeth, he said things like "I seen." He was nothing like my father. But that wasn't why I hated him. I hated him because every time my mother chose to be with him and not me, it was like he was taking her away all over again.

My father pulled onto the shoulder of the highway. We would wait there for Brad's plane to land so we wouldn't have to pay for parking. He said he'd know which Air Canada jet my brother was on, and that once it flew over, we'd walk to the terminal to get him.

My father caught my eye in the rearview mirror. "At least I'm getting you away from your drug dealer."

"You don't think they have drug dealers in London? Because I promise you, I'll find them."

Behind me, everything that hadn't perished in our house fire the year before was once again packed up in cardboard boxes. Somewhere back there were my old Christian books. I'd glimpsed *The Late Great Planet Earth*, which my father had brought even though he ridiculed it for predicting that the world would end in 1988.

"There's Brad's plane!" My father took the key from the ignition.

"How can you tell it's his?" I demanded. I slid over to the door all the same. At least my brother still cared about me. As I got out of the van, I grabbed the doomsday book. I would dump it in an airport garbage can. The rest of the Christian books I would throw out when we got to my uncle's.

It turned out that it hadn't been Brad's plane after all; his had come in much earlier. Fortunately, he was still at the gate, scanning the terminal for us. Standing there with his suitcase in his hand, he looked small and frightened.

"Brad!" I waved. His hippie locks were gone, replaced by a short, little-boy cut—my mother's doing.

"Are we going back to the house first?" he asked my father, ignoring me. "I want to say goodbye to my friends."

"No, son. We're going straight to your uncle Don's."

"To the hellhole," I said.

For a moment, I pitied Brad, caught between the two tornadoes that were my father and me. Then I went back to feeling sorry for myself.

"Come on, son." My father picked up Brad's suitcase. "We're going to have a big adventure—thanks to your sister."

I gave my father my dirtiest look.

"Brad, let's sit in the back," I said when we got to the van. "Far away from the old man." I rolled the sliding door open.

"No thanks," he said. "I'm sitting with Dad."

He was angry with me. Brad, who never complained about anything, never made a fuss, was angry with me. I was shocked.

My father started the van.

A sweater flew over from the front seat and landed on me. "Mom asked me to give that to you," Brad said. "She knit it."

I deposited the sweater on the floor by my feet.

As the VW rumbled onto the highway, I leaned against the cool glass and felt the vibrations on my cheek. We were heading southwest toward the city where my parents first met. We passed Lake Ontario, and the turn-off to Kincardine, the town my mother had run away from. London was only a two-hour drive from Brampton, but it felt like the end of the world.

Every turn of our wheels was taking us farther away from our beautiful house.

My fear of losing my home had come true. But it wasn't the government who was taking us away.

"I hate you," I said, looking at my reflection.

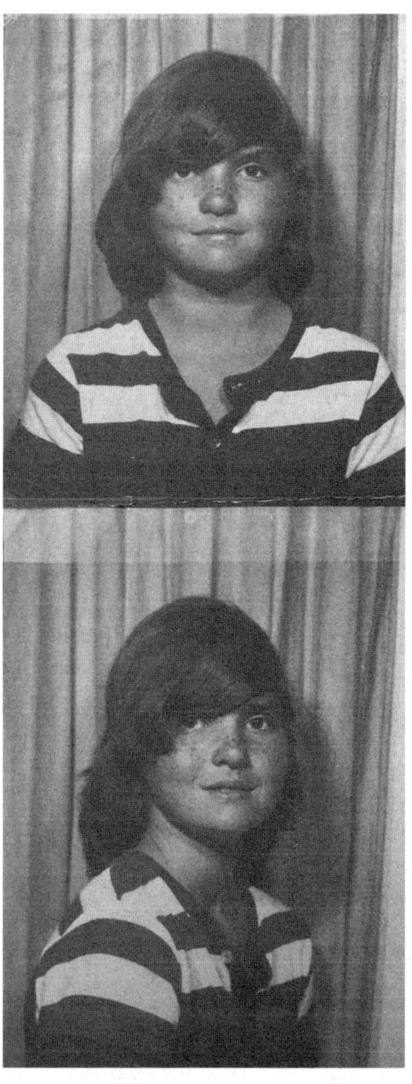

Brad, Brampton, 1973

CHAPTER 23

THE SHACK

LONDON, 1973

MEADOWLILY ROAD—THE NAME EVOKED wildflowers and green pastures. Instead, we turned onto a dirt track lined by spindly trees and ugly, neglected houses.

"Here we are, kids," my father said, his tone flat. He must have known there was no use trying to drum up any excitement as we juddered down the long driveway, which was potholed and muddy from a recent rain. We stopped outside the shabbiest house on Meadowlily Road.

"Make yourself useful," my father said to me. "Carry something inside."

I climbed down from the van. My white Adidas shoes sank into the mud as far as the stripes on the sides. "Oh, great," I said. "You made us leave our home for *this*?"

"If I were you, I wouldn't complain." I wasn't sure if he said that because I was the reason we were here or because grumbling was one of his few red lines.

In this family, we don't complain. You don't like something, change it.

But I was fifteen; what could I change? My father was acting like he had done something loving by moving me out of Brampton, but I was planning on making my disagreement clear.

I picked up a box of clothes from the back. Carrying the lightest load I could get away with, I purposely tracked mud into the house. *You clean the fucking floor*, I thought.

I had never been to the house my uncle bought after his wife left, so I didn't appreciate how bad things were until my eyes grew accustomed to the dark. Then I saw that, inside, our new home was even more of a construction site than outside. The walls were bare boards with strips of pink insulation tacked on. Plastic was stapled over the windows. The floor was raw planks.

"Dad, you've got to be kidding," I whispered as he came in behind me, stepping in my mud. "This is just a trick to scare me, right? And now we're going back home?"

He put the boxes down. "This is the bed you made, sis."

At that moment, I would even have gone back to Kirkland Lake. Anywhere but here.

"You and your son can sleep on the pullout couch," my uncle said by way of welcome. He had the same long nose as my father, same stocky build. I remembered him as always speaking in a gentle, almost meek voice, but he seemed to have grown hard. "As for you, young lady, Cal is giving you his bedroom upstairs. You might want to thank him."

I wasn't in the mood to thank anyone. I was just about to say so when my cousin Cal grabbed my arm.

"C'mon," he said, dragging me away before I made a scene. "Let me show you my room."

Cal had a round face, like me and Brad and most of the cousins. His hair was short and parted on the side—more A student than hippie. We went up the narrow staircase to where his room was tucked under a slanted ceiling. It was little bigger than his single bed, but at least it had a door. I looked to him with gratitude. But I was still too angry to say thank you. I think he understood.

Suddenly, he put his finger to his lips. "Keith's in there," he whispered, motioning to the door across the hall. "I'd keep out of his way if I were you."

I was fine with keeping out of Keith's way. I remembered Cal's older brother as a glowering, moody man.

"Cal, where will *you* sleep?"

"I'm staying with my girlfriend's parents till I finish high school." He was three years older than me.

"Don't you mind giving me your bedroom?"

"Listen, I'll tell you a little secret. I don't want to be here any more than you do."

The minute I finished eating dinner that night, I got up from the table, craving the refuge of Cal's room.

"Come back and carry your dishes to the sink," my uncle ordered. He used to hide candies around his house for Brad and me to find. He used to be *that* kind of uncle.

I'd changed as well. "You can't tell me what to do."

"I sure as hell can."

"Lori, Don, calm down," my father said. "You'll disturb the neighbors."

"What neighbors?" I snorted. "One of those other shacks?"

Keith's chair scraped along the floor, and he loomed over me, dark and angular. "What are you even doing here, you ungrateful little bitch?"

"You leave my daughter alone, you nutcase."

"Don't you call my son a nutcase."

"Don, why do you let him act like this?" My father wedged himself between me and Keith. "Stop being such a milquetoast."

The vein in Keith's neck throbbed. "Don't you call my dad a milquetoast." He pushed himself up against my father's chest.

"Son, son," my uncle Don said. It was like trying to placate a hurricane.

Keith was bristling. "You get out of my face," he said to me.

"Gladly," I shot back.

He walked out, slamming the door so hard, the plastic on the windows shuddered.

Brad, who had left the table as soon as the trouble started, turned the volume up on the television.

"This is the worst thing you've ever done," I said to my father, then ran up the stairs to Cal's old bedroom. I put *Goodbye Yellow Brick Road* on the turntable and dropped the needle into the groove. Keith hadn't come back, so I cranked it up. The music drowned out the sounds of my father and uncle arguing below—and my thoughts of Brad in front of the television trying to make himself small.

It was late August: time to register for classes. Brad went along like a good little soldier, but I dreaded being the new kid in yet another school. To get us ready, my father bought Brad a sweater, jeans, and a T-shirt. For me, he organized a pair of contact lenses and a packet of birth control pills.

"I don't need the Pill," I said to the doctor my father had found. "I'm a virgin—and I plan to stay one."

With better foresight than mine, my father asked her to write me a prescription anyway. It would turn out that contraception was the only type of insurance he believed in.

Now that I'd replaced my glasses with contact lenses, I stopped lowering my head to cover my face with my hair. But the confidence of contacts had come too late. I no longer cared about making friends: I wasn't planning to be around for long. As for drugs, I didn't know who to buy them from or who to do them with—so in that way, at least, my father had been right.

From the start of grade ten, I skipped as many classes as I went to. My marks, which had begun to wobble in Brampton, now went over a cliff. I blamed my father—and whoever had talked me into signing up for Latin. I was angry at everyone, except for Brad. Him I felt sorry for. His life had been ruined, too.

My father didn't realize how much school I was missing. He was busy working an angle, as he called it. He'd managed to buy an old black pickup truck, and now he was advertising his services to cut down trees (where did he learn to do that?), deliver firewood (from those same trees), and haul away junk (or, as he called it, "unwanted household items"). Soon he was colonizing my uncle's kitchen table with slips of paper scrawled with phone numbers and no other identifying information as he tried to remember whose number that was and why he'd written it down. I didn't know how he made any money like that.

And if he wasn't making money, how were we ever going to get out of here?

If not for Keith, life at Meadowlily Road might have been close to tolerable. When he was angry, he'd prowl the house itching for a fight: *What are you looking at, you little bitch?* But when he was happy, it was worse. Wired up, boisterous, he'd find me reading quietly and belt some pop song right into my ear. I couldn't wait to grow up so that I could get away. You were supposed to be eighteen to leave home. But how could I last three more years?

That week, when I was making one of my rare appearances at school, my social studies teacher handed me a note. Usually, a note meant being called in to see the principal. I unfolded the paper with trepidation. I wasn't being sent to the office; I was being sent to the school psychologist. I shoved the note into the pocket of my jeans and planned to play hooky on the day of the appointment.

My cousin Cal also knew I was in a bad place, and he gave me the address of a party he'd heard about, probably so I could make some friends.

"Don't you want to come with me?" I asked him.

"Nah. I'm having dinner with my girlfriend's parents."

It was either another Saturday night with Keith, who didn't appear to have any friends at all, or a party where I didn't know anyone. I decided to go. Maybe there'd be some drugs.

My father was lying on the couch watching television with my brother when I came downstairs in my best outfit: a black satin shirt, bell-bottom jeans, and a new pair of silver slingback shoes.

"I'm going to a party."

He sat up with a grunt. "I'm glad to see you're finally making some friends. Have fun."

"Why don't *you* ever go out, Dad?"

"I've got my kids. What more do I need?"

I thought it an odd thing for him to say, considering I barely talked to him anymore.

I took the bus into town and found the address Cal had given me. The door was opened by a tall Cree who was one of the popular kids in my high school. Chogan had high cheekbones and honey skin. I gave him a wide smile even though I knew he was out of my league.

"You can leave your shoes here," he said, pointing to a collection on the floor.

"I have to take off my shoes?" I looked slimmer with the extra height my heels gave me.

"I'm just following orders."

I peeked into the living room and saw that everyone was in their stocking feet. What kind of preppy party was this? Sighing, I dropped my silver shoes on top of the pile. Now that my feet were bare, I wished I'd shaved the wisps of hair on my big toes.

But no one noticed me or my hairy toes. The other kids were sitting, probably stoned, on one long couch or talking in clutches in the kitchen, drinking out of red plastic cups. I tried to join a group standing by the fridge; their eyes flicked over me before they went back to talking to each other. *Fuck it.* I decided to go home.

The pile at the door had grown. I began to root around for my shoes. But my hands kept coming up empty. I took out every pair and lined them up. That's when I got frantic.

I found Chogan in the kitchen. "My shoes! They're gone!"

"They can't be gone," he said. But they were.

"How can you steal someone's *shoes*?" I'd lost things before, but this felt like a violation.

I should have asked to use the phone. My father would have come to get me in a heartbeat. The rest of the time, he was probably in over his head with me, but this was the kind of parenting he knew how to do: pick me up, take me places. I was getting the crazy idea, though, that I was going to make it through this mess on my own.

In every other way, my life was out of my control. But now I saw something I could do. I could get myself home in my bare feet. It excited me, thinking how I would manage it. My father had always said I could do anything, and now I was going to prove it.

The minute I hit the sidewalk I realized my stupid mistake. The pavement was a shock of cold, and I felt every piece of dirt on my bare soles: the grit and cigarette butts, the dog turds and chewing gum. I tried to avoid as much as I could, but everywhere was filthy. I felt naked and defenseless.

The bus stop wasn't far. I told myself if I could just get on the bus, I'd be fine.

"Hey—" the bus driver said when I boarded with my dirty feet. I hurried toward the back before he could stop me. The rubber floor felt even worse than the pavement outside. Something gunky stuck to my soles. I didn't want to know what it was.

The bus stopped where the dirt road to our place began. As I stepped down, the cold mud of Meadowlily Road oozed between my toes. My jeans dragged in the muck. Trudging up that dark road, I had never felt so alone in my life.

But I'd also never felt a deeper sense of satisfaction than when I finally made it to the back door. It was hard, but I'd gotten myself out of that situation all on my own. Maybe I *could* do anything, like my father said. I turned the handle and went inside.

"You're home late," said a voice in the dark.

My heart thumping, I snapped on the light.

My uncle Don was sitting there on his own, in the quiet of the sleeping house. He studied my face. "Is everything okay?" He was speaking in the gentle voice he used to use.

"I'm okay now," I said. And it wasn't a lie.

He and I would have more fights—though not as many as Keith and me—yet that one moment of concern made me feel that I had got my old uncle back. Many years later, Cal would email me to say his father was fading fast. I would fly across the ocean to see him. There, in the hospital room he would never leave, my uncle Don was frantic. "I can't find my keys. Help me get my keys."

My uncle's last wish would be to get back to Meadowlily Road. At fifteen, what I wanted most in the world was to get away.

CHAPTER 24

ESCAPE FROM MEADOWLILY ROAD

LONDON, 1974

AFTER I'D PROVED TO myself that I could manage without shoes on my feet, I felt stronger. I decided to keep my appointment with the school psychologist after all. If I was ever going to escape the mess my life had become, I needed to change.

It was a dull gray day, the sky the color of our school lockers. Dr. Sweetland's office, though, was warmly lit by a lamp on her desk. The way she wore her hair up made her look middle-aged, but I think now she was younger. She gestured for me to take one of the two empty chairs.

"How are you?" she asked. It was a simple question, yet it made tears come into my eyes.

I was eleven the last time an adult woman had shown me any warmth. I might have planned to put on a tough act, but it was like she pulled one thread, and everything came undone. It all spilled out: my dreams of going to university—her eyebrows shot up at this; I was failing every subject—and everything that had happened since my mother's boyfriend crossed our path in his garbage truck.

We talked for fifty minutes every Tuesday. But Dr. Sweetland kept going back to one thing: "Tell me about your mother leaving."

"She was gone when I came home from school. That's all." She was on the wrong track. I was over my mother. My problem was Meadowlily Road.

"Describe the scene to me when you realized she wasn't there," she insisted.

"I don't know," I said. "The kitchen was clean. She didn't bother leaving a note, but she had time to tidy up."

"So, you feel you weren't important to your mother?"

"I don't know. I guess, no."

"Let's pretend your mother is sitting in that chair. What would you want to say to her?"

"I don't want to talk to a chair."

"That's your mother."

"I don't want to talk to her, either."

I hated role-playing. But that fall, just to please Dr. Sweetland, I faked it. I would ask the chair the same question over and over, not realizing that it was truly the one thing I wanted to ask my mother in real life—and the one question I never would. As I made up answers for her in session after session, I heard myself saying things I didn't even know I knew.

Why did you leave?
I didn't love your father.
Why did you leave?
I was alone.
Why did you leave?
Men were always chasing me.
Why did you leave?
I met Art.
Why did you leave?

I had to.

It's not that I forgave her. That would turn out to be a hard place for me to get to. But in Dr. Sweetland's office, I stopped believing I was the only one who had driven her away.

Just before our sessions broke for the Christmas holidays, Dr. Sweetland asked me to think about a question: "Why do you believe that the message you think you heard from your mother—that you're not worth anything—is the only message she gave you? There are other messages in your life that you may not be hearing." She leaned forward across her desk. "Your father thinks you are worth loving. How can you learn to hear that?"

At that point, I wasn't receptive to anything my father had to say. As I started to blame my mother less, I started to blame him more. When I came home after my last session with Dr. Sweetland and saw him lying there on the couch, again, I erupted.

"You're not even trying to get us out of here."

He opened one eye. "I'm resting. I just delivered a load of firewood." He closed his eye again. "You try doing that yourself."

I nudged him with my foot. "Well, you're looking pretty comfortable now. But what about Brad and me? Don't you care about us having to live in this hellhole?"

He sat up. "It's all your daddy can afford right now."

"Then try harder. You know how horrible Keith is."

"Just avoid him."

"You don't get it!" I screamed. "You need to do something." Every shred of grief and anger was coming out of me at the same time.

I could see from his expression that he was going to say words to pacify me. And that was the moment it struck me. Like the night my shoes were stolen, it was going to be up to me.

The next day, I got a job at the Orange Julius down at the mall. By the end of January, I'd saved enough for a deposit and the first month's rent.

"Dad, I'm moving out."

"Like hell you are."

"I am, and I'm not coming back. I found an apartment for two hundred and twenty dollars a month. I make enough for half the rent, and I have a roommate to pay the rest. Adrienne, Paulette's sister, is moving down from Kirkland Lake. Remember, she used to live across the street from Bev's?"

"You're not moving out. You're only sixteen."

"Well, actually, Dad, I'm fifteen. Thank you for noticing."

"Christ, fifteen. And how old is that Dupuis girl?"

"She's twenty. And could you not call her 'that Dupuis girl'? She has a name."

"It doesn't matter. You're not moving in with her."

"Thanks for sharing your opinion, but I already paid the first month's rent. And there's no way I'm staying in this nightmare one minute longer."

My father sighed. "What do you want me to say?"

"Nothing. Anyway, fifteen is not so young. You left home when you were my age."

"Those were different times," he said. "Besides, if you remember, I was sent off to reform school."

In the end, my father helped me scrounge some old furniture from the same junk stores that had bought his "unwanted household items." Adrienne contributed the dishes and utensils. With pretty blond hair cut at her shoulders and big breasts—which, back then, marked you as easy—she had picked up a job waitressing within hours of getting off the bus from Kirkland Lake.

After I left home to live with Adrienne, I didn't go wild: I did the opposite. Now that I could blame only myself if things went wrong, I stopped skipping school and poured myself into my homework. But spring break was coming up: even though I'd never had many restrictions, now I had none, and it was time to take advantage of that.

I waited for Adrienne to come home from work. "Let's hitchhike to Florida."

"Florida?" She dumped her tips onto the coffee table. "What about school?"

"I've got two weeks off."

"I guess I could quit and get another job when we come back, but I've got dick all for money." She pointed to the pile of quarters, dimes, and nickels. "I've probably got, like, twenty-four bucks."

"I've got twenty bucks. That's enough to get us to Florida and back."

I don't know why a twenty-year-old thought a teenager's plan was even remotely sensible, but Adrienne agreed.

A couple of days later, I walked out of school to see my father's black pickup idling at the curb. Standing next to it, he looked like two people in one body. I had to laugh. From the waist up, he was a businessman, with a gray trilby hat and a leather coat. From the waist down, he was a laborer, with dirty work pants tucked into steel-toe boots.

The tailgate was down flat to accommodate all the junk he was hauling. "I thought you might need a chair." He pointed to a fringed armchair teetering on a pile of pipes.

"I don't need another chair, Dad," I said, eying the stained old piece of junk he'd brought me. "But how are you doing?"

"Well, I should get a good buck for this here copper," he said, which didn't answer my question. "You sure you don't want that chair?"

"Yeah, I'm sure. How's Brad?"

"He misses you. You doing your schoolwork?"

"'Course. Things calmed down at home?"

"No offense, Lori, but it's certainly quieter without you. Still, I'd like to get the hell away from Keith. Sunday night, I almost had to call the cops."

Until this moment, I hadn't given much thought to Brad. Even though he was not on Keith's radar, it wasn't a good environment for him. "Do you want to stay at my place?"

"Move in with you?" His voice immediately brightened.

"No, Dad, definitely not. You are *not* moving in. But you and Brad can bunk there for two weeks, while Adrienne and I are in Florida."

"You're not going to Florida."

"Let's not start that again. Do you want to house-sit my place or not?"

"Well, I guess I can't stop you from going."

"Nope."

"Well, then, don't worry. Brad and I will keep your abode safe until your return."

That weekend, Adrienne and I presented our birth certificates to the guard at the Canada–United States border, then we hitchhiked down the slushy highway, jumping out of the way so we wouldn't get sprayed when cars pulled up beside us. Two young women with backpacks, we never waited long to be picked up. Ride after ride, we kept going until the roads cleared, the sun came out, and the surf nearly touched the asphalt. While, up north, our country was under ice and snow, we felt kissed by luck to be here, catching our first rays on a beach in the Florida Keys.

When the sun went down, we unrolled our sleeping bags on the sand, using our parkas for pillows. In the morning, some other campers took us out back of a grocery store to show us how to dumpster-dive for food. So far, I hadn't spent much of the twenty dollars in my purse.

A few evenings later, I met Richard. He was a high school math teacher from Michigan, also on spring break. When he joined us by the campfire, my first thought was more of a wish: I wished we had teachers like him in my school. Richard had shoulder-length blond hair and was shirtless under a white linen suit—a look of crumpled sophistication. I had just enough confidence to let my eyes linger on the V of his chest hair.

The crowd around the fire grew. The joints and the guitars came out. After a while, Richard stood up. I felt a pang of disappointment, assuming he was making a move for Adrienne. But instead, miracle of miracles, he came to sit next to me. My smile was exactly what my father meant when he said I wore my heart on my sleeve.

"Is that your sleeping bag?" Richard pointed to where Adrienne and I had slept the night before.

I nodded.

"Go on, grab it. Let's go for a walk."

As he led me into the forest, I was charged with the sense of my own power. I was only fifteen, and a high school teacher had chosen *me*!

It was a balmy, full-moon evening. The strumming of the guitars faded away, and soon all we could hear was the crashing of the waves. Richard found some yellowed palm fronds, dragged them into a pile, then laid my sleeping bag down on top.

"Have a seat," he said, patting the bed he'd made.

I didn't hesitate, seeing no virtue in safeguarding my virtue. Coming to Florida was about blowing through every guardrail in my life. I was free. And I was in charge of my own real estate.

Richard pulled my T-shirt up over my head. My confidence evaporated as I tried to cover my stomach with my arms. He pulled them away. Then he unzipped my jeans and worked them down over my hips. I was trembling now.

"It's okay," he whispered as he lowered himself over me.

The penetration was sharp. Then it was all over—more quickly than I'd expected and with less fanfare. But afterward, I felt special as he held me in his arms, my head on his shoulder, my fingers interlaced with the hairs on his chest. In my mind, he was already my boyfriend. I would hitchhike to Michigan, wherever that was, so we could spend weekends together. I was excited about our future. He drifted off to sleep.

Sometime in the night, I woke. The moon was shining down through the trees, lighting up pockets of the forest. I sat up and shivered. I was naked and all alone.

"Richard?" I called.

There was no answer. I called again.

He wasn't there.

Suddenly, I was ten years old again. The emptiness filled me with dread, the same dread I felt when I realized my mother was gone and I was alone. I jumped up, panicked. Grabbing my sleeping bag, I ran toward the sound of the surf, where Adrienne and the other campers were.

The campfire had gone out. "Adie," I sobbed, kneeling by her sleeping bag. "He took off."

Groggily, she sat up and gave me a look that said, *What did you expect?*

But I hadn't expected that.

I lay awake thinking. I wasn't the same girl who'd gone into the woods with Richard. Returning to that old place of vulnerability was like discovering I was walking around without any skin. I had every freedom in the world but no way to protect myself from that freedom.

With the first light, I hitchhiked to Fort Lauderdale with Adrienne. She was growing tired of my weepiness. After a couple of days, she suggested we keep heading north. We made the journey to Canada in one long stretch, catching what sleep we could in the cars that picked us up.

On a snowy afternoon, we walked back into our apartment to find it had been thoroughly colonized by my father. Clothes were strewn about the living room; the dining table was covered in papers. The kitchen had his trademark tornado-torn-through-it look. Adrienne had a pissed-off expression, but strangely, I wasn't even exasperated by the mess. I was just glad to feel Brad's arms around my waist, to hear my father's grunt as he got up off the couch, to see the relief on his face that I'd made it home unharmed.

If only he'd known.

I didn't have the heart to send my father and Brad back to that shack with my cousin Keith, so instead, I said, "It's late. Why not go tomorrow?" Adrienne shot me a dirty look, but my father and brother, who hadn't made any effort to pack up their affairs, looked happy at the prospect of another night of comfort.

A week later, they were still in no hurry to get back to Meadowlily Road.

Adrienne was barely talking to me now. "You've got to do something," she hissed at me one morning while we both waited outside the bathroom for my father to finish.

"I can't kick my family out."

The toilet flushed, and my father emerged. "Bacon and eggs?" The day before, he'd used his old trick of placing the plate of food in my hands to wake me up for school. When he tried the same technique to get Adrienne up for her shift, she yelled at him.

The next day, I walked into our apartment building just as Adrienne was coming out with her backpack. She looked angry. "I'm going home to Kirkland Lake," she said. "I didn't come here to shack up with your family. If your dad had woken me up with breakfast one more time, I swear I woulda killed him."

When I went inside our apartment, I saw the contents of my father's pockets strewn across the dining table. There were crumpled receipts, some loose toothpicks, and an open pack of Rolaids covered in lint. Next to that he'd smoothed out a half dozen pieces of paper with just phone numbers on them.

He nodded hello to me as he picked up a paper and dialed the telephone.

"Excuse me, ma'am, but why do I have your number in my pocket?"

I was used to hearing him make calls like that, but the woman on the end of the line clearly thought he was a crank.

"No, no, wait," he said. "Maybe you called me because you want some junk removed? No? Or perhaps you need some firewood delivered? I have the finest alderwood, perfectly dry . . . Or could it be that you have a tree to cut down?"

I had to smile. I'd evolved in so many ways—because of my barefoot walk, because of Dr. Sweetland, because of Florida—but here was my father, the same as ever.

He had always said that if I didn't like something, I should change it. And I did. I was proud that I'd managed to leave home.

The only problem was that home had followed me.

CHAPTER 25

BEGINNING AGAIN, AGAIN

LONDON, 1974

MY FATHER HELD OUT a plate. "Who wants Crab Dacker for breakfast?"

"What's that?" Brad asked. Still in his pajamas, he was sitting cross-legged on the carpet. In front of him was a chessboard where he was setting up his pieces. He wrinkled his nose. "It looks weird."

"It's not weird. It's an English muffin, poached egg, crabmeat, and Daddy's hollandaise sauce."

"Can I just have cereal?" Brad asked.

"Sure, son, whatever."

"Dad, can we get back to the rent?" It was past due, and I'd already had two calls from the landlord. "When can you give me your half?"

"I'll get it. You know your old dad."

"That's why I'm worried."

"Look, I just haven't found the right thing this month. Picking up junk is a piss-poor way to make a living."

"Yeah, I noticed."

He handed me my crab. Not having rent money was no reason not to eat well.

"Anyway, it's probably time we got the hell outta Dodge," he said. I think we were all disappointed with our lives in the city. I had made no friends here, and this time, Brad hadn't, either.

"Groovy. We're moving," I said. "But where?" We'd made the rounds of my father's siblings: Aunt Dixie in Kirkland Lake, Uncle Brian in Brampton, and now Uncle Don in London.

While he reflected, I noticed my father's Hemingway beard was sprinkled with bits of crab.

"Brad, what say we move?" he asked.

Brad barely looked up from the game of chess he was carrying on with himself; he was the only one who knew how to play. "Whatever you guys want."

"So, what's your brilliant plan, Dad? School starts in five weeks. And apparently, we don't have any money."

"Well, we've worn out our welcome with my brothers." He added his plate to the dishes in the sink. "I guess we'll have to go back to my sister's."

"Aunt Dixie's?" I had once believed we had only to get out of our small town to have that bigger life I dreamed of. If anything, things had gotten worse since we'd left. "At least Bev's there." I hoped she had forgiven me for last summer's acid party. "But we still need money."

"I'll figure something out," he said. "Your old dad's going to be a Somebody, you know."

"Far out. When?"

A week later, we had sold the black pickup for a handful of postdated checks and were back in our old Volkswagen van with my mattress and box spring teetering on the roof.

"Dad, that's going to fall and cause an accident." Brad's tone wasn't accusatory: he sounded as if he thought that would be an interesting development.

"Don't you worry, son. I've got it tied down." The rope holding the mattress in place was threaded in through one window of the van and out another.

I pointed to my father's handiwork. "You realize you've tied the doors shut."

"Lori, quit bellyaching and go crawl in from my side. Brad, you can climb in through the window, can't you?"

I shimmied around the gearshift sticking up from the floor. On the passenger side, Brad hoisted himself up to the window and then let himself fall in headfirst. When he twisted himself right way up, his long hair was all over the place.

"You're such a hippie kid."

He stuck his tongue out at me.

"Come on, you two." My father turned the key in the ignition. Black smoke from the tailpipe enveloped us. I held on to the rope above my head: it was the only thing keeping my old bed from flying off. We hadn't been able to sell it along with our other thrift store belongings, so now we were taking it to the dump—our last stop before leaving the city forever.

We had started too late in the day. Stretching ahead of us was an eight-hour drive—or longer, with all these cars heading for cottage country. It was already dinnertime when we pulled off at Webers roadside stand.

"Daddy, where are we going to sleep?" my brother asked as we set our trays down on the picnic table.

"You can settle into the back while we drive, son." Now that his psoriasis had calmed down, Brad could go to bed without the drama of my father applying cream to the crevices in his feet.

"I mean where are all of us going to sleep? It's almost dark."

I laid my cheeseburger down on its wrapper. "Yeah, what time will we get to Aunt Dixie's? Won't everybody be asleep?"

"Maybe we should get a hotel in North Bay," my father said. "That's about halfway to Kirkland Lake."

"We can't afford a hotel," I pointed out, and stole a fry from Brad.

"I have those postdated checks from selling the pickup."

"But we should save that."

"Then let's go to a campsite."

I raised my eyebrows. "*You* go to a campsite. Take me to a youth hostel. I'll sleep there."

"Can I come?" Brad asked me.

"No."

The real reason I wanted to go to a youth hostel was that I knew hostels attracted hitchhiking boys, and I was boy crazy. It had been full on for the last few months. Every entry in my diary carried the names of three or four boys who'd looked my way. "I like Paul, Rick, Sam, and the guy who works in the shoe store, in that order." I had written those words without any irony. The next day, the names changed, but the hunger remained. I was famished for the attention of not just a single boy, but every boy, all the time. It took only one boy showing interest in me to make me feel worthwhile—for about two minutes. Then I'd need someone else's attention to execute the same trick. Moving out of Meadowlily Road and surviving Florida had made me feel stronger, but nothing could take away the feeling that I was unlovable.

Now that I was sixteen, I was learning how to catch a boy's eye. Contact lenses, lipstick, and short shorts seemed to help, along with my natural tendency to bestow a big smile on everyone, but especially cute boys.

A couple of hours later, we had reached North Bay. So eager to help me find the youth hostel, because it would make me happy, my father asked for directions from the first people we saw, even though they were in the middle of crossing a street.

"Dad, you're going to get somebody killed." A half minute later, I rolled down my window so I could ask a woman on the sidewalk.

It turned out the hostel was just a block away. My father pulled a U-turn into an empty spot. He took one of the parking tickets lying on the dashboard and reached out the window to tuck it under the windshield wiper. "Brad and I will sleep right here," he said. "So we'll be close to you."

I wasn't sure if that was his real reason or if he was trying to save money on a campsite.

"G'night, Dad. G'night, Brad." I hurried out of the van before anyone got the idea of walking me to the hostel.

"Wait—what's the rush? Do you need any money?"

"No, I still have thirty bucks left from Orange Julius. Someone told me youth hostels cost two bucks."

"Is that all? Then maybe we should come with you."

"Don't even *think* of coming in. Anyway, you're too old."

"Okay, okay." He gave a sigh of pretend-hurt feelings. "See you in the morning. Be good."

"Bye, sis." Brad had already crawled into the bed he'd made for himself in the back. He was an intrepid traveler by now, visiting our mother as often as Art would let him.

I had just crossed the street when my boy radar started tingling. A cute guy was driving toward me, his motorcycle helmet slung over his arm in case the cops came around. I flashed my smile. He slowed down. I walked past. His head turned to keep me in sight.

A moment later, there was a crunch and the tinkle of broken glass. Watching me instead of the road, the cute boy had rammed the car ahead of him. Now his motorcycle lay on the ground. With an embarrassed look, he righted the bike, shoved on his helmet, and sped away.

I skipped to the youth hostel. A boy had had an accident because of me!

The girls' dorm had six beds. As I put my bag into one of the metal lockers, I heard voices floating up the stairs. Because it sat on the intersection of Highway 11 and the Trans-Canada, the nearly five-thousand-mile-long route from coast to coast, North Bay was popular with hitchhikers. I hurried down to join them.

Entering the common room felt like coming into a party of explorers. Maps were spread out on tables scattered around the room. By watching their fingers trace a path, I saw that a couple of kids were traveling east, to Montreal or Halifax, but most seemed to be hitchhiking west, to Winnipeg, Calgary, or Vancouver.

Ignoring the girls, I made a beeline for the best-looking guy. Because hitchhiking boys far outnumbered girls, I figured tonight my chances were good.

He was sitting at the end of a ratty couch, nearest the light. As I eased myself down next to him, he looked up at me with dreamy green eyes. His hair fell in kinks all the way to his waist. He was mending a tear in his backpack with a large darning needle.

"D'you need help?" I asked him.

"Thanks, man, but this canvas would be too hard for you to work with." He took a Swiss Army Knife out of his pocket and used the flat side of a blade to push the needle through. "There. I just need the stitches to hold until I get out west. Then, like, I'll have my own place, and I won't need this old pack anymore."

Corky was older than me, a university student. After lights-out, I slipped from the girls' dorm to meet him in the common room. But rather than romancing me, as I had hoped he would, he told me about Vancouver. His face grew animated as he described a city lapped by the Pacific Ocean, dotted with beaches, surrounded by islands and mountains.

"And you know the weirdest thing? It doesn't snow there."

"What do you mean? It's in our country, and it doesn't snow?"

"Yeah, man. Microclimate."

I was stunned that no one had ever told me. "Is there a university there?"

"Like, of course. Two. I'm going to UBC."

It suddenly hit me how limited I had been in imagining my future. This was so much bigger than my dreams. And to think I had almost gone back to Kirkland Lake.

"Take me with you."

"What?"

"You said it's hard for a guy hitchhiking alone. I'll come with you." Despite my vows to protect myself, I was as open and eager as a puppy.

"Sure, okay, whatever." He shrugged.

"I just need to get my things tomorrow morning." I leapt up. I couldn't wait one more minute to get a start on the new life I'd just glimpsed.

I found Corky after breakfast, as everyone was being shooed out of the hostel for the day.

"I just have to get my stuff from the van," I reminded him, "and then I'll come back."

"Hey, why don't you meet me on the highway? It's just off Algonquin."

"Okay. I'll hurry. You'll wait for me, won't you?"

"I'll wait." He gave a little jump to hike up his backpack.

"Promise you'll wait?"

"Like, promise, man."

Part of me hadn't been sure it was a good idea to leave my father and brother behind to hitchhike thousands of miles to Vancouver, but I was getting more excited as my plans took shape. I'd find a part-time job, finish high school, then go to university.

But how would I tell my father?

I needn't have worried. When I got to the van, only Brad was inside.

"Where's Dad?"

Brad pointed in the direction of a pancake house. "He's gone over to use the bathroom."

I was relieved. My father wasn't going to get a chance to talk me out of this. I went inside the van to get my suitcase.

"I'm going now, Brad."

"What? You're going? Where?"

"I'm going to hitchhike to Vancouver. I'll call you guys at Aunt Dixie's. Tell Dad, okay? I'll call you."

My suitcase was heavier than I'd expected, but I was so juiced up about my future that I didn't let the weight slow me down.

The ramp to the Trans-Canada was flat. On both sides of the highway, hitchhikers in groups of two or three held their thumbs out. I walked along the line heading west, scanning every face. I recognized a few people from the youth hostel, but Corky wasn't one of them. I ran across the highway and checked out the people heading east. He wasn't there, either.

He'd gone on without me. I was crushed.

I hauled my suitcase to the yellowed grass of the verge and sat on top of it. I had been such an idiot to think he'd wait for me. Even though I vowed

I'd never get hurt again, my tears told a different story. I would have to hitchhike now, but to where? North to catch up with my family? Out west by myself?

Behind me, I heard wheels cutting across grass. Then came the familiar "Ah-ooh-ga!"

I could have cried with joy.

My father, leaning out his window, yelled, "What the hell do you think you're doing?"

He'd come back just when I needed him. But I didn't know what to do. I'd glimpsed a future grander than my dreams, and I couldn't go back. I wanted a bigger life so much that I would have hitchhiked to the West Coast with a guy I'd just met.

"I'm not going back to Aunt Dixie's," I said. "I'm going to Vancouver. The city has beaches and mountains and two universities. And it never snows!"

"Get in the van," my father said.

I shook my head. "Dad, there's got to be more to life than Kirkland Lake."

"We'll all go. Together."

"What do you mean—where?"

"To Vancouver. To the tropics of Canada!" He turned to my brother in the back seat. "Change of plans, son." Then he gestured to me. "Now, come on. Put your suitcase in the back."

When I climbed in, he shook his head and said, "How could you even think of going on without Brad and me?" With a roar of the old motor, we bumped over the verge and onto the highway heading west to a new life.

CHAPTER 26

TRANS-CANADA

CROSS-COUNTRY, 1974

WE MADE IT THREE hours out of North Bay. Then, halfway up a hill with two thousand miles yet to go, the life went out of our van. The motor stopped. We began to roll downhill.

"Dad!"

"Shush."

We were gathering speed. My father looked over his shoulder. Driving backward, he steered to keep us out of a ditch. I looked back, too. The rear window was blocked by our boxes; I couldn't see a thing.

Suddenly, I felt a jolt. I grabbed the dashboard and looked up at my father. He was smiling so hard his eyes were crinkling.

"Gave you a good scare, didn't I?"

He'd popped the clutch to get the engine started. Now we were once again climbing the hill. My eyes met Brad's, and we exchanged a look of relief.

"It's that damn regulator," my father said. "I knew I should have stopped at that last town."

"If you knew the regulator was going, why didn't you get it fixed?"

"Don't worry. It'll all work out."

"Dad, we need to get that regulator looked at!" I was almost certain I smelled something burning. "We can't just hope we won't have to climb another hill. Ever heard of the Rockies?"

Just then, we passed a sign that read WAWA 10 MILES.

"D'you think we can make it to that town?" Brad asked.

"Of course we can." But my father was watching the dials more than the road.

"I should've hitchhiked," I said.

We took the next fork off the Trans-Canada, followed by our own cloud of smoke. The marker for the township of Wawa was a surreal three-story-tall Canada goose.

"Over there!" Brad cried out. He pointed to a Canadian Tire store with two kayaks leaning against the front.

"I don't see a gas station," I said irritably.

"The sign says go behind." Brad's voice was still high, but now it had an authority that said he wasn't a little boy anymore.

Out back of the Canadian Tire, my father signaled to a young mechanic who was smoking by a pump. He wore a coverall with a wrench sticking out of his side pocket. He didn't need to look under the hood to tell us what was wrong.

"See that gas, eh, dripping down your tailpipe?" He pointed with his wrench. "That's your first clue your regulator's shot to hell."

I gave my father a furious look. He shrugged.

The mechanic tapped his wrench on the tailpipe. It dropped to the ground. "That's your muffler gone, too." He leaned down to extract the coat hanger that had been holding the exhaust pipe in place. "How far did you say you'd come? Amazing that thing was still attached."

"What's it going to cost to fix the regulator? Forget about the muffler—we don't need it."

"Dad!"

"Okay. What's it going to cost for both? Your best price."

"It's not my price you need to worry about. It's your parts, eh. With this old vehicle, we have to get a shipment in from Toronto." He pronounced it *Tarana*.

"How long's that going to take?"

"Two, three days, if my dealer has the parts in stock and puts them straight on a Greyhound."

Brad shot me a look reminding me that this road trip was my fault. I hoped Wawa had a youth hostel.

We followed the mechanic into the office. He opened a thick catalog and then ran a dirty fingernail down the pages until he found the reference numbers.

"I have to get my kids in school," my father said, as if that would move the parts onto the bus more quickly. "We're on our way to Vancouver."

The mechanic looked up so sharply, he lost his place in the catalog. "West Coast, eh?" He gave a low whistle. "You'll never make it."

To get the money for the repairs, my father took his packet of postdated checks to the Wawa branch of the Royal Bank. He'd put on his best suit. Meanwhile, Brad and I looked like hippie kids, he with his long hair, me in the farmer's overalls I'd sewn into a blue jean dress.

"I hope this check doesn't bounce higher than a kite," my father said as he approached the counter, speaking loud enough for the bank teller to hear.

The teller was a raven-haired woman with dark First Nation eyes. A familiar look crossed my father's face.

Oh no, I thought. *Here it comes.*

"Do you find being so beautiful an asset or a handicap?"

I kicked his foot.

Usually, my father would get a laugh as a reply, but the teller pondered the question seriously. "It's, I don't know, an asset?"

Now he was stymied. His chat lines never got him anywhere, so he had no follow-up for this one. Instead, he watched her count out the new bills while he worked on a response. Suddenly, his face lit up.

"Young lady, do I have your permission to fantasize about you?"

"Dad!" I kicked him again.

"Lori, why are you kicking me?"

"What is the point of kicking you if you say it out loud?"

As we left the bank with the money, my father faked a limp. He forgot it as soon as he spotted a bakery. "C'mon, kids. Let's get ourselves a treat."

The bell above the door clanged as we entered. A young man came from the back room wiping his hands on an apron. "What can I do ya fer?"

"Do you have any day-olds?"

We exited the bakery with a bagful of discounted pastries. "Let that be a lesson to you," my father said. "Never pay full price unless you have to." He took a bite of a lemon Danish. "You see? Still perfectly good." He handed a sugar donut to my brother, who took a dubious nibble. "Come on, Brad. There's nothing wrong with it."

That evening, in the common room of the Catfish Lake youth hostel, I learned we weren't the only ones stuck in Wawa.

"It's a vortex, man," said John, the cutest guy there. I'd noticed his wide smile and aw-shucks good looks right away. Like Corky, he had long, wavy hair parted in the middle; it was a thing back then. "Hitchhikers get stuck here for days," he continued. "I heard of this one guy who was here so long he married a local waitress."

"What about you?"

"Day three, man, day three." He shook his head. "But you gotta love us." He laughed. "All those hitchhikers out there on the highway every morning, politely waiting their turn. So Canadian."

If the spare parts arrived in time, I hoped we could move some boxes in the van to make room for John.

The garage had towed the van here to Catfish Lake so my father could camp outside the youth hostel while Brad and I slept inside. A couple of evenings later, my father was frying three breaded veal cutlets on our Coleman stove. On the second burner, he switched back and forth between potatoes and creamed corn.

Nicola, who was also staying in the hostel, was standing behind me braiding my hair. I closed my eyes, enjoying her light touch. When she was finished, she turned to my brother. "Hey, Brad, want me to braid your hair, too?" He shook his head self-consciously and slunk over to the lakeside.

"Don't go far," my father called out. "Dinner's almost ready." Then he turned to Nicola and Tony, her boyfriend, who was sitting cross-legged on the grass wearing an embroidered Indian tunic and loose white pants.

"Are you two hungry?"

Both nodded emphatically.

Leaving the potatoes at a rolling, musical boil, my father lifted the hatch at the back of the van. He returned with two more cans of creamed corn.

"Plenty for everyone," he said, then cut the veal into pieces so we could all have some.

I told Nicola and Tony about our plans to drive to Vancouver for the start of the school year—which was getting closer all the time.

"Vancouver's a big city, man," said Tony. "Trust me. You don't want to go there."

"Victoria's where you should go." Nicola accepted a plate of food from my father. "It's as beautiful as Vancouver, but smaller and mellower. And it's on an island, so that's super groovy."

"Does it have a university?" I asked.

"Of course." Nicola laughed. "Victoria has everything."

"Does it snow there?" My brother sounded hopeful that the answer would be yes. While my father and I had had enough cold winters to last us forever, Brad would always miss the North.

"It doesn't really snow," said Nicola, dashing his hopes, but raising mine. "It's just ninety minutes from Vancouver by ferry, so it has the same microclimate. But you can ski in the mountains; they're close enough."

"And the rents are cheaper," added Tony.

My father paused his fork midway to his mouth. "How much cheaper?"

The next morning, I watched John execute that backpacker's jump to hike up his load before he began to trudge in the direction of the highway. I waved goodbye, then ran back to where my father was lighting our stove.

"Dad, come on. We have to get the car fixed now!"

"Don't rush me, Lori. The parts are in; they're not going anywhere. Let's just have a nice breakfast. I'm making poached eggs."

"We have to go this minute and pick up our friends hitchhiking. If not, they'll be stuck in Wawa for weeks." My father probably thought I was thinking of Nicola and Tony, but I meant John.

"In that case, they'll still be on the highway when we get there." With one hand, he broke an egg into the pan.

It seemed like the mechanic would never finish tinkering. Finally, late afternoon, he was done. With his dire warnings echoing in my ears—*You'll never make it*—I directed my father to the Trans-Canada. Lined up along the highway, there were maybe twenty-five backpackers in all, mostly singles, with some couples. They were just as orderly as John said they'd be. Nicola and Tony weren't among them, so they must have gotten a ride, but there, at the head, was John.

"Dad, we have to stop."

"What?"

"Dad. Stop. Here!"

The tires sprayed gravel as we screeched next to John. When he recognized us, he flashed his big smile and pulled off his backpack.

"I guess we can take one more," my father said.

Thanks, I mouthed, as I squeezed closer to make room in the front seat.

"So, Dacker, what are you going to do out west?" John asked. To hear my father above the racket of the van, which not even the new muffler had rectified, he was leaning across me. "Have you got a job lined up?"

"A job? Hell, no. I'm going to start a business."

"Oh, what kind of business?"

I looked over at my father, curious to see how he was going to answer. We'd never discussed how he was going to support us once we got to where we were going.

"I'll figure something out," my father said. "I've been living off my wits since I went to war at sixteen."

"Sixteen?" John whistled. "How'd you manage that?"

"I said I was eighteen. I wasn't even old enough to shave, but the recruiter let me through."

I'd heard the story so many times, I can imagine the chaos on that day in 1940. Inside Charlie's Hotel, young men are filling out recruitment forms while a scar of miners, coming off the night shift, cut through on their way to the Beverage Room. Presiding over it all, wearing his trademark bowler hat, is Charlie Chow himself, rich from taking early mining stock in exchange for a room and a hot meal.

"The army sent me to Camp Borden," my father told John. "They assigned me and the other boys from Kirkland Lake to the employment platoon. That name alone should have tipped us off. Instead of rifles, they issued us tent mallets. I was pretty cheesed off when I realized they were training us to be workers, not soldiers."

We'd gotten to the part where my father convinces the other fourteen Kirkland Lake recruits to go AWOL. They spend a two-week holiday in their hometown, fêted like the war heroes they are not. And least not yet. On their return to camp, they fully expect to be disciplined.

"But you know what? Those bastards headed off to war without us." My father smacked the dashboard. "They left one officer behind who told us to go report to our captain at the train station in Toronto. We found Captain Adams just as the troops were boarding trains for Halifax. He was drunk as a skunk. 'Get aboard, boys. We're all going the same way,' he said. In the morning, he denied ever seeing us and told us to get off at the next stop or he'd have us court-martialed."

"Wow, Dacker," said John, "That's quite the story."

"Are you kidding? That's only the beginning. We stay on the train, thinking we'll be sent back when we get to the ships at Halifax Harbor, but you won't believe what happens next. At the top of the gangplank, the sergeant in charge is none other than our former chief of police. He arrested me many a time. So, he waves us aboard, saying our travel orders will catch up with us. But of course, they won't, because we aren't supposed to be there. So, anyway, we get to England. We're taken with the other soldiers to Camp Aldershot. But being stowaways, with no official papers, once we get inside the gates, we can't get out again. We're prisoners of war."

My father laughed even though the joke was on him.

John leaned in. "So, what did you do?" He seemed genuinely taken with my father's tale. I looked over at Brad to see if he was listening, but he was looking out the window. We could recount this story by heart.

"We would have spent the war trapped there, except for this girl. She worked in the canteen. I was in love with her, but she was mad about a sergeant major. One night, I got so jealous—remember, I'm just sixteen—that I hit the officer right in the kisser. And that got me sent to the stockade."

My father had described the scene so many times, how the next morning, two burly military police frog-marched him across the camp. The sergeant major he punched was following behind, bellowing orders: "Prisoner and escort, halt!"

"When they bring me to the camp commander, he takes one look at me and goes, 'Sergeant Major, dismiss the guard.' Then he says to me, 'For Christ's sake, how old are you, son? And what are you doing over here?' He says if I don't tell him the truth, he'll kick my ass all over camp. Begging him not to send me back, I wipe away my tears and tell him the whole story. And that's how I got to join the war."

"Your old man is so cool," John said to me. "I wish I had a dad like him."

John stayed with us for seven hundred miles, until Winnipeg. The whole time, he had eyes for just one person. It wasn't me.

We were more than halfway across the country. Covering a couple hundred flat prairie miles a day, we could make it to British Columbia in less than a week. But the closer we got, the more I worried. Would we be able to find a place to live before school started?

My father had long given up the pretense of looking for a campground. At each new town, he parked the van outside the youth hostel and cooked dinner for us on the Coleman stove. One evening, he noticed some back-packers watching us.

"Look at them," he said. "They probably haven't had a proper meal for a week."

The next day, he went rooting around the back of a grocery store refriger-ator. "Bingo!" He was looking at the expiry date on a packaged T-bone steak.

"Dad, it's gone bad," Brad said.

"That meat's not bad. It's just high."

"Then why is it green?"

"It's not green, son. It's brown. That means it's well aged."

He looked for some more of the same, then carried his purchases to the cash register. "This meat's off," he said to the cashier. "What kind of discount can you give me?"

She looked flummoxed. "You can just get something fresher."

"No, this will do. How much?"

We left the store with a cardboard box of T-bone steaks, plus some yel-lowing broccoli. "Tonight, we feed everyone!"

Two nights later, when we arrived in Moose Jaw, word must have gotten out. I counted fourteen backpackers waiting for us.

My father didn't give any thought to conserving our scant resources. "Look at them, Lori. They're hungry."

"If you keep this up, *we'll* be hungry."

In the smallest concession to my concerns, he began making spaghetti sauce for his dinners, because hamburger meat was cheaper than even "high" T-bone steaks. Every evening, he cooked up a new pot of sauce, oily bubbles popping on the surface.

"Here, kidlings," my father would say. "Start handing out the paper plates."

When we got to Banff, near the border between Alberta and British Columbia, a small crowd started gathering.

"Sheesh," my father said. "How can we feed all these kids?"

In Banff's municipal park, against the backdrop of the Rocky Mountains, we claimed two picnic tables placed among the fir and poplar trees. My father set the Coleman stove on one table and prepped another for a serving area. On one end, he piled the plastic utensils and paper plates. He unraveled green garbage bags and handed them to two young hippie women who were hanging around, giving them the job of garbage pickup.

As they waited for my father to cook their dinner, the kids congregated nearby, some playing guitars, some stretched out on the ground. A couple were throwing a Frisbee. Between them, a dog wearing a bandanna around its neck tried to catch it.

"Man, this is so beautiful." One of the girls who was supposed to be on garbage duty had put her bag down and was grooving on some drug. "I just dig your dad so much." She was watching my father stir the spaghetti sauce, a tea towel hanging at his waist.

I started counting the group behind her. "Dad, there are forty kids waiting. We can't feed that many!" Even worse, not a single one of these people looked familiar. Where was John, not to mention the other hitchhikers we'd been meeting all the way across the country?

"Forty?" My father frowned. "Brad, get me all the day-old bread that's in that box on the passenger seat. Now, this is what we're going to do," he said to us as we took our places beside him. "Brad, you give each person one slice of bread with margarine. Not two. One slice. Lori, I'll serve the spaghetti, then you give each person a spoonful of tomato sauce. Just this big, no more." He dipped his wooden spoon into the sauce to demonstrate.

He turned to the girl who had been grooving on him earlier and held out a green container of Kraft Parmesan to her. "You can't trust them not to take the whole damn thing," he said. "Just give them a sprinkle." Behind her, people were pressing in.

The kids had formed a line, and now they were jostling to get to where we were serving. A guy at the front with a long beard and holey jeans stopped at Brad's serving station and grabbed two slices of bread.

"Hey," my father shouted. "One only. We don't have enough for everyone to take two."

"Bummer," the guy said, shoving both pieces of bread into his mouth. My father was still glaring at him when the next guy in line stuck his own fork into the pot, trying to take out more pasta.

"Leave something for the next person," my father said, annoyed.

At the back of the line, the pushing was turning serious. Two young men had their fists up. "Lor, watch the spaghetti," my father said. "Come on, you two. No fighting." He shook his spoon at them.

We were now facing around sixty hungry hippies. I wondered how my father's magical thinking was going to feed this mob. Suddenly, people surged forward and started helping themselves.

"Dad," I called, but he was still trying to keep the fighters apart.

"I need two servings." A wiry guy was reaching past me into the pot. "I got my dog, too, man."

By the time my father made it back through the crowd, the pots were empty. The girls on garbage duty were nowhere to be found. A dog was licking the paper plates strewn around on the grass.

"That's it," my father said to the group milling around. "Show's over."

I was still fuming as we pulled up in front of the Banff youth hostel. "Dad, we have to stop this."

"What?"

"We have to stop feeding strangers. You almost caused a riot. Plus, we need to save our money to rent somewhere. School starts in two weeks."

"It'll all—"

"Don't tell me it'll all work out. It won't work out if we're broke." I jumped down from the van and slammed the door.

The next day, a chastened version of my father took the wheel. That version lasted about ten seconds. "Hey, kids. Ever seen mountains so beautiful?"

Growing up in Ontario, of course we hadn't. But I wasn't willing to give up my anger yet, not even for the Rockies.

Two days later, we were driving onto a narrow spit of land for the final leg of our journey. Ahead of us, the towering ferry that would take us to Vancouver Island was straining at the ropes that held it to the dock, churning the sea with its engines. We clattered over the ramp to park on the lower car deck. As the ship beneath us rumbled out of the harbor, I announced that I was going up to the observation deck.

"Hold on," my father said. "We'll all go together."

At the top of the ferry, I pushed against the wind to open the door, stepped over the ledge, then ran to the railing. Not even my dreams had prepared me for my first real sight of the Pacific, where diamonds of sunlight glinted off the waves like a glittering promise. Boats crisscrossed ahead of our hull, leaving foamy trails in the water. Above our heads, seagulls with outstretched wings rode the wind drifts, showing their snowy white undersides. Islands covered in rainforest rose from the water.

I turned to my father and saw my sense of awe reflected in his face.

Ninety minutes later, we drove off the ferry onto Vancouver Island and followed the highway signs to Victoria, our new home. We slowed just enough to exclaim at the baskets of flowers hanging from the old-fashioned streetlamps, which gave the city a quaint English look, then kept going. Only when we were about a mile past downtown did my father turn off the engine.

"We made it, kids."

Brad and I looked around in surprise.

"Made it where?" I asked. In the falling dusk, I could make out a line of cliffs ahead of us. They dropped straight off into the Pacific Ocean, roaring below.

We got out. Brad pointed to a plaque. "It says here we're at Mile Zero."

I thought then that my father had wanted to conclude our long journey at this spot—the end of the Trans-Canada, or the beginning, depending on how you looked at it. Now, with the ocean straight ahead of us, we had to go either left or right. I looked at my father expectantly.

That's when I knew he'd stopped here because he didn't have a plan.

It would matter later, but in that moment, I didn't care. I felt a rush of gratitude. My father had driven us across the country to save me from hitchhiking with a boy whose face I couldn't even remember now. The wind off the ocean was pulling the tears from my eyes across my cheeks.

"My emotional daughter," my father said as we got back into the van. Then, showing us that some things never changed, he leaned out his window to ask someone halfway across the street for directions to Victoria's youth hostel.

Our journey was over. Or so I thought.

CHAPTER 27

TEN DIMES

VICTORIA, 1974

TO GET TO THE youth hostel's front desk, we had to walk through the common room. It smelled like patchouli. My father was wearing a brown plaid suit and a trilby hat. Amid the beads and backpacks, bushy beards and bell-bottoms, he looked like a shabby narc.

"Hey, do you think my dad could stay here with us?" I asked the hippie working the desk. Since we'd set out from Ontario, my father hadn't slept anywhere other than the back of the van. And we might be there for a while.

"Of course, man. He's, like, your *dad*," the hippie said. "I can give you your own dorm room. But, like, we're only open for another week. Summer's over, man."

I gave my father a sharp poke with my elbow.

"What?" He raised his eyebrows. "We'll find something."

Inside our dorm, there were two sets of bunk beds and a bank of metal lockers. After we ate dinner outside in the van, I sat on one of the beds—the room had no chairs—and pulled out my diary, leaning my head forward so I wouldn't clock myself on the upper bunk. Above me, Brad was laying out his chessmen while my father washed his underwear and then draped it to dry over the bars of his bed.

"Now what do we do?" I asked my father.

"Tomorrow, we find a place to live." He made it sound so simple.

"You heard what the guy at the front desk said. Victoria has a one percent vacancy rate."

Brad leaned over from his bunk, looking at us upside down. "Yeah, Dad, and he said we need references and a deposit, too." My brother swung himself down the ladder, holding on with one arm like a monkey.

"How many times do I have to tell you not to listen to the naysayers? If we did that, we wouldn't even be here."

That was less reassuring than he meant it to be.

The next morning, we trooped to the bank. Everything now hinged on money. We couldn't register for school until we had a place to live. We couldn't get a place to live without paying the first and last month's rent—plus a security deposit. And all we had left was one check to cash.

My father handed the teller the check, and we all watched as she studied it. "This is from out of province." She wrinkled her nose. "I'll need to get my manager's signature."

I looked over at my father, silently imploring him not to trot out one of his chat lines and give the bank reason to doubt his credibility.

Just then, a woman waiting behind us tapped my father on the shoulder. "Is that yours?" She pointed to an envelope on the floor.

"Yes, that's mine," he said. Too quickly, I thought. I didn't remember him holding an envelope. I watched him gauge its thickness before he shoved it into his pocket.

"We have to wait for your check to clear," the teller was saying. "It could take a week or ten days. Do you bank here?"

After opening an account, my father hurried us back to the van. He took the envelope he'd picked up off the floor and shook it upside down over the driver's seat. Brad watched with wide eyes as twenty-dollar bills floated down like snow.

Despite his early start in life as a thief, my father was now, in his own words, "honest to a goddamned fault." But this time, I figured we were safe. There was no return address on the envelope, so my father's honesty couldn't get in the way of our keeping that money.

He put the bills inside his wallet, then crumpled the envelope into a ball. Suddenly, he uncrumpled it. "Hold on a second." He fished inside and extracted a piece of paper. He gazed at it with sorrow. "It's a stub from a pension check. And it has the old lady's name and address."

With Brad and me still in shock, my father retraced his steps into the bank. He spent $2.50 of our diminishing reserves to buy a money order so he could mail the full amount back to the pensioner.

My father had done the right thing, but it was hard to keep that in mind when school was starting in days and we still had no place to live.

"Don't you kids worry. Your old dad will figure it out."

"I'd better get a job," I said.

"You don't have any faith in me, do you?" My father reached into his pocket for a handful of change. "See this?" He separated out the dimes and held them in his open palm. "I'll get us settled with these ten dimes."

"Yeah, ten dimes," I scoffed.

"Ten dimes, ten phone calls. You watch me. Maybe you two will learn something."

The next morning, I went downtown to look for a job. Brad tagged along. While he looked at jeans we couldn't afford in a store called the Bootlegger, I went up to the cash desk to ask for an application. The cashier reached under the counter for a form and a pen to fill it in. I studied the paper with dismay. The first thing it asked for was my address and phone number.

"Can I bring this back later?" I was ready to help support the family, but first we needed a telephone.

When Brad and I got back to the youth hostel, my father told us he'd already visited two houses. Both were gone by the time he got there.

The constant worry that formed the backdrop to my life was turning into gut-churning fear.

"Who needs a house anyway?" my father asked. "What say we live on a boat?"

The following day, the three of us went down to Fisherman's Wharf. We had just stepped onto the floating dock when Brad cried out, "Look, a seal!" He pointed to where a head was rising straight out of the water. The seal moved up like a periscope, but had tender brown eyes.

Maybe a boat wouldn't be so bad after all, I thought. Just then, I noticed a row of float homes bobbing on the water, brightly colored with flower boxes and rooftop decks.

"Which one's going to be ours?" I asked with rising excitement. It would be a dream living here.

My father pointed in the opposite direction, to a metal tugboat. It had a For Rent sign in its window.

"*That's* where we're going to live?"

"Yeah, that's the one," said my father, ignoring the horror in my voice.

The gray tugboat was sitting low in the water with bumpers at the front made of old tire strips. When we boarded at the back, it dipped down. A man in rubber overalls came out of the cabin below and waved us in.

Stepping over the lip of the doorway, I could smell the brew from a tin pot burbling away on a miniature stove.

"Would you like a coffee?" the captain asked my father.

"I don't even like people who like coffee," he answered, a line that was never as funny as he thought.

"Hookay, then." The man put the coffee down. "Let me tell you 'bout the boat. It's got an aluminum hull, sleeps three—"

"Where do three people sleep?" I interrupted, glancing around in astonishment.

"There's a double bed fore." He pointed to where two steps led down to the V at the front of the boat. "And this here table becomes a single bed."

Directly above the stairs was a platform with a captain's chair. Surrounded by salt-crusted windows, it was the only properly lit part of the boat. Brad immediately climbed up and pretended to rotate the wheel while the captain finished his tour, standing in one spot and pointing.

"Dad, no," I whispered as we stepped back onto the dock so we could "think about it."

"I know, Lori. You don't have to tell me."

"We still have seven dimes left," Brad piped up.

The next morning, my father took his coins and the classified section of the newspaper to the phone booth across the road from the youth hostel.

I was too anxious to write in my diary. We'd be out on the street when they closed this place down. And where else could we go for six dollars a night?

My father came back into our room.

"That was fast," I said. "Did you use up all your dimes?"

"I think I found our dream home."

To get there before someone else rented the house, we took the coastal road but immediately got stuck behind a convoy of retirees. We finally broke free at a gated community called Uplands, then cut across the University of Victoria. I promised myself I'd study there one day.

Beyond the campus, a dense, dark patch of rainforest gave way to dramatic cliffs dropping to the waves below. We'd arrived in Cordova Bay.

On the right side of the road, a line of peeling arbutus trees hid the ocean view and the million-dollar homes that enjoyed it. On the other side, a long driveway led to a white turn-of-the-century farmhouse in the middle of a field next to a barn. Farther back, we could make out the uniform houses of a subdivision, but right here, it felt like we were in the country.

The front door was unlocked. The real estate agent had told us to go right in.

In a state of yearning so intense that my breath constricted, I walked through the big country kitchen to the living room, which had a real fireplace, then through to the four bedrooms and, finally, to the sunroom at the front of the house. I'd never wanted to live anywhere so badly in my life.

"Dad, please. We have to get this place." My heart was burning in my chest.

"Yeah, Dad," Brad added. "It's great."

"But how can we get them to rent it to us when we don't have any money?"

My father smiled. "You just watch me."

The real estate office was in a shopping mall in town. "We're all going in together," my father said. "We're going to play the sympathy angle." Of all my father's "angles," that was the one I liked the least.

We were ushered into an office where a real estate agent wearing oversize aviator eyeglasses sat on the other side of a vast desk. "My assistant says you like the house," he said. "And what do you do for a living, Mr. Thicke?"

"I'm a businessman."

"Oh, what kind of business?"

With my eyes, I pleaded with my father not to mess up.

"You name it. I've been in every kind of business."

The real estate agent looked like he was weighing a follow-up question. Instead, he slid the application form toward my father. "If you could just fill this out with your last address, how long you were there, your references, your employment history—or, in your case, your business history—and your bank details."

My father handed me the form. I put our names at the top of the page, then stopped. What could I possibly write that wouldn't kill the deal? Last address? References? He had to be kidding.

"We just moved out here after our house burned down in Ontario," my father was saying. "We lost every damn thing we had in the world." The sympathy angle.

"A fire, eh," said the agent. "That's too bad."

My father neglected to mention he'd let the fire insurance expire. That could have been a deal-breaker right there. I noticed Brad feeling around the back of the cushions. I wondered if he was looking for more dimes.

The real estate agent leaned back in his chair. "What's your current income?"

My father ignored that question. "My wife left me with these two young children." He pointed to Brad and me as if it hadn't been obvious that we were with him. "I've been bringing them up on my own."

I did my best to look pathetic.

"I see. But we'll still need the first and last month's rent and a security deposit."

"Let's talk man-to-man." My father leaned across the desk with a confidential air. "Are we competing against anyone else for the house?"

"No," the real estate agent admitted. "It's too far out of town for most people, and too big."

"And with the house empty, you're losing out on rent, am I right? So, you don't get any commission?"

The man seemed to be waiting to find out where this was going, so my father went on. "We can move in right away."

"With the first and last month's rent?"

I noticed that he'd dropped the security deposit.

"We can get that to you later. For now, I suggest we take the house right away and start paying rent. It's a win-win. You won't lose any commission waiting around. And I'll be able to get the kids registered for school."

"You haven't got them enrolled yet?"

"No, we need an address for that."

The real estate agent was wavering. Now was the time to ratchet up the pressure. "Dad, we have to get signed up for school!"

Whether it was us two motherless children or the lack of other prospective tenants, the agent agreed to let us have the house—if we came back the following week with one month's rent.

"You see that, kids? Only four dimes spent, and look at us now!"

"But Dad, what about the rent?" He still couldn't see the hurdles ahead of us the way I could. He never would.

"Just watch me—I've got six more dimes to raise the money."

That evening, I joined my father and brother in watching a show in the common room.

"So, you doubted your old dad?" my father boomed, without seeming to notice that people were trying to hear the television.

"What do you mean?" I whispered.

"I've gone into the wood business."

"The wood business?" I was so surprised, I forgot to lower my voice. "What wood do you have? And how would you deliver it? Not in our van!"

One of the bearded hippies in the room walked over to turn up the volume on the television.

"I put an ad in the paper looking for firewood, and I got a response from a farmer who's been clearing his land. He'll deliver the wood, so all I do is get the customers and give him the addresses. They pay me, I pay him, and I don't have to do a damn thing. I just take the orders, and the money will come rolling in."

"Dad, since when has money ever come rolling in? Besides, we don't have a phone—how are customers going to call you?"

He lifted his shirt so I could see the pager on his belt.

"Tell her how many dimes you used," Brad interjected.

"Three," my father said with pride. "I'm not counting any callbacks I get on my pager out of the ten calls." He handed me a napkin that was covered in his writing. "By the way, I put some other classified ads in the paper."

With his random capitalization and big printed letters—he hadn't stayed in school long enough to learn cursive—he'd written, "Room and board in a rural setting (ladies only)." He turned the napkin over to show me the second ad: "Free pickup of unwanted appliances and household furniture by single father with 2 young children."

"Dad, please don't tell me you really put that in the newspaper."

"We need furniture, don't we? And whatever we don't use, I'll sell. I'm telling you, the sympathy angle works."

The next day, when I went downtown to put in some job applications using my father's pager number, I noticed a hand-printed Help Wanted sign taped to the corner of a storefront window. It was the first time in my life I'd seen a vegetarian restaurant. As I opened the door to go in, I was hit with the smell of curry and marijuana.

Inside the Veggie, the one waitress in evidence was standing as if paralyzed by the crowd of diners. Just as I was about to speak to her, she ran to the back of the restaurant. I followed her into the kitchen as she picked up a joint that had been burning in an ashtray.

"I saw the sign out front and, well, I used to work as a waitress." I didn't tell her I'd been fourteen at the time and had stayed only long enough to buy myself a transistor radio. "Is the manager here?"

"I'm the manager," she said, passing me the joint. "I'm Barb."

Out of politeness, I took a toke. I hadn't touched drugs since leaving Meadowlily Road.

Barb was heavyset, with curly brown hair. She picked up a plate of salad with sprouts on top and held it out to me. "Can you start right now? Everyone else was too stoned to come in to work."

I was elated. "What do you want me to do?"

"Deliver this."

"Where?"

"You'll figure it out," she said and took another hit of the joint.

With no instructions on how to make a smoothie or how big to cut the carob brownies, I somehow made it through the lunch service. When I went to the back of the restaurant where Barb had disappeared to, I saw her at a table cleaning the most marijuana I'd ever seen at one time.

"You didn't ask about the pay," she said to me.

I hadn't dared.

She pulled out seeds and stems and put them to one side. "Just get your money from the till and leave a note for how much you took."

"How much *is* my pay?"

"Just pay yourself what you think you're worth."

"Seriously?"

"Yeah, we don't go in for that capitalist bullshit. It's more like a cooperative here." Rolling herself a joint from the pile of cleaned buds, she lit it up and passed it to me.

I shook my head. I was still trying to get my brain around all this. "But what if I take too much?"

"Well, then, you must be worth it."

"Uh, okay. So, what shifts do you want me to work?"

"Come in when you want. Leave when you want. We're not your fucking parents here."

"Far out." Given that I hated being told what to do, I couldn't believe my luck in finding the Veggie.

My father was washing our socks in the sink when I got back to the hostel. "Dad, I got a job! It's the coolest restaurant in the world. And I can help with the house because I paid myself today."

"What do you mean you paid yourself?"

"We just take our pay out of the till."

"What the hell kind of business is that?"

"Dad, it's a beautiful business. There's no capitalist bullshit." I held out twenty dollars.

"Well, I hope you don't mind if I use a little capitalism to get our rent. I already have a dozen orders for firewood."

The next day, I showed up at the Veggie for the lunch service, and the door was locked. Barb arrived fifteen minutes late to open up.

Back at the hostel that evening, my father was looking satisfied with himself. "I found us two boarders," he said. "I told you I'd get us set up in ten calls, and I still have one dime left."

"How can we have boarders if we don't even have a place to live?"

"Don't be a Negative Nellie. We'll get that house." He laughed. "We have to: I already took a deposit." He held up his last dime. "I'll use this one to get our new phone installed."

In a matter of days, with thirty-eight orders for the firewood and two boarders who'd paid their first and last month's rent, my father had enough money to get us the keys to the house in Cordova Bay. As we stood in front of the door, I feared something might go wrong. Miraculously, the key worked, the door swung open, and we were home.

"Kids, this is the Year of Dacker."

I felt like it was going to be my year, too.

The next day, I went with my father and Brad to the garbage dump to get some furniture. Several people were already driving back out through the gates, so we eagerly climbed down from the van to see what they'd discarded.

"Here are some gloves," my father said, handing a pair to Brad and to me. We knew the drill: if something looked valuable, into our van it went. If it turned out we didn't need it, we'd sell it later.

We found an overstuffed chair and a TV stand for the television we'd get one day. Just as we were loading up a perfectly fine dresser, a long Cadillac Coupe DeVille drove in. While an elderly woman waited in the passenger seat, a man got out, opened his trunk, and deposited neat little bundles of newspapers onto the ground. Just as they were about to drive away, the woman's voice floated out her window.

"Did you see that family picking through the garbage?"

We were the only family there.

"Disgusting. Doesn't that man give any thought at all to what he's teaching his children?"

CHAPTER 28

NORMAL

VICTORIA, 1974

I WAS IMPATIENT TO jump into my new life. It was the first day of school, and we should have left ten minutes ago.

"Lori, sit down and eat your breakfast."

"Sit down?" A normal parent would have been hustling us out the door. *You'll be late for school.* But normal wasn't how things worked in our family. "C'mon, Dad. We have to go!"

My father gave me a long-suffering look. "Okay. Grab your toast. You kids can eat while I drive."

We climbed through a hole in the fence to the cul-de-sac where we'd parked our truck. It was paved, and we'd already had a taste of the mud that came from Victoria's seasonal rains.

"Your coach, milady." My father stretched his arm out with a flourish.

I climbed in, followed by my brother.

"We'll drop you first, son."

Brad seemed relieved that at least *he* would be arriving on time. He didn't like breaking rules. He had that in common with our mother. Brad would probably leave us in a heartbeat to go live with her if her husband would let him.

A couple of minutes later, there was a break in the trees, and Brad's new junior high school popped into view.

"Do you want me to come in with you?" my father asked.

"I'm okay," Brad said. He climbed down from the truck and walked away from us to be the new kid once more, a little taller this year, but still small for his age.

"Now let's get you to that school of yours." Claremont Secondary School was up a steep hill. "I think we can make it."

"You *think*?"

We arrived after the bell—which saved me from making my grand entrance in the smoking, overheated pickup truck that replaced our old VW van. Inside, the hallways were quiet, classroom doors closed to contain the hubbub within. I took a deep breath, then followed the signs taped to the brick walls. My homeroom was on the second floor. At the front of the class-room, students were greeting one another as long-lost comrades. I waited for someone to notice me, but when no one did, not even the teacher, I took a seat next to the window and looked out.

Back in Kirkland Lake, there was a limit to how far you could see: to the end of a lake, to the mine shaft, to a ridge of scrub pines. But sweeping from the shores of Cordova Bay all the way to Washington state was an endless sea of turquoise. The view wasn't just breathtaking—it was a revelation. It was like my old dreams had had borders around them; now my future as a sixteen-year-old in this new land seemed as infinite as the ocean. My father always said I could do anything. And in that glorious, awe-filled moment, I believed it.

At lunchtime, the cafeteria was hosting presentations for the various clubs. I put my name on the sheet of yellow foolscap for the entertainment committee. Heady with the feeling that anything was possible, I also signed up for the yearbook committee, which was canvassing for writers.

My high school photo with the eagle feather, Victoria, 1974

The following morning, brushing my hair for school, I spied the eagle feather I'd stuck in the corner of my mirror.

It doesn't matter what people say about you, my father always said to me. *As long as they talk about you.*

I laced the eagle feather into my long, dark hair. *Let them talk.*

After school, the entertainment committee was meeting backstage in the auditorium. Behind the curtain, where the walls were painted black, a group of students waited among the pulleys and spotlights. Sitting on a ladder was a guy whose light brown hair was brushed out into the biggest Afro I'd ever seen.

"Nice feather," he said to me, raising one theatrical eyebrow.

"Nice hair," I volleyed back.

"Yeah, too cool for school." He gave a sheepish smile. "I'm Fred."

After the meeting, during which we'd discussed the upcoming school dances, Fred said, "Let's get out of here." He aimed his forefingers at his temples like two pistols. "These student council rats are giving me a"—he sang the word—"*headache.*"

We walked down Claremont Hill together and then turned right onto Cordova Bay Road, where the closest store was. On the way down, I learned that Fred was one grade ahead of me. At the store, he got a Coke, I got a Canada Dry, then we went behind the building to the public beach. We sat on the same driftwood log, digging our shoes into the pebbly sand. Coming from Ontario, I couldn't stop marveling that wherever we went on this island, we were never far from the ocean and its boundless promise.

"I haven't actually slept with anyone yet," Fred was saying in the instant intimacy that had sprung up between us.

"I lost my virginity last year." I didn't mention how I'd woken up in a forest naked and alone.

"I don't want it to be just sex," he said. "I want a guy who cares about me. Otherwise, it's just going to make me feel like shit about myself."

"I know what you mean." I was a bit surprised that it wasn't just girls who felt that way. "It's like if we can get someone to love us, that makes us worthwhile."

"That is so fucked up."

"But you feel it, too?"

"Shit, yeah." He threw a rock into the ocean.

As the sun went down, Fred walked me to the bottom of our long driveway but declined to come meet my father. "Parents don't usually get me." By the way he said this, I wondered if he meant *his* parents.

The next day, Fred was waiting for me in the cafeteria. A pair of popular girls from the student council were making a presentation. I got the feeling that everyone in the school knew them. Laura appeared to be from the rich side of Cordova Bay. Her hair was perfectly blow-dried, and she held her fine fingers as if her nail polish were still wet. A cashmere sweater was tied casually around her neck. But even Laura faded into the background next to Elizabeth, dark-haired and as vivacious as her red lipstick. She was the funny one. Right now, Elizabeth was holding court in front of the other students.

"They think they're so cool." Fred pulled me to the back of the lunchroom, where we could sit by ourselves. "You know what? Most of these kids are going to peak in high school. But high school's not our time. The future is ours."

I looped my arm through his, hoping he was right.

Fred was camp in an era when being gay was something you hid. I loved that my new best friend was as fabulously freaky as me.

That evening, I went to my job at the Veggie and immediately felt the buzz in the air—I could almost track the news traveling from table to table. Even stranger, there was no smell of pot in the restaurant. I went back to the kitchen to ask Elvis, the cook, what was going on.

"They're closing us down, man," he said.

"Who?"

"The city."

"Why would they do that?"

He shrugged and sprinkled some sesame seeds onto a salad that he then handed to me to deliver. Later, he brought out his guitar to play for the customers who had stayed on to bid the restaurant farewell.

I told my father my job was over while he was mending a pair of Brad's gym shorts.

"Don't worry," he said, though I hadn't until that moment. "We'll figure something out."

I took that to mean he had been counting on my salary.

"It's okay, Dad. I'll get another job. They're looking for waitresses at that event place." I had been hoping that losing my shifts at the Veggie would give me more time for my writing assignments, but I didn't tell him that.

Not long afterward, Fred took me to Sappho's, a gay club with deejay music, a big dance floor, and a disco ball.

It was the beginning of a new phase for me. Now that I was seventeen, I wasn't trying to find myself anymore; I was trying to invent myself. And listening to Helen Reddy sing "I am woman, hear me roar," I knew exactly who I wanted to be.

My father had always said, *You're in charge of your own real estate.* Now I interpreted that to mean that I could sleep with anyone I wanted, male or female. That freedom hadn't come with a user's manual, though. And my father certainly hadn't given me one. My mother might have, but I had long ago stopped listening to her. So, it didn't occur to me that there were good reasons to say no once in a while. The only word I knew was yes.

Allowing someone inside my body had made me feel vulnerable. It opened me up, filled me with longings, made me insecure. So, I developed a rule to protect myself. I could sleep with whoever I wanted, but I would leave them before they left me.

That was how I became my high school's ambassador for yes.

One day, Fred and I were on our way to the back of the lunchroom, as usual, when I overheard Laura and Elizabeth debating how old you should be before losing your virginity. Laura seemed to think it was something you saved, like money in the bank.

I stopped at the end of the long table where they were eating their sandwiches. "You sound like we're in the Middle Ages."

Elizabeth looked around to see who might be listening in.

"Why shouldn't we sleep with whoever we want?" I went on, energized by their shocked looks. "We're liberated women. Sex should be on our terms, and with whoever we want. The more lovers, the better."

Looking back, I hope to God no one took my advice.

That spring, Fred asked me to be his prom date. "We can show this school who's really cool."

Although he was one year ahead of me, I hadn't thought about him moving on. Now I felt a sudden sense of sadness. For the first time since Bev, I had a real friend. And when he graduated, Fred would be leaving me behind.

"If you'll be my date, it'll get my parents off my back," he added.

From what I could tell, Fred's Italian parents, who ran a grocery store, were strictly old country. He was too afraid to come out to them.

"I just wish they accepted me for who I am." He sighed.

"Your parents shouldn't just accept you—they should celebrate you!" That's what my father did. Though, sometimes I wasn't sure if he was celebrating me or the parts of himself he saw in me.

When the time came for Fred's prom, I volunteered to buy him a corsage. The student council had arranged discounts, so I went to Elizabeth's house to pick up a coupon.

She answered the door in curlers. She was also in grade twelve, so it was her prom, too.

"Just give me a sec," she said and shut the door.

I looked through the window, curious to see life in one of the subdivision houses. The scene I witnessed that morning was like a dream of the ideal family. Elizabeth's mother was leaning over her sister and brother with a jug of orange juice. Her father was pouring himself a cup of coffee before coming back to his seat with a book under his arm. Her mother sat down and said something to her husband, and he put the book away.

I'd always said I didn't want to be like everyone else, but I felt a sudden longing to have what Elizabeth had. I envied her for having a normal family and all the trappings: a driveway that didn't muddy your shoes, a car that started when you turned the key, furniture that didn't come from a dump. And rules! She had them; so did Fred. I hated rules, but freedom was sometimes confusing.

When Elizabeth returned with the coupon, I still ached from wanting something I would never have.

Back at home, my father stretched the wall phone cord as far as it could go while stirring a pot on the stove. He was telling his caller that the check was in the mail. Then he plucked an envelope out of a pile of unmailed letters, slid it into his pocket, and hung up the phone. Soon, the check really would be in the mail.

"Why can't you just have a job like other dads?"

He looked surprised at my outburst. "Why would you want me to be like other dads?"

I didn't have an answer for that.

That evening, Fred showed up at my door wearing a yellow ruffled shirt and a green tuxedo with velvet lapels. I told him about how I'd felt at Elizabeth's place, that I wished I had a normal family like hers.

"Normal's just a setting on a washing machine," he scoffed. "Anyway, why be normal when you can be"—he pointed both index fingers at himself and sang the word—"*fabulous*?"

I hugged him, then pinned the corsage on him. "For the belle of the ball," I said. Maybe convention *was* overrated. I didn't want to be a total freak, as I sometimes felt, but I did like being a *little* different.

Later that evening, out of breath from our disco dancing, Fred and I collapsed on a bench outside the gymnasium. "We are definitely the funkiest ones in this school," he said.

We had stolen a couple of glasses from the soft drinks table, and now he topped them up from a mickey he pulled from his back pocket, barely bigger than a flask but enough to get us in trouble.

I cooled my sweaty back against the wall. "So, have you decided what you're going to do now?"

"I'm going to go full-time at Bootlegger. I need the money to get my own place."

"Don't you want to go to university?"

I was stunned when he shook his head. I thought everyone dreamed of university.

"All I want to do is meet a great guy and settle down." Fred was more conventional than I was.

I held up my glass. "Here's to next year—and to me surviving without you." We both had tears in our eyes.

He held his glass out. "And here's to our big, fat futures."

Yet he seemed sad, as if he couldn't see his future at all. I realized then that it took more than a view over a limitless horizon to make you feel like anything was possible. You needed someone to believe in you. I may not have had a normal life, whatever that was, but at least I had a parent who believed in me.

CHAPTER 29

LIKE FATHER

VICTORIA, 1975

EVER THE OPTIMIST, my father tried to hand me the mop.

"Perhaps Her Majesty would deign to wash the floor?"

"Dad, no, I'm studying."

He sighed as he started to swish the mop around. "So what did your last servant die of?"

The truth was that I didn't need to study that much; I was back to being an A student. To me, though, the point of homework was to avoid housework.

I was in my last year of high school. Bev had come for the summer and taught me to drive, but she was back in Ontario, and I'd lost Fred to Vancouver, where there was a proper gay scene. Now my only friend was my creative writing teacher. Mr. Munch had sandy-colored hair and a coppery beard and always wore blue jeans and a corduroy jacket with elbow patches. The first time he handed me back an assignment, he said, "Nice. Keep writing." With his encouragement, I expanded to short stories and to essays about women being able to do anything a man could—beliefs my father had primed me for. I was going to be a famous writer and travel the world.

My father, however, had his own plans for my future. "I don't know why you always need to be studying," he said that day, pushing dirty water around on the floor. "You're going to end up in business, like your old daddy."

"Never!" I roared. "I'll *never* go into business."

"Never say never." He gave that knowing chuckle of his, which infuriated me even more.

My brother came ambling into the room. His hair was still long, and he wore a chain of puka shells around his neck.

"What are you shouting about?" he asked with mild curiosity. My shouting was not an unknown occurrence in our house.

"Oh, forget it," I said, turning to the books on my lap.

"What about you, Brad? Aren't you going to be a businessman?"

"Sure!" At twelve years old, Brad didn't seem bothered by having his future laid out for him.

Not long afterward, I was in Mr. Munch's writing class when suddenly the intercom crackled to life and my name came blasting from it. I froze, pen in hand, not knowing what to do.

"Go on," Mr. Munch said, looking concerned; it was never a good thing to get called into the principal's office.

I raced down the hall. Flinging open the office door, I startled the school secretary.

"It's your father." She passed me the phone.

"Dad? What's wrong?"

"Lori, I have to get you out of school right now," he said. "Pretend you're upset."

"What?"

"Make like I'm giving you bad news. Look sad."

"What's going on?"

"I'll tell you when I pick you up. Just say you have to leave."

When I got outside, my father's pickup truck was idling in a cloud of its own exhaust.

"Is Brad okay?" I asked, breathless.

"Brad?" My father looked puzzled. "Of course Brad's okay. He's at school."

"Then why did you call me out of class?"

"Look in the back."

Behind him, spread out from the pickup's cab to the tailgate, were boxes of long-stemmed carnations. They lay in loose bundles, organized by color: red, white, yellow, pink, and blue.

"What's all this?"

"What does it look like?"

"You got me out of school because you bought some flowers?"

He looked at me like I'd insulted him. "Not bought, scrounged. I was at the dump when some men threw out a whole load of perfectly good carnations. As fast as they chucked them off their truck, you can believe your old daddy was picking them up. Now let's go."

"Where?" I climbed into the passenger seat. If I went back to class now, it would be too hard to explain.

"You're going into the flower business."

"Dad, I have school."

"Forget school. You're going to be a businesswoman."

"No, I'm not. I'm going to be a writer." I should have pushed back harder. But the flowers were already there. "Okay, just this once."

There is a turn where Cordova Bay Road leaves the coastline and heads inland. That was where my father deposited me. It was one of those warm fall days that always made me appreciate the West Coast. My father stood the flowers up in white buckets he'd already filled with water. He handed me a roll of plastic wrap, a box of elastic bands, and the sign he'd already made for me: CARNATIONS, $2 A BUNCH.

"Come back and get me in fifteen minutes," I called after him. The back of his pickup was still visible when the first car pulled up beside me.

"I'll take two."

I rapidly assembled the bouquets and passed them through the window.

The driver gave me five dollars. "Keep the rest," he said—which was lucky, because my father hadn't thought to leave me any change. As that customer swung back onto the road, another car took his place.

"This is perfect," said the woman in the Lincoln. "I'm on my way to see my mother."

I had just wrapped up her bouquet when a motorcycle stopped up ahead. I grabbed a bucket of flowers and ran forward, sloshing a bit of water onto my leg.

Two hours later, my father came to get me.

"Dad, I can't believe it. I sold all the flowers!"

"That's wonderful, darling." He loaded the empty buckets into the back. "How much did you make?"

I counted the money. "A hundred and three dollars!"

He raised his eyebrows. "Wow, you're a natural at this."

"Here, Dad. I'll give you half." I was remembering our fifty-fifty split with the Christmas trees back in Kirkland Lake.

"Don't be silly. That's yours. Now you can invest in more flowers." He eyed the wad of money, then reconsidered. "I'll just take something for expenses." He peeled off a few bills for himself.

"Take more, Dad. You need the money for the rent."

"I'll get the rent somehow. Don't worry. It's more important for my daughter to learn about business."

I felt rich. I'd always associated business with losing money—that's how it often worked for my father. But now I saw you could actually end up with more money than you started with! I was beginning to get the attraction.

A few days later, we were downtown, sinking into the plush seats of Harpo's Cabaret. With my father urging me on, I outlined my plan to Michael, the young bar owner. Instead of selling old carnations for two dollars a bunch, I would offer his customers fresh roses for two dollars a single stem.

"You want to sell flowers inside my club?"

I nodded.

"And take photos for your customers," my father added.

"Hmm. I guess you could come by tonight and feel out the crowd."

As the owner went to the bar to get a Tom Collins for me and a Drambuie for my father, I whispered, "Dad, I don't think he knows how old I am." The legal drinking age in British Columbia was nineteen.

"Well, just don't volunteer anything."

I decided to call my company Lori's Flowers and Photos. Before I'd made a single sale, I was spending money at a print shop on Fort Street, ordering five hundred business cards and two hundred sheets of headed paper. The letterhead was pink; the cards were high-gloss red with a raised black rose. I'd not only inherited my father's outlandish taste, but also picked up his lifelong habit of investing in cards and stationery before figuring out if a business would fly.

But it did fly. I just did the opposite of everything my father had taught me about business, and I was fine.

Sashaying from table to table with a basket of long-stemmed roses turned out to fit the outgoing personality I'd picked up from my father. Six nights a week, I'd hit the bars and restaurants with my flowers. All along my route, the buzz would build. A romantic dinner, a birthday, a girls' night out—wherever I went, there was always someone waiting for the flower girl. In a matter of months, I had saved five hundred dollars to buy a clunky station wagon that I christened the Red Rocket, though it was more red than rocket.

One day after school, Brad and I were doing our homework at the kitchen table, elbow to elbow, with the occasional jab. Brad's love wasn't schoolwork as mine was; he was more sports oriented and had been recruited for the school tennis team. He hadn't yet entered his rebellious phase, so if he figured he had no choice but to get down to his homework, he did.

When the wall phone rang, Brad beat me to it.

"It's for you," he said. He let the receiver fall so that it twisted on its cord down the wall. "Some man."

I pulled a face and picked up the phone. The kinks made the cord so short that I had to stand with my cheek nearly touching the dial.

"I'm callin' from the *Times Colonist.*"

"I'm sorry, is that bill late?" A chip off the old block, I had already run up one or two bills with the newspaper. I gave Brad a dirty look for passing me the phone. We had a protocol for collection agencies: *No one's home.*

"Nope, not a bill." Now I realized that with his clipped way of speaking, the man on the other end of the line couldn't be a bill collector; they always started out friendly. "You the high school student with the flowers?"

"Yes, that's me." I hoped he wasn't investigating me for selling in the bars while underage or not having a business license or not charging sales tax—my father was full of good ideas like that.

"I'd like to interview you."

"Really? That's fantastic!"

The journalist wanted to get a photo of me selling flowers, so we made an appointment to meet the next day at the Red Lion Inn, one of those hotels in Victoria that boasted of being more British than Britain. My father insisted on tagging along. We took my Red Rocket.

"You're going to let me do the talking, right?" I said to my father as I maneuvered the car onto the road.

He twisted his thumb and forefinger in a sign of buttoning his lips. "I won't say a word."

Inside the lounge, it was nighttime at three in the afternoon. A red glow coming from behind the bar illuminated the sole customer, a compact older man. On the table beside him was a camera.

"Are you the photographer from the *Times Colonist*?"

"Couldn't swing a photographer." He pulled a notebook out of his back pocket. "Doin' everything today."

My father reached out with a take-charge handshake. "Where do you want to start?"

The journalist turned to me. "How'd you get into this business?"

"You see, I was at the dump that day . . ." my father began.

"Um, Dad. Maybe I should answer that."

The journalist looked from my father to me, a surprised expression on his face. "Yes, tell me in your words."

It went on like that, the journalist trying to steer the conversation back to me as my father jumped in to answer or add a flourish to something I'd already said.

"Lori, why are you kicking me under the table?"

Later, driving back to Cordova Bay, I growled at my father, "Why did you do that?"

"What?" He raised his eyebrows in that innocent look of his. *Who, me?*

"You said you were going to keep quiet."

"You can't blame a man for promoting his darling daughter."

"But Dad, what if he believes that stuff you said?"

When the article came out, it was even worse than I'd feared.

I bought four copies of the *Times Colonist* that day, then sat on a log at the public beach where Fred and I used to hang out.

At the top of page five, there I was, under the headline "Entrepreneur, 17: 'Think Big or You'll Never Make It.'" "Think Big" was something I'd said about my dreams and how if you aimed for the sky, you might at least reach the clouds—things my father had taught me and would always himself believe, despite all evidence to the contrary.

Entrepreneur, 17: 'Think Big Or You'll Never Make It'

By AL FORREST
Times Staff.

Claremont High School student Lori Thieke plans to make her first million before she's 25 — and she's well on her way.

At 17 she is president of Lori's Flowers and Photos, a registered Victoria company that employs 50 girls between 19 and 23 years of age.

The flagship of her many enterprises is a flower and photo service for dining lounges but her company also supplies waitresses for private parties, models and referrals to the Victoria Escort Service.

"The girls who work for me are all older than I am but they all seem to accept me," she said.

"My goal is to make one million dollars by the time I am 25. I don't think I will ever be as wealthy as Christina Onassis but you have to think big or you'll never make it."

She came from Toronto 11 months ago and began earning pocket money by purchasing and selling used furniture. Then she began to branch out into antiques and then flowers.

Lori ran a roadside flower stand at her Cordova Bay house on the honor system but had to close the stand when some customers proved less than honorable. They not only stole the flowers; they took the cashbox.

She attends school by day and over the dinner hour has a meeting with her four regular flowers-and-photos girls, handing out cameras, flowers and their routes for the evening.

She takes a route herself on weekends when it is busy.

She guarantees the girls $3 an hour or commissions, whichever is higher. The company works on a low-price, high volume basis with a bouquet of flowers selling for $2 and a picture for $3. With photographs costing $1.40 each to take, one mistake and the profit is just about gone.

Lori recently sent 10 girls out to act as waitresses at a private party in Sidney and hopes to expand this side of the operation.

"Right now the supply of workers exceeds the number of orders. There are a large number of girls available for work in Victoria. Every time I place an ad, I get a large response."

She said most Victorians seem to like the idea of flowers and photographs in a cabaret.

"I think it is a nice European touch. Every now and then we will find a place that has a very English atmosphere and people don't want to be bothered with pictures and flowers. But I think this idea is changing in Victoria, especially among the younger generation. Most people are very friendly."

Lori Thicke sells flowers at cocktail lounge

My first time in the press—with my father posing as a

customer, *Times Colonist* (Victoria), October 6, 1975

Below that was a grainy picture of me, with my round face and long dark hair. A wicker basket of flowers was looped over my arm. My father was in the frame as well. Facing away from the camera, he was pretending to be my customer.

"Claremont High School student Lori Thicke plans to make her first million before she's 25—and she's well on her way." I liked that. "At 17 she is president of Lori's Flowers and Photos, a registered Victoria company that employs 50 girls."

Hold on, I thought, *fifty girls?* When my father told the journalist I had fifty employees, I'd kicked him under the table.

That night, at least one customer in every restaurant had read the article and wanted to congratulate me. I was still smiling when I walked up the steps to Harpo's. The bar where I'd kicked off my business six months earlier was my favorite stop of the evening. Wearing a black dress and a pair of shoes that were hurting my feet, I waved to the bouncer and then reached for the door.

But he blocked my way.

"I'm just going in to sell my flowers."

"You can't come in here."

"Why not?"

"Because you're seventeen."

"I come in every night!"

"You're underage. Good article, by the way."

Harpo's was one of my most lucrative stops, and I had no one to send in my place. Despite the newspaper saying I had fifty employees, it was just me.

At breakfast the next morning, my father handed me a sheet of paper with an ad typed on it. The letters were striped red and black, which meant he'd gotten his typewriter ribbon twisted again. Now the red was on the top.

I handed it back to him. "I can write my own ad."

"But you don't want just any employee. You want the right kind. Here's what you write." He read from his own paper. "Attractive, fashion-conscious young ladies wanted to sell—"

"Why 'fashion-conscious'?"

"You don't want hippies."

I'd only recently stopped identifying as a hippie. "Are you sure we can put 'attractive' and 'young ladies' in an ad?"

"Sure, you can put that. Why not?"

It was 1975. The ad went in as written by my father. Despite how often I railed against him, he was still the person I looked up to. We'd had our ups and downs, but things had always worked out, just like he said they would.

I hired my first two employees, Luki and Jacquie, sisters. Luki had a more relaxed style, wearing her blond hair down to her shoulders, while Jacquie, with pure elegance, often pinned her hair up. At seventeen and eighteen, respectively, the two were as underage as I was, but I figured that unless the *Times Colonist* interviewed them, we'd get away with it. Reading from my father's playbook, I hired Luki and Jacquie under the table, which meant that for the longest time, I knew only their first names and that they lived on a sailboat. One night, as we were putting the unsold flowers back into the Red Rocket, I discovered that the sisters were Bohemian—not in the sense that my father was, but in the sense of European nobility from the Kingdom of Bohemia.

Luki, Jaquie, and I had a routine. I would do the restaurants in the early part of the evening and then pick the two of them up in the Red Rocket to cover the nightclubs I could no longer get into. Because I was following in my father's footsteps, I paid them out of the handfuls of cash they gave me. Even after I bought a green ledger book to tally up expenses and earnings, I still ended up throwing my receipts into a brown paper bag. Like father, like daughter.

When another newspaper, *The Victorian*, asked to interview me, once again I believed my father's promise to keep his lips buttoned. Once again, he exaggerated, this time adding to my supposed roster of fifty employees the real European countesses Luki and Jacquie. The *Victorian* article was followed by one in *Success Magazine*, which—making a big deal of my age and my "chutzpah"—put me on the cover. When Air Canada's in-flight magazine called, I left my father at home and downgraded my business to only four employees. The article was still flattering enough to earn a call from my uncle Brian in Brampton. Last he'd seen, I was failing at school but succeeding at pilfering his drug samples. He thought I'd never amount to anything.

"It's a good thing I was strapped into that plane," my uncle said. "Or I would have fallen out of my seat." Rising in the estimation of a family member who'd thought so little of me was my sweetest victory.

You weren't supposed to believe your own publicity, but I didn't know that. I was beginning to feel like Fred's hair: too cool for school. I started skipping classes to study at home, then show up just for the tests. The one class I never missed was Creative Writing, with Mr. Munch.

One day, we were all working on a writing exercise in silent concentration. It was so quiet, we could hear our own pens scratching on our papers. I was writing a piece about feminism that I hoped to sell to a newspaper. Suddenly, there was a boom like a cannon. Everyone jumped.

My pager! I leapt for my purse, which I'd draped over one of the coat hooks at the entrance to the room. The pager I used to run my business was blaring out a message somewhere near the bottom of the bag, where I couldn't reach it. I felt myself turning red. Finally, I got the pager and silenced it.

Mr. Munch put his hand on his chest as if I'd given him a heart attack. "Well, that was exciting."

After that incident, I started asking myself if business and high school were compatible. I felt different from the other students. Older.

I was changing. Now that I had an income, I decided it was time to tackle the family finances. I called my father into the kitchen and shooed Brad from the table.

"Dad, you need to be more responsible. Can you show me all the bills you have to pay?"

"Why? I can't pay them anyway."

"I can help."

"Since when did you become the parent in this family?"

"Someone has to be."

"Very funny. Anyway, you can save your breath. I don't know where all the damn bills are. We can do this another time." Stalling was his usual tactic for dealing with anything organizational.

"There's never another time. What if we go bankrupt?"

He sighed. "You're being dramatic."

"Dad, just bring me the bills."

With good-natured capitulation, my father brought in a paper grocery bag from his truck. He emptied the contents onto the kitchen table.

"You've got to be kidding me!"

"There's probably some more. Let me look through my pockets."

He pulled out a handful of crumpled bills and threw them onto the pile. "Is that it?"

"Just wait." He felt around the top of the fridge. That yielded one more bill.

I flattened out the crumpled papers, then started putting them in alphabetical order. Some bills were handwritten.

"You bought a terrarium?"

"I'm selling it on consignment."

Others came in triplicate, like the ones for the classified ads in the *Times Colonist* marked PAYMENT DUE.

"Hey, wait. What's this?" I peered at one of the Final Notice bills. "This one is made out to me." I turned to my father, incredulous. "You used *my* name?"

"I had to. I was over the limit under mine."

"I'm not even out of high school, and you've already wrecked my credit rating!"

"I'll pay that bill first. Put it on the top of the pile."

"The letter says it's going to collection." I checked the date. "Three weeks ago! They're going to come after me."

"Don't panic. They can't take you to court if you pay something—anything." He got his checkbook out. "Here." He wrote out a check and handed it to me.

"Five dollars? They want fifty."

"Trust me, they can't sue if we pay something."

"How do you know things like this?"

"It's business."

"Business?" Suddenly I was furious. "You have no idea how to run a company!" I was yelling now. "You're disorganized, and we are always in trouble, and now you're going to ruin my credit."

I looked at Brad. He was squeezed over to the farthest corner of the couch as if trying to avoid stray bullets.

"Maybe we should go into business together," my father said. "That way you can keep track of the bills."

"Never!"

I couldn't pay all the bills I'd found, and neither could my father. I worried that Brad and I were in danger of losing our home again.

I was four months away from graduating when I went to see the guidance counselor. I wanted her to talk me out of quitting school. It seemed the smartest thing would be to work full-time on my business and make sure we had enough money coming in. But that's not what I wanted to do, really.

The guidance counselor's office was homey and warm, with low lighting. It made me think of Dr. Sweetland. As I settled in across from the counselor, she examined me over the top of her reading glasses.

"Nice article."

"Which one?" Despite feeling scared and confused about my future, I couldn't help showing off.

She laughed. "More than one? That's good." She placed her glasses in her drawer. "So, what can I help you with today?"

"I'm thinking I should quit school."

"I can understand that."

"You can?" That was not what I was hoping she would say.

"Well, certainly it must be a challenge for you to stay on top of your studies with fifty employees."

"I only have four."

"Oh, okay. Four, then."

"Actually, two. It's just that I don't have enough time for my schoolwork *and* for business. So I feel I have to choose." Now it seemed I was trying to convince her that I should drop out, which was the last thing I wanted to do. I changed tack. "But quitting would be crazy, right? It was always my dream to go to university. I mean, it *is* my dream."

"You know, it's okay if you feel that quitting school is the right thing for you."

"But isn't it your job to tell me to stay in school?" Did she think I wasn't university material?

She shrugged. "If you're meant to go to university, you will."

That evening, I sat staring out the bank of windows from the kitchen table. When my father came in, I said, "I quit school today, Dad. I'm going to devote all my time to my business."

"Okay, then," he said, and went silent as he digested this. "But you didn't do it because of me, did you?"

"No, Dad." But I didn't know if that was true. All I knew was that my old dreams were gone, and I didn't know what would take their place.

CHAPTER 30

DACKER & DAUGHTER INC.

VICTORIA, 1976

BEING A HIGH SCHOOL dropout left me with a lot of spare time. In the evenings, my flower business kept me occupied, but the days were another matter. With hours to kill before it was time to load my flowers into the Red Rocket, I would lose myself in self-improvement books. Meanwhile, my father was hard at work on his dream: Dacker & Daughter Incorporated.

One afternoon, it was just my father and me in the house. At the long table overlooking the orchard, I was rereading a section of a pop psychology book, *Games People Play*. The description of people who bicker to create space when a relationship is too intense seemed eerily familiar. It could have been describing my father and me.

"Mind if I join you?"

"Dad, I'm reading."

Ignoring my irked tone, he set his gray Underwood onto the table and set to work. With his thick index fingers, he hammered the keys. *Clack clack clack.* He swung the carriage over to the next line to bang out a few more words. *Ding.* I pretended I wasn't curious and went back to my book. Undaunted, my father yanked the paper out of the typewriter and, with a dramatic sweep of his arm, handed it to me.

"What's this?"

"Just read."

LADIES AND GENTLEMEN.

Would you like to enjoy a fine dinner, dancing, theater, cabaret, and get paid for it with no risk of embarassment? Consider going out on the town as a paid escort. Strictly an above board operation with no hanky-panky permitted. If you are attractive, outgoing and conversant, call Kanda Entertainment Agencies, 388-6275, page 712, leave message for return call.

"Just so you know, *embarrassment* has two *r*'s, and that's not what *conversant* means." I didn't admit that it wasn't a bad effort for someone who had only a grade-eight education. "And what the hell is Kanda Entertainment Agencies?"

"It's our new business."

"Dad, this is an ad for an escort service."

"Don't close your mind. Think of a man—or a woman—who only wants someone attractive as a dinner companion, nothing more."

"Come on. Escort agencies are just a front for prostitution."

"Not ours. It'll be strictly upper class. We'll make everyone sign an agreement that there'll be no hanky-panky."

"Right, and that's going to work." I professed skepticism, as I always did, but that was more to needle him. The truth was that I had a daughter's bottomless faith in him, so I was easily convinced that a piece of paper would prevail against hanky-panky.

Despite my father's saying women customers would be clamoring to use our new service, the only people who gave us business were men. We contracted with a half dozen escorts, whom we sent out regularly. When a nineteen-year-old friend from school said she needed work, I added her to our roster. Not long afterward, I sent Lynn off in her new black dress to meet her date in the restaurant of the hotel where he was staying. Around ten p.m., just as I was putting my leftover flowers away, the phone rang. Lynn was calling from a pay phone in the lobby.

"He says I'm supposed to sleep with him!" She sounded shaken.

"Are you serious? Wait, is he still with you?"

"No, he's gone to his room. He thinks I'm going to follow him."

"Quick. Just get a cab out of there. I'll pay you back."

My father had fallen asleep on the couch. I woke him up to tell him what had happened.

"Come on. You're not blaming me for that?" he asked, incredulous. "I didn't know that was going on."

Suddenly, it occurred to me why none of the other women had complained of advances—and that my father had just reached the same conclusion: our escorts were making their own deals.

We *were* running a front for prostitution.

The next day, we went downtown to officially close Kanda before we got arrested for pimping. As we signed the papers, my hands were shaking. I thought, *Was this what I quit school for?*

Not long afterward, my father's Underwood came out again.

"I'm afraid to ask."

He pulled the sheet out of the typewriter. "It's an application form."

"For what?"

"You know my friend Peter, who owns the Queen Victoria Inn?"

"You have a friend?"

"Okay, not a friend, but a man I know. Anyway, he says we can rent the penthouse on weekends for an after-hours nightclub. We'll make a fortune selling booze."

"Dad, how on earth would we do that legally? You have to have a liquor license."

"Not if you sell to club members, Miss Know-It-All." He handed me the sheet of paper he'd typed up. "Here's the application form we'll use."

Applicant must be of good character, be of legal age

not be of a belligerent nature or rowdy when drinking

must be respectful of establishment rules

must be respectful of the feelings and the personal privacy of their fellow persons.

"'Their fellow persons?' Oh, dear God, Dad. You've got to be kidding with all this."

"Why would I be kidding?"

Just then, Brad came running in from school swinging a tennis racket. "Hey, Dad, I made the elite team!"

"What team?"

"Hullo—do you notice what I have in my hand?" Brad mimicked a Björn Borg serve.

"Right, of course. Good for you, son."

My father didn't sound overly interested, and Brad looked disappointed.

"Hey, that's great, Brad," I said too late; he was already heading back out the door. When, after a while, he came in for supper, I didn't think to ask him any more about it. My father and I were already in deep discussion about our plans. We were starting a bar—before I was even able to be in one legally.

Our "Nite-People Society" was a hit with the waiters and waitresses coming off their shifts. As word got around town, the line grew outside the penthouse elevator. My father had a table at the door, where they could fill out his application form and then pay the five-dollar membership fee so we could sell them alcohol. Besides having the run of the top floor, my father had arranged it so members could go down to the pool in the basement, strip off their clothes, and skinny-dip.

Brad was thirteen at the time. Now that my father and I were away on Friday and Saturday nights, he'd either sleep over at a friend's or sit in a corner of our nightclub sipping a root beer until it was time to go home. If he ever took himself off to the pool to see the naked swimmers, I never noticed. On a few weekends, he went off on trips to distant tennis tournaments. Frankly, we were relieved when he did go away; then we didn't need to think of him at all.

With the first handfuls of cash, I paid off my father's outstanding bills. But before long, new ones started piling up: alcohol, mix, napkins, ice. I wasn't convinced that our drinks prices were taking into consideration all these costs, not to mention the nightly room charge. Without keeping books, we could judge what we were making only by seeing what was left when my father emptied out his pockets on Sunday morning. But we never seemed to be as far ahead as I expected.

"Dad, we need to make more money."

"Hmmm. We have a captive audience in our members. How about if we put together some tour packages?"

While we were making plans for our new travel agency, Brad spent more time away from the house. Perhaps to bring him back into the fold, my father spent money on a present for him: a mini motorcycle. I felt that such a big expense would spoil Brad. Since quitting school, I was trying to put money into my father's pocket, not take it out. On top of that, the motorcycle meant Brad was away even more often, tooling down the trails between our house and his school and then coming back with his hand out for gas money. I made no secret of my feelings, which Brad didn't appreciate.

Brad on his motorcycle, 1976

After some wheeling and dealing, my father and I flew down to Las Vegas. Circus Circus had given us two hotel rooms for free after we proposed selling gambling junkets to our private club members. The hotel-casino was betting that our tours would take off and generate some income for them. My father was that convincing.

"I've never seen a pair like you and your dad," the manager said to me when we were checking out. "I can't tell if you'll be wildly successful or go nowhere, but we will certainly remember you."

Our travel business ticked the second box: it went nowhere. We never got enough people signed up to launch a single tour. And now our after-hours club was showing some cracks.

We had always acted as our own bouncers at the door, but now a rougher crowd was starting to show up. It soon became clear that we had no idea how to keep people from getting out of line. Despite signing a document claiming they would "not be of a belligerent nature or rowdy when drinking," our members were turning out to be exactly those things. Once again, my father had put his faith in a piece of paper—much as I had put my faith in him.

One night, I felt a strange ripple run through the penthouse. A hush of anticipation. In the center of the room, a circle had gathered around two men. I pushed my way to the front just as they squared off. One man's fist sailed through the air and landed with a crunch on the other man's face.

I'd never seen violence up close. There was an ugliness to it that shocked me. I ran away from the scene. My back against the wall, I slid down to the floor and began to sob.

My father jumped out from behind the bar, torn between stopping the fight and coming to my rescue.

"You," he pointed to someone. "Break them up."

I couldn't stop crying. It was all out of control.

"Lori, calm down. I need you to help me clear this joint. Someone's going to call the cops."

"Dad, the bar!" Behind him, people were helping themselves to our unguarded booze. Glasses were so full that the hijacked alcohol was sloshing over the carpets.

I wiped my face and helped him herd groups of customers into the elevator. Finally, the last couple of drunks downed their drinks and left.

I looked around. The penthouse was a disaster.

My father pulled out two chairs for us. I took my shoes off to rest my aching feet.

"Dad, we don't know what the hell we're doing," I said.

"Sure, we do, Lor."

"No, we don't. We really need to close this place down."

"We're making money."

"We can't keep a lid on things. And we're not making that much. Not really."

He sighed. "Oh, well, we'll probably get kicked out anyway."

It had been a long night. With my father at the wheel, we drove through the darkened city. In the silence, I thought how far I was from the kind of life I'd dreamed of up on that ridge above the old farm. How had I gotten here? Running an illegal after-hours club and an escort service? My father's desire to create a successful business for us had pushed him to pursue ideas that could only get us into trouble.

It was clear I was not a good influence on my father. I had to stop encouraging his schemes before they devoured him *and* me, but how?

A few days later, I was gathering my flowers into bouqucts—a calm, repetitive job that gave me space to think—while my father stirred salt into his split pea soup at the stove.

"Dad, shouldn't you have made me stay in school?"

"Since when could I make you do anything?"

"Yeah, I guess."

"But are you thinking of giving it another try?"

"I really messed up by quitting. I should be graduating now."

"You can always go back."

"I feel about twenty years older than the kids in high school. I can't go back."

"There's no such word as *can't*. My daughter can do anything she sets her mind to."

Before I could explain to him why he was wrong, the back door opened and Brad came in supported by a friend. He was hopping on one leg.

"What happened to you?" My father put down his spoon.

"He was playing tennis," his friend said.

I ran to my brother's side to help him sit down. "Are you okay?"

"My knee hurts really bad. I turned—I think I tore something."

Brad, the one who had commanded none of our attention, suddenly needed all of it.

"I'm taking you to the hospital," my father said.

I grabbed a packet of frozen vegetables. "Let's put this on your knee." I bent down to do so, but my brother took the bag from me.

"I can do it myself."

Brad needed knee surgery, plus a few days in the hospital to recover. After his operation, my father and I came into his hospital room just as he was being scolded by the nurse for having too many visitors. Teenagers I'd never seen before—except for the one friend who had brought him home—were clumped around him, with a couple sitting on the edge of his bed.

"Half your friends will have to go."

My father laughed and said, "Come on, Lori. Let's leave Brad to his admirers."

"I'll catch a bus home, Dad. Brad, do you mind if I just hang around?"

"Do whatever you want. It's a free country."

"I'd just like to stay with you. I won't bother you. I've got my book."

His friends—where did he get so many of them?—stayed until the nurse came in again. This time, she shooed them all out. When they were gone, I settled into the chair beside Brad's bed.

"I'm tired," he said. "Can you pull the curtain around me?"

I hadn't had time for my brother, and now he didn't have time for me. I wondered if it was too late to repair our relationship.

"You sleep, Brad. I'll be right here."

When Brad first went into the hospital, I'd written in my diary that he was the most important person in the world to me—but was he really? I'd always been more focused on taking care of my father and on myself. The result was that Brad didn't care if I sat with him or not.

When Brad's dinner tray arrived, I was still there, and remained until the end of visiting hours. Over the next few days, from the moment the hospital let visitors in until they kicked everyone out, I stayed with Brad. My father came and went, and Brad's friends appeared for a few hours after school, but mostly I sat quietly beside my brother, reading.

I often wondered what I was doing there. Brad acted like I didn't exist. I was sure that I'd wasted my time. But as he was being discharged, he turned to me.

"Thanks, Lor."

"For what?"

"For hanging out."

When the school year finished, I had to accept that I would never have my own graduation or my own prom. But Brad was happy: he was going to spend the summer with our mother. She and her husband had moved across the country to Campbell River, where Art worked in a mine and my mother had a job as a bookkeeper in a supermarket. They were just 150 miles north of us now on Vancouver Island, no ferry required.

The bus would have been hard for Brad to manage on crutches, so I drove him. Even though we arrived an hour late, our mother was waiting at the window of her mobile home. As I parked, she flew out the door and crushed my brother to her chest. Seeing his face as he squirmed away in pleasure, it occurred to me that at the end of the summer, he might not want to come back to us.

My mother gave me a timid hug. "You sure you have to go, Lor?" In the year since I'd seen her, she hadn't changed much. At forty-nine, she still wore her hair in short, loose curls, but now it was salted with silver.

"Yeah, Mom. I have to work my flower business tonight."

"Well, at least let me give you this." She held out a bag. Inside was a sweater she'd knitted for me, in red. It was my favorite color.

"That's great, Mom," I said. I didn't sound like I meant it, even though I did. I knew she was trying. I just didn't know how to acknowledge that or let her in.

Sunday morning, as usual, my father and I took the Red Rocket to the Western Speedway. Each week that summer, he had managed to find something to sell at the flea market so he could have the table next to mine. Now in the back of my station wagon were buckets of my unsold flowers and a box of antique books he'd found cleaning out someone's old junk. After the nightclub and escort service fiascos, working at the weekly flea market with my father was enough Dacker & Daughter for me.

That day, I was setting up my flowers next to my father's leather-bound books when I heard a voice behind me. "Heyyyyyy."

It was Danny, a flea market regular. He was around six feet tall, with shoulder-length red hair. He was wearing blue jean overalls and a bandanna around his neck, and he had just finished unloading books of stamps from the back of his Karmann Ghia. He walked around to where I was taping prices onto my buckets and gave my shoulders a squeeze. He was always just a little too happy to see me, so I felt relieved when he ambled over to talk to a couple of early birds.

I looked across the oval of the racetrack to where dishes and bric-a-brac, car parts and kids' toys, were laid out on tables and on the ground, then back to where my father and I were working. I couldn't help but see how much my life had gone downhill since I quit school. From my classroom window, I had once seen a vast sea of possibilities. Now selling other people's junk seemed to be all that lay ahead for me. *Think big or you'll never make it*, I'd said to the journalist. Was this thinking big?

One table over, my father gave me a funny look. "Lor, are you stinking thinking?"

"No."

Yes.

That evening, when we got back to the farm in Cordova Bay, I said to my father, "I should've listened to you." He looked startled; I didn't usually credit him for being right. "Maybe I should figure out how to go back to school."

"Did I say that?"

"You said I could do anything I set my mind to."

"Of course, yes. But I thought you felt too old for high school."

"I do. But I could try to get into community college, to finish grade twelve."

"Look where I've gotten to with only a grade-eight education," he said. He didn't realize he had just made the case for me. "Anyway, go ahead if you want to go back to school. I've got a new deal that you wouldn't be the least bit interested in."

I laughed, taking the bait. "Really?"

"Yes, really, Miss Smarty-Pants. Scrap prices are going through the roof. I can make a fortune on old cars."

"A fortune, eh, Dad?"

"You wait and see. I'm going to surprise you."

I wondered briefly what it would take for my father to surprise me. The next morning, I drove to Camosun College to pick up an application form.

CHAPTER 31

COMBUSTION

VICTORIA, 1976

MY BROTHER WAS SUPPOSED to stay with our mother until the end of August. In July, she called me to come get him.

"The trailer is so small, you know, and it's hard for Art, with Brad around all the time."

"What does Brad think about that?"

"Oh, you know, he understands. That's just how Art is."

Yeah, that's how he is, I thought. Since Art lost his job in the mine, he had been spending his days in front of the TV, expecting my mother to clean and cook the moment she came in from work. It made me hate him even more.

On Saturday, after a three-hour drive, still fuming about Brad being sent away, I pulled up in front of my mother's mobile home. She was there, as usual, waiting at the window. I could see her excitement in the way her body became animated when she caught sight of my car. She came running out. Brad followed, without his crutches now.

"I can't stay," I told her, even though I had to go to the bathroom. I preferred peeing by the side of the road to seeing Art's uncouth face.

"Oh, okay." She turned to my brother. "All ready for your trip, Bradley?"

Her jaunty tone seemed forced. It wasn't the first time I had the impression that she was hiding a broken heart. There was a sadness to her life that I couldn't bear to think about.

Brad shrugged and put his bag into the back seat. Like my mother, he also hid his emotions.

But I hid nothing. "That fucking Art," I raged as we drove away. I was mad on my brother's behalf and mine. Once again, Art had come between us and our mother.

"It's okay," he said. "I was missing my friends and my motorbike." Then he added, "And of course, you and Dad."

We drove the rest of the way in silence. Years would pass before my mother finally told Art to get out.

"I never should've left you children," she would say to me.

"But why did you stay with him for so long?"

"I had to. Because I left you and Brad to be with him."

In some weird way, she'd suffered through with Art because of us.

"Oh, Mom."

"He never understood how hard it was to leave you. When he asked me to go away with him, he said, 'I'm leaving my six children—you can leave your two.'"

As if love could be measured in numbers.

But on that summer day when I picked up Brad, I didn't know any of this. Except for the six children Art had left behind, along with his pugilistic wife.

As soon as Brad and I got home, my father tossed me a manila envelope. "I believe this was the mail you were expecting?"

I tore the envelope open, overjoyed when I saw the contents. It was an acceptance letter and a course catalog for Camosun, the community college with a campus nearby. I could not only finish grade twelve, but I could also take some university courses, like psychology and creative writing. I opened the catalog at the kitchen table and began picking my classes.

It felt like I was on my way again. My life was back on track.

Not long after I sent away my registration, my father came into the living room with a bad-news look on his face.

"Kids, we have to move."

I jumped up. "What the hell are you talking about?"

"We have to leave Cordova Bay."

"I don't want to move again," Brad said. "I have my friends here."

"Dad, I love this house."

"We have no choice."

"No one ever asks me what I want to do." Brad's voice was so fierce, it was almost like he was crying.

"Why do we have to leave?" I said. "I don't want to move, either."

"Our landlord defaulted on his mortgage, so they're putting the house on the market. We need to find a new place to live. Unless we want to take over the payments and buy it ourselves."

Since our farm had burned down, my father had never expressed any interest in homeownership. "You want to buy this house?" I asked.

"Yeah, let's buy it," said Brad.

"Hell, no," my father said. His tone implied that owning your own house was a crazy idea. "Who wants to be *married* to a house?" In his book, being married was about the worst thing that could happen to a person.

To avoid being "married" to our house, my father found a bungalow to rent not far from downtown. Our lives would have turned out differently if I'd had another source of investment information: we were leaving behind the only significant parcel of undeveloped land in the whole of Cordova Bay. It would soon be worth millions. We could have had that land simply by taking over the mortgage payments.

But at least we were free.

A couple of days later, my father was packing up boxes to go to the new house. I'd made my decision. I told him I wouldn't be going.

"What?"

"I'm renting my own house."

"Don't be silly. How would you pay for that on your own?"

"Luki and Jacquie will move in."

"The countesses who sell flowers for you?"

"Yes—they're tired of living on a sailboat."

"You don't need those girls. Brad and I can come with you, help you pay the rent. I'll cancel the lease on the other house."

"No way!" I felt like I was fifteen again and escaping Meadowlily Road, only to have my father and Brad move in with me.

"You sure? I don't see why we need to pay two rents," he grumbled.

"Dad, it's not about the rent! I'm eighteen. I need to live my own life."

"Oh, well." He sighed. "Just do what you have to do."

I found a house not far from campus. I was on my way to that bigger life I'd dreamed of. No more Sunday mornings at the flea market for me.

As for my father, he started a business that didn't involve me—buying up old junker cars to sell by the pound to the scrap metal yard in Vancouver. I felt liberated, even if certain details of his business confused me.

"But how will you get all those cars to Vancouver?"

"When I'm ready, they'll send over their mobile compactor. It's a machine that compresses them into little cubes. Then I'll just ferry the cubes across to the mainland."

What could go wrong? I thought. At least it wasn't illegal.

Just before college was to start, I visited my father in the lot he'd rented in the industrial part of Victoria, far from all the tourist attractions. As I came up over the bridge, his cars were already visible on the horizon. Dozens of junkers—not so different from some of the cars we had owned—were stacked one on top of the other. Looming above the wooden fence, the top row of wrecks was an eyesore even in this area reserved for eyesores.

I let myself in through the gate, then followed the trail wending through the car carcasses teetering above me. I heard my father's voice and entered his office.

"You can go rub salt in your ass!" he was shouting into the receiver. "I'll do it myself." He slammed down the phone.

"What's up?" I asked. I wasn't overly concerned: he regularly told people to rub salt in their asses.

"Damn scrapyard tells me I have to wait three months for the compactor."

"Three *months*?"

"Apparently there's so much demand, you're supposed to reserve in advance. I can't pay the rent on this yard for three more months, so I'll just have to crush them my way."

"Your way?" I didn't like the sound of that. "How can you get all these cars across on the ferry without compacting them into cubes?"

"You'll see, Miss Negative. Come back tomorrow."

The next day, the gate was gone and the fence around it had been flattened. Inside the yard was a giant Caterpillar bulldozer; rather than try to fit it through the gate, he had mowed the fence down.

My father was seated high up in the cab. He fired up the bulldozer and headed straight for one of the old wrecks. There was a crunch of metal and glass as the Caterpillar crawled over the car's hood, onto the roof, and then down over the trunk.

The car was flat now, but it wasn't the neat cube the compactor would have made: the doors were spread-eagled, and the fenders were hanging off at odd angles. My father climbed from the Caterpillar's cab onto the top of its rusty track and then jumped down to the ground. He was shirtless in the heat, with a pair of rainbow-colored suspenders holding up the blue jeans hanging just below his belly.

"You can do this one now," he called out. A welder who'd been smoking behind the wrecks came over. I knew him from his work on one of my father's other projects, a machine for extracting gold dust.

"Hey," Sammy said. It sounded more like *Hnnngh*. His jaw had been wired shut from an operation to give him a square jawline.

Lighting his torch, Sammy began to neaten up the wreck. He sliced through the wayward metal with a blue-and-orange cutting flame.

"You really think this is going to work?" I asked my father.

"There's more than one way to crush a vehicle."

"It looks like a lot of effort." I glanced around at the dozens of cars still stacked up in his yard. The bulldozer would have to drive over each one.

"I don't have a choice. I've got a semitrailer booked for tomorrow to take these cars to the scrapyard in Vancouver."

"By ferry?"

"Of course, by ferry. Did you think I'd fly them there?"

I couldn't imagine the contents of his yard fitting onto a semitrailer, but I shrugged. My father never spent much time thinking of ways things could go wrong. He only thought of ways they would go right.

The next evening, lost in the pleasant task of setting up my new house, I'd all but forgotten the cars when the phone rang.

"Well, that didn't go as planned."

"Hi, Dad. What happened? Did you get the cars all loaded onto the semitrailer?"

"Yeah, that part we did."

"And you got them to the ferry?"

"Yeah, we did that, too."

"And you got your money?"

"There's sort of a funny side to this."

"I'm afraid to ask."

"You remember Sammy cutting off the doors with his welder's torch?"

"Yeah."

"Well, some sparks must have gotten into the upholstery. And when the truck was going down the highway, the wind must've whipped them up."

"Oh my god, Dad, whipped up the *sparks*?"

"The truck got onto the car deck all right, but then the whole damn thing burst into flames."

"On the ferry?" I gasped. "Was anyone hurt? Did the boat catch fire?"

"Luckily the ferry hadn't left yet. They were able to evacuate."

"Oh, Dad. Are you in trouble?"

"No, but I'm banned for life from the BC Ferries."

I felt dread drop like a stone to the bottom of my stomach. I was about to start college. Was it a mistake leaving my father to his own devices?

The next morning, I was in a panic. It was my first day at Camosun College, and driving up and down the neighboring streets, I couldn't find a single place to park. I checked my watch again. I was going to be late. Ignoring the signs, I pulled the Red Rocket into the parking lot reserved for faculty, my father's motto on my mind: *Rules are for other people.*

I found a spot near the clock tower, then raced up the steps. I got to my Psychology 101 class just as the instructor was writing his name on the blackboard. When he turned around, I felt my cheeks burn.

My new professor was Danny from the flea market. He smiled, as always just a little too happy to see me.

CHAPTER 32

BREAKFAST IN BED

VICTORIA, 1977

DANNY WAS THE KIND of professor who wore blue jeans to teach and who let you call him by his first name. But beyond that smile of recognition when I walked into his classroom, he treated me like any other student. I hated that.

Over the summer, I'd avoided Danny because he liked me too much. I wasn't attracted to older men, and he was at least thirty. But now the flea market tables had turned. Since Danny had stopped showing interest in me, I suddenly found him irresistible. I didn't realize there was something else going on—namely, the false belief that if I could win over someone who mattered the way a professor did, that would mean I mattered, too.

I was determined to make Danny mine. To do that, I would use the two things I was good at—banter and sex.

My new house on Bay Street had three bedrooms on the main floor and one in the basement. Luki and Jacquie, who were selling flowers for me in the evenings, took two of the upstairs rooms; they had been dreaming of sleeping on something that didn't rock like their sailboat did. Because the basement room would be harder to rent out, I took that one for myself. Now I would turn it into a bedroom for seducing Danny. I opened the *Times Colonist* and started scanning the classifieds for what was synonymous with sex in the seventies: a waterbed.

Setting up the waterbed was harder than I'd expected. Even when empty, the mattress was so heavy that it took two men to haul it downstairs. After filling it with hundreds of gallons of water from the garden hose, I lay down—and discovered the other thing they don't tell you about waterbeds: they're fricking freezing. I put the mattress cover on it and tried again. It was only marginally warmer. Already regretting my purchase, I moved on to the rest of my plan. I put on the red satin sheets. I mounted sheer curtains all around the bed. I placed a mirror sideways on one wall. (The view from the ceiling didn't seem that appealing.) Then I stepped back to see the room as Danny would see it.

I had taken today's sexual revolution back to a nineteenth-century bordello.

Between running my business and going to college, I had little time to meet men, so I spent every psychology class scheming to get Danny into my bedroom. I flirted with him. I dressed for him—in skirts and, once, a wide-brimmed hat that I imagined made me look sophisticated. Yet, for all my efforts, he seemed more amused than interested.

Then, one day after class, I got a call on my pager from my wholesaler. My father had forgotten to deliver my check, and now they were refusing to release the flowers for tonight's rounds unless I paid up. I had a fifty-minute break, but my car was a twenty-minute walk away—four parking tickets in a row had convinced me to abandon the faculty lot.

Desperate, I came up with an idea.

Danny was just walking into his office when I asked to borrow his little Karmann Ghia. He parked it right next to the school.

"You know how to use a stick shift?"

"Of course." The Red Rocket was an automatic, but Bev, when she visited, had taught me to drive a manual.

"Okay, I guess." Danny slowly reached into his drawer, then handed me his keys.

I was elated. This proved I was more than just another student to him.

I was at the door when he called me back. "By the way, I had a problem with the brakes the other day. They should be fine, but just be careful."

I easily found his Karmann Ghia. Getting in behind the wheel, I placed my purse on the passenger seat. As I maneuvered out of the space, re-familiarizing myself with a stick shift, I pumped the brakes. They seemed to work fine, so I swung the sports car into the street.

After I delivered the check to release the ransomed flowers, I headed back down the long, straight stretch of Shelbourne Avenue that would lead me to Camosun College. Suddenly, I heard a honk. I looked over my shoulder to see Elizabeth, from my old high school, driving beside me. We weren't that far from Cordova Bay, where she still lived with her parents. I waved back.

Up ahead, I saw the light at McKenzie had turned yellow. I wasn't close enough to run it, so I pressed the brake—and my foot went straight to the floor. Ahead of me, the light turned red, but I couldn't slow down. Cars crossed in front of me. I was speeding into a busy intersection with no brakes. To my right was a gas station. I turned the wheel hard. The car went up over the curb, and I swerved to miss the gas pumps. There was no way to stop, but ahead was a brick wall. I deliberately drove into it.

The front of the sports car folded like an accordion. I couldn't move—not from injury, but from shock. Beside me, I heard banging on my window.

"Are you okay?" It was Elizabeth. She'd seen the whole accident.

"I think so," I said, dazed. "Oh my god. I've wrecked Danny's car."

"At least you're alive."

"He loves this car! You have to come with me to tell him."

"Who's Danny?"

"My psychology prof."

Elizabeth looked surprised but agreed to come. We left the Karmann Ghia scrunched up against the wall.

When we got to Camosun, Danny was in his office marking papers.

"Your car," I said, and took a breath. "The brakes went."

"She was so fast-thinking," Elizabeth added loyally.

"Wait, what about my car?"

At that moment, announcing the worst thing I'd ever done to anyone, I started to giggle. "I crashed it."

He looked at me as if I were speaking another language. "You did what?"

"I don't know what happened. I'm so sorry." I still couldn't stop the nervous laughter. "It was the brakes."

Danny looked at my slashed pantyhose and the bright red mark on my knee. "Did you hurt yourself?"

"No, the nail polish from my purse smashed."

"Were you doing your nails while driving?"

"Of course not," I said, indignant, although truthfully, that *was* something I had done before.

"Did you try downshifting to cut your speed?"

"Oh no, I didn't think of that."

"Are you sure you didn't confuse the clutch for the brakes?"

"But you said the brakes were bad."

"Not that bad."

"You have insurance, right?"

Danny looked anguished. "Yes, but not for collision."

"I'll pay you back," I told him.

"Of course you will. But right now, I need a car."

"You can have mine."

The Red Rocket was a beast of a vehicle: slow, heavy, and a gas guzzler. Danny was not happy with the trade, so I offered to sweeten the deal with five hundred dollars.

Despite destroying his car, I was convinced I still had a chance to seduce Danny. Rather than give him the money I owed him at school, I would take it to his property. He was building a house on a ten-acre lot in the highlands, which is why he had been moonlighting at the flea market.

That night, I drove out to Danny's property in the old Buick I had just bought. I had five one-hundred-dollar bills tucked into my red garter belt.

"I brought your money," I said to him, opening the door of the car. Even though I was shivering in the crisp fall weather, I swung my legs out. Then I slid my dress up so he could see my garter belt with the bills. "Come get it."

Danny looked down at me as if weighing what to do. He came close. He slid my dress higher. Shutting my eyes, I felt his breath on my cheek. I leaned back as he tugged the money out of my garter belt. Then I felt a chill. I opened my eyes. With a smile that was wryer than usual, he shoved the bills into his back pocket.

"See you in class tomorrow," he said as he walked away from me. "And don't forget your essay."

At the time, none of this felt remarkable—trying to seduce my teacher, crashing his car and giving him mine in return. Lacking a frame of reference for how people usually behaved, I found all of it perfectly normal.

Still, the constant rejection was painful. In December, even though I loved psychology, I made the decision not to enroll in Danny's class the following term.

And then, the most surprising thing happened. In the end, what seduced him was not the red garter—it was my *not* being his student. When I dropped Danny as a professor, he picked me up as a girlfriend.

Around this time, my father called to say that Brad had been caught skipping school again. It had been weeks since I'd spoken to my brother. I felt guilty; I knew he needed the kind of mothering my father couldn't give him. Maybe I could? I still had an extra bedroom.

"Dad, I think Brad should come and live with me."

"Why do you say that?"

"He's been caught skipping school like how many times?"

"As I remember, you missed a lot of days yourself."

"Brad's not like me. He needs rules and regular hours and someone to go talk to his teachers. You know that's not your thing."

"I believe in letting you children make your own decisions."

"But, Dad, kids make stupid decisions!"

"Just do what you need to do." My father sighed. "But you'd better ask Brad first. I don't think he'll want to leave his old daddy."

By then, I was suspecting that my father's freewheeling approach to parenting was not as good for Brad as it had been for me. Things a parent should have warned me about—religion, drugs, sex—I had had to figure out for myself. Even so, I felt lucky that my father gave me the values to make my own decisions. But what about Brad? What did he feel? What did he need? He seemed to be struggling. I invited him to come live with me and my roommates, hoping I could be a better sister to him. He said yes right away. I wondered if he was hoping to find something that was missing at home.

I enrolled Brad in a nearby junior high, where he made new friends, a group of four boys. He no longer played tennis, but he and his friends shot a lot of pool. He even brought them home on occasion, which was new. Perhaps I was less embarrassing than our father. But as I tried to put some structure around my brother—rules neither of us had ever had—I discovered that I didn't know how. And enforcing the few rules I did try to institute, like asking him to be home by a certain time, seemed more trouble than it was worth.

In the end, the only thing I could give Brad was what I wished I'd had from our father: I took an active interest in his education. I didn't have to start on my flower rounds until six, so every day when Brad came home from school, I would be there telling him to do his homework.

It must have been a shock for my brother, who'd never been constrained in any way. "You're not my mother," he would yell, and then take off, sometimes not coming back until late.

I was out of my depth. Brad would cut class, disappear to shoot pool with his band of friends, and come back only to sleep. I was worried about what he would become if he messed up his education. I made an appointment with his high school guidance counselor. When I knocked on the door, a bearded man looked up from his desk.

"Can I help you?"

"I have an appointment."

The counselor seemed taken aback. When the secretary wrote my name down, he must have assumed Brad's mother would be coming in. "You're the guardian?" he asked.

"Not officially. But my brother lives with me."

"What about your parents?"

"Divorced. I thought Brad needed more structure than my dad could give him. The problem is, I can't seem to make him care about school."

I'd put my brother on the guidance counselor's radar, which Brad added to the list of things he blamed me for. On top of that, it didn't work.

A month after Brad moved in with me, my father announced that he was giving up his bungalow. "What's the point of living in a house by myself, without my kidlings?"

"So, where are you going to live?"

"I'll just sleep in my car."

"In your station wagon?"

"You know me. I'm a free spirit. I don't need much. I'll just park in your driveway so I can use your bathroom."

"Dad, you can't sleep in a car in my driveway!"

"I'll be fine. All I need is to use your bathroom. But if that's too much trouble, I'll just go to a gas station." I could hear the hurt in his voice.

"Oh, for god's sake, you can't go to a gas station."

That night, before Danny fell asleep, I told him what my father was planning. He flipped over, making a wave that nearly threw me off the waterbed.

"Never a dull moment with you," he said and ruffled my hair.

In a matter of days, my father held a yard sale and sold everything he had accumulated since we moved west. Then he packed his clothes and shaving kit into his Impala station wagon. I left my Buick on the street so he could park in my driveway to sleep.

I should have known better. After I finished selling my flowers that evening, I came home to find Brad's note on the door:

Dad is going to spend the night in your bed, because it is too damp outside for him to sleep in the car.

I Left your sleeping Bag on the couch.

I Love you
Brad

The next morning, I woke up groggy from a spotty sleep on the couch to see Luki and Jacquie standing in front of me.

"What's up?"

"Your father."

The smell of bacon was permeating the house. On cue, he poked his head through the alcove.

"Finally, you're awake. I'm making bacon and eggs for the girls. Do you want some?"

When he went back to the kitchen, Luki said, "We didn't leave our own family to live with yours."

Where had I heard that before?

"He said he was going to sleep in the car." I couldn't help but hear how naïve that sounded.

In a repeat of the situation with Adrienne, Luki and Jacquie soon packed up and left. My father moved out of his car and into my house.

The truth was, I thought it wasn't a bad thing to have him under my roof, where I could keep an eye on him. But a niggling little voice wondered, *Will I ever be free?*

One morning not long afterward, I was sleeping beside Danny when I heard a knock at my bedroom door.

"Lori, Danny, wake up."

"Dad, we're sleeping."

The mattress cover had slipped off the waterbed, and now it was cold on my back. I pulled the red satin sheets up until they touched my chin. The water made a slurping noise.

Danny raised himself up on one arm. I gave him an apologetic kiss on his temple, where his red hair was going gray.

Just then, the door opened, and in came my father. "I brought you two breakfast in bed." He set a tray in front of us. In the middle was one of my flowers from the night before, sticking out of the honey jar.

Danny turned to me as soon as my father left my red satin boudoir.

"Does any of this seem normal?" I knew he meant my father moving in with me, then serving the two of us breakfast in bed.

I would soon leave Danny. I couldn't stand for anyone to criticize my father—that is, anyone other than me. But in that moment, with the waterbed sloshing beneath us, I told Danny the truest thing I could say.

"It's normal to me."

CHAPTER 33

& SON

VICTORIA, 1979

I MOVED INTO A house with a basement suite, where naturally my father and brother took up residence. The fact that I didn't say no—never a word I was good at—encouraged my father to think that once this writing kick was over, I'd go into the family business, whatever that happened to be at the time.

"Never!"

Brad, for his part, seemed more like our father every day. When he dropped out of school at sixteen, I knew who to blame.

"He's just following in your footsteps."

"What can I do?" my father protested. "You can lead a horse to water."

"He's not a horse. And he should've stayed in school. He's a smart kid."

"I only went to grade eight, and look at me."

I *was* looking at him. He was living in his daughter's house. And he was perpetually broke. Any money he managed to scrounge, he was pouring into his invention: the machine to pull flecks of gold from river sand—gold so fine it had until now slipped through every known method of capture. For someone from Kirkland Lake, this was the Holy Grail—and equally mythic. Since the ferry fire, I had a new awareness of my father's capacity to create train wrecks. Still, I didn't want to burst his bubble. "Yeah, Dad, you're doing fine. It's just that I really thought Brad would graduate."

"I trust your brother to make his own choices."

I hit the same wall with Brad. "I don't know why you're getting involved," he said. "You should just butt out."

Brad found a job with a scrap metal dealer he'd met helping our father. Soon he was coming home dirty and tired after a long day's work sorting metal. Meanwhile, after two semesters at community college, I was accepted at the University of Victoria. I sold my flower company for four thousand dollars, enough for tuition and living expenses. I was done with business, I thought.

As for my father, he opened a junk store. I was thrilled because now he would clean up the mess outside our house. We had become *that* family, the one with an old car up on blocks in the yard—though in our case it was an army generator, a row of rust-bitten school lockers, and a centrifuge to sift sand for hidden gold.

I thought the shop would keep him out of trouble, but almost as soon as he opened, the city began trying to close him down. It wasn't just that he'd lined the sidewalk with his detritus: the generator and school lockers as well as a wringer washing machine, some marine buoys, and a banana-seat bicycle. Or even that you had to walk past his junk to get to the luxury yacht dealership behind him. It was the location. The store sat right on the Trans-Canada Highway. Everyone going anywhere—up island, to the ferry, or to downtown Victoria—passed right by his disorderly door.

My father had created an epic eyesore on Victoria's busiest street.

"There goes the neighborhood," Brad said as we watched our father nail his hand-stenciled sign above the entrance: WE $ELL ¢HEAP, YOU $AVE $.

Ignoring this, my father pointed to the three new yachts displayed next door. "Kids, when I make it rich, I'm going to buy us one of those boats. Which one do you like best?"

My brother and I rolled our eyes at each other.

Despite the city's attempts to shutter the shop, my father convinced Brad that this was a viable business. So, my brother quit the scrapyard to work in the store alongside our father. Now, thank goodness, it would be Brad incarnating our father's dreams, not me. Dacker & Daughter had become Dacker & Son.

But my father and brother were like the odd couple. Soon, customers were remarking at their explosive arguments, which they made no attempt to conceal.

Why don't you ever do what I tell you to do? (My father, hands on hips.)

You're standing right there. Do it yourself. (My brother, stomping away.)

I'd never heard people in a shop argue openly like the two of them. I assumed some employees argued with their bosses—just in private. But private wasn't how we did things in our family.

Brad and my father somehow carried on without killing each other. During my second year of university, my father added an auto glass business. At first, he was the one replacing broken windshields under a tarpaulin out back. But the customers complained: either the windshield cracked when he was putting it in, and then they had to wait while he ordered another one, or it leaked with the first rain. Then Brad took over, turning out to be something my father wasn't: meticulous.

Stopping by the store on my way to university around lunchtime one day, I was surprised to see a boy of around fifteen adding items to my father's blight on the sidewalk.

"Who's that?" I asked my father when the boy went inside.

"That's Kenny, my new employee. I caught him breaking into the warehouse where my gold machine is."

"What? He was breaking in . . . and you hired him?"

"Not just like that. Give your dad some credit. I recognized the kid when he ran away, so I went to his home to talk to his foster parents."

"I'm still trying to get my head around this. You *hired* him?"

"Lori, it was heartbreaking. He's living in that house, the one with the demolition notice." He pointed to a pink stucco bungalow, the only home left in this commercial area. "His foster parents took me to his bedroom, and he was lying on the bed staring at the ceiling. There was nothing else in his room, just that bed."

"But you caught him robbing you!"

"Look, no one ever gave me a chance. They locked me up in reform school. So, I told him, 'I'll give you the chance I never had.'"

"Oh, Dad," I groaned. "Why can't Brad help with the store?"

"Your brother doesn't like how I do business. Speaking of Brad . . ." My father cupped his hands around his mouth. "Kenny!" he called. "Would you give Brad a hand out back?"

A flurry of sound came from the office. A drawer slammed shut and then Kenny emerged smoothing down the pockets of his jeans.

"Yeah, sure," he said.

Kenny was nothing like Brad. He wore a black biker shirt and had tattoos on his arms. But he still had freckles and was so slight that his chest was concave: maybe in him my father saw the boy *he* had once been.

Inside the store, my father's office was a tiny room dominated by a kitchen counter. His gray Underwood typewriter sat next to his makeshift cash register, which was an adding machine above the silverware drawer. Five-, ten-, and twenty-dollar bills were lying in the grooves meant for forks, knives, and spoons. This was a step up: my father's cash register used to be his pocket. I hoped that having a new employee would mean more organization for the store. Brad certainly wasn't interested in finances; he just wanted to fix things.

I followed my father outside, where the traffic made a constant rumble. He took off his suit jacket and slung it over the handle of a lawn mower, covering up a sign that read WORKS GOOD.

My brother came loping up the hill from behind the shop. At seventeen, he had turned into a handsome young man, long-legged and tall. At six foot four, he was like a giant compared to my father and me.

"It's a wise man who knows his own son," my father said, watching Brad approach.

I jabbed him hard with my elbow. "Why would you say that?"

"It's just a joke."

"It's not funny." I hoped Brad hadn't heard him.

"Kenny's going to give you a hand," my father told my brother.

"I don't need a hand."

"You should give him a chance," my father said. "He's a good kid. And he helps with the customers."

"What customers? As far as I can see, I'm doing most of the business here with my windshields."

My father brushed this aside. "I'm investing in the future."

"You're paying him for nothing."

"Brad, let's not worry about nickels and dimes—once I get my gold machine working, we're going to be rich. This is going to be the Year of Dacker."

Back in the office, my father reached into the cutlery drawer. Pulling out a twenty-dollar bill, he handed it to Kenny. "Here—why don't you get us some chicken across the street. Lori, Brad, white meat or dark?"

While we waited for Kenny to come back, Brad felt around in his pocket for his cigarettes. My father opened the back window for some air.

"I wish you'd get it that we really don't need Kenny around here," my brother said.

"Now, son, you could have worked in the office if you'd wanted to."

"It's not that, Dad." Brad lit his cigarette. "I just don't get why you hired him."

"The kid needed a break."

"You don't appreciate anything I do around here, then you hire that kid and think the sun shines out of his ass." Brad threw his match out the window and walked outside.

Kenny should have been back by then. My father and I went to the front and saw him on the other side of the Trans-Canada, holding our lunch. Cars were whizzing by, except for the odd one slowing down to gawk at the store. My father gestured to Kenny to cut right across the four lanes of traffic, but understandably he hesitated. Not seeing the rushing cars as a good enough reason to hold up our lunch, my father stepped into the road and put his hand up. Cars screeched to a stop. Kenny ran across.

There was more chicken than we could eat because Kenny had spent the whole twenty. My father pulled out enough for us and handed him the bucket with the rest. "Here, why don't you run this down to your foster parents?" Kenny shrugged and took off. "I was in their house the other day, and there wasn't a goddamned thing to eat," my father confided to me.

We brought Brad's plate down to where he was getting ready to work on a windshield.

"Have you talked to Kenny's probation officer lately?" my brother asked.

"No. Why should I?"

Brad grabbed a chicken leg. "I guess I should tell you this. I met a guy last night who told me Kenny spent six months in juvie."

"Brad, you've got to stop bringing up a man's past," my father scolded. "I was in reform school, too, you know. And look at me now."

"Oh, forget it," Brad said.

I glanced at my watch; I had to go to class. "Thanks for the chicken, Dad." I gave him a kiss on the cheek. "Don't work too hard, Bradley," I yelled to my brother.

He made a face at me.

That evening, on my way home from university, I drove past the store again. All three of them were out front. My father was jabbing a finger in Kenny's direction. I could tell he was shouting. Kenny's head was down. Brad was towering above both of them with his arms crossed over his chest. I slowed down to see what was going on.

Behind me, a horn honked. I pulled a U-turn and parked around the side of the store and watched unseen as the argument continued.

"I counted four hundred dollars this morning, and we've made at least a hundred bucks since then," Brad was yelling. "Now there's only three hundred." He balled his hands into fists.

"Kenny, I trusted you." My father shook his head in disbelief. "I was giving you a chance."

Kenny said nothing.

"I've never even checked the cash—you could have been doing this to me all along. When a man trusts you, you don't screw him." All the wind seemed to have gone out of my father.

Kenny looked up. "You're not going to tell my probation officer, are you?"

Brad thrust himself closer to Kenny. "That's all you care about?"

My father put his arm out to stop him. "It's okay, Brad. Reporting Kenny won't do any good." He took his suit jacket from the lawn mower and put it on. "Just go home, Kenny," he said in a beaten voice.

Kenny tore down the hill toward his house. Suddenly, Brad wrapped his arm around our father's shoulders. In that one tender gesture, all their arguments were washed away.

It would be the last time I'd see them embrace. Everything was about to change.

CHAPTER 34

CRASH

VICTORIA, 1982

THE DAY AFTER THE incident with Kenny, Brad and my father went back to arguing. I could hear their raised voices as I came up the hill by the yacht dealership. My father was leaning out the back window while Brad worked on a car below.

"Son, you can't spend all day on that windshield. We're trying to make a buck here."

"If you're so concerned about money, why didn't you order the right windshield in the first place?" Brad threw down his polishing cloth. "I spent half an hour on that sucker before I figured out why it didn't fit."

My father slid the window closed. Brad picked up his cloth and began to remove the bits of glue from around the windshield. A light rain was starting up. Some droplets were wetting a T across my brother's broad shoulders and down the center of his back.

"Should you be doing that in your good clothes?" I asked him.

"Yeah, well, I'm meeting someone after work."

"Someone?"

"Can I please have some privacy in my life?"

"You have loads of privacy. Ever since you moved out to live with your friends, you don't tell us anything. I suppose you have a girlfriend, but if you do, I've never met her."

"You think I'm going to let her meet my crazy family?"

"Me? What's wrong with me?"

When Brad didn't answer, I turned on my heel. I was going to check on my father and, as usual, tell him what he was doing wrong. The sidewalk outside his store was still littered with unsightly castoffs. So far, the city council had been unable to shut him down, but not for lack of trying.

My father emerged from his tiny bathroom shaking water off his hands.

"You should put a proper towel dispenser in there," I told him.

He ignored me, as usual. He padlocked the front door, then walked down to his car, which was parked beside the latest gold-extraction machine. Any money he made from the store was going directly into the pockets of the welders he hired to get the machine to churn out pure Midas dust. *You can take the boy out of Kirkland Lake . . .* I thought.

We bought some fish and chips, and he took me to Clover Point, where we sat in his station wagon. With a light rain tinkling on the roof, we ate looking out at the sea. On his dashboard was the usual clump of traffic tickets. But, oddly, in the back seat was his Underwood typewriter.

"What's that doing here?" I asked him.

He reached into the back, nearly upsetting his fish and chips, then handed me a sheaf of papers. "I'm writing a book."

"You are? When did you get that idea?"

"I thought it was time I put down my war stories."

I flipped through the pages he'd handed me.

"You realize you're copying me," I said.

"You're not the only writer in the family. Don't forget, my father was a poet. If anything, I'm following in *his* footsteps, and you're following in mine."

Except that I wasn't following in anyone's footsteps. I wasn't writing anymore.

My father's efforts should have inspired me, but over time I came to see writing as impractical. I was just about to graduate from the University of Victoria with a combined psychology and English degree, and that was also impractical. I didn't want to be a psychologist or teach English—I'd simply studied what I loved. But now I had no idea what to do. The things I'd dreamed of, like being a writer and traveling the world, were just that: dreams. Where would I find the money? Anyway, I needed to stick around to keep an eye on my father. I was constantly worried about him. Who knew what he'd get up to if I weren't around? It was bad enough when I was.

I was right to worry. A few evenings later, I got a call from my brother. He never phoned me without a reason.

"Dad's in the hospital."

"He can't be," I said.

"There was an accident. I'm going there now."

I don't remember driving to the emergency room, just that, suddenly, I was there. And everything had gone quiet. It was like my concern for my father wiped out my sense of hearing. The staff were moving from bed to bed, hooking and unhooking machines, wheeling people in and out of cubicles. It was like I could *see* the noise but couldn't hear it.

Then Brad was there, taking my arm. The sound came back on. He pulled aside a curtain that encircled a gurney. My father was lying there. His eyes were closed. His skin was ashen. Even his tattoos were faded.

I turned to my brother. "Is he all right?"

My father opened his eyes. "Of course. What did you think, I was dying?"

I rushed to his side. "What happened. Where are you hurt?"

"My leg," he said. "Motorcycle."

"Dad was selling a windshield in the middle of four lanes of traffic," Brad said. "He saw a car at a red light with a crack. He was halfway across when the light changed. That's when the motorcycle hit him."

"Do you want to know the worst part?" my father asked in a woozy voice.

"This isn't the worst part?" I gestured toward the emergency room beyond our cubicle.

"I didn't get a chance to give out my card."

"Dad, don't make me laugh. You're lying here hurt."

"Oh, he's not feeling too much pain," Brad said. "I think he's flying on painkillers right now."

"Higher than a kite," my father said.

"So then, after someone calls nine-one-one, Dad borrows a quarter from the guy who hit him and asks for help to get to the phone booth. He had to call the insurance company to see if the ambulance waiting for him was going to be covered."

We all laughed too loud at this.

When we stopped, my father dabbed at his eyes with the corner of his sheet and said, "This is embarrassing, but I have to tell you. You know how they always say to wear nice underwear in case you're in an accident?"

"Yeah."

"Well, I just happen to be wearing the worst pair I own."

Our laughter exploded again. I think we were getting a little hysterical.

A nurse bustled in, glared at us, then snapped the curtains closed.

"How can you laugh, Dad?" I whispered. "Doesn't it hurt?"

"Are you kidding? I've never been in such pain in my life. My goddamned leg's split open."

We'd come so close to losing him. "Don't you ever do anything that stupid again."

"But of course, he would.

A couple of days later, my father was back at the store, hobbling around on crutches. He pointed to where Brad was putting in a windshield. "Go talk to your brother."

"Why?"

"He's mad that I'm not at home resting. But if I did, who the hell would run the store?"

I went to where Brad was working. Even under an open tarpaulin, the smell of windshield sealant was in the air. "Hey," I said.

He glanced up, then went back to his work as if I weren't standing there.

I started to walk away. "Nice talking to you."

"Wait," he said. "As long as you don't want to talk about Dad right now, you can stay. Besides, I have something to tell you."

"That sounds serious."

"I know it's bad timing to bring this up now, but I'm planning to move to the Okanagan Valley."

"What? That's hundreds of miles away!" Brad had been moving away from us for a long time, but at least he'd been here physically. I always thought we'd win him back one day, but now . . .

"First, I almost lose my father, and now you're telling me I'm about to lose my brother?" I felt a sadness in my heart.

"I knew you'd get all dramatic," he said. "It's nonstop fun around you two. But seriously, I can't take Dad's chaos anymore. Not that you would even notice it. For you, it's just regular life."

He had a point. I didn't understand what Brad's problem was. This was how we'd always lived.

"Dad's not going to be happy about you moving away," I said.

"He'll still have you. You've always been the special one to him." Brad's voice was bitter.

"That's not true." But he was right, and it hurt me to know he knew that our father's eyes always shone brightest for me. I had a sick feeling that once Brad got away from us, he'd be gone forever.

"I wish you weren't leaving."

"I'm not going right away. I'm going to plan it out, wind down the windshields. I'm not like you and Dad, always rushing into everything. But I just thought you should know."

"Have you told Dad yet?"

"I told him just before his accident. Jesus." Brad smacked his hand on his thigh. "I hope that wasn't why he was so anxious to get me another windshield."

"I wouldn't put it past him, trying to keep you around a little longer. That's exactly why I worry about him. He sees the opportunity, never the danger."

In a few weeks, my father was able to do without the crutches. But the effects of his injury lingered on—in me. I couldn't get over the fright his accident had given me. Then, one evening, my worst fears came true: there were flashing lights outside my father's store. I tried to see what was going on, but a police cruiser blocked the road. I pulled over at the bottom of the hill and raced to where a group of people had gathered.

I pushed my way through the crowd to see a gaping hole in the chain-link fence that surrounded the yacht dealership. A truck had rammed through it. Its back end was still on my father's property, and its front end was buried in the side of a yacht. Two other yachts that had also been up on blocks lay on the ground beyond the first one. The hulls were split open, the metal railings bent, the windows smashed. The truck must have pierced the chain-link fence, then knocked the boats over, domino style.

I ran up the hill, searching for my father. I found him up top, talking to a policewoman. As she walked down to look at the yachts, I went to his side.

"Dad, what happened?"

"Well, I bought this truck at a livestock auction—"

"Wait, that was *your* truck?"

"Yeah, I just bought it. I parked it out back, but I guess the emergency brake didn't work."

"Didn't you try it out before you bought it?"

"I was going to get it checked out right after I got the insurance."

"What? You didn't insure the truck? Do you even know what those wrecked boats are worth? You are so fucking irresponsible!"

"Don't swear."

"You're telling me not to swear when you just destroyed three new yachts?"

"These things happen, Lori. That's why there's insurance."

"But you didn't have any!"

"That's true. But the yacht company must have insurance."

"Against a truck knocking over their boats? How do you insure for that? Anyway, don't expect me to fix this."

My father looked puzzled. "You're not responsible for me."

"Yeah, right."

"I'm a grown man."

"But look at the damage."

"It could have happened to anyone."

"No, it couldn't! Who buys a vehicle at a livestock auction?"

"Well, that part, maybe. But how was I to know the parking brake didn't work?"

"Why do these things always happen to you?"

His face showed momentary confusion. I could see he didn't think *he* was the problem here. Then his expression shifted, as if he suddenly realized I didn't just mean that this insanely expensive accident was his fault. I meant that *everything* was. Everything that had happened to us.

He lowered his shoulders and started to walk away. But then he spun around and glared back at me. "You listen here, missy. Maybe I wasn't lucky enough to get an education like you, but I've managed to support you and your brother just fine. Did you ever go hungry? No. Did you ever want for anything? Never. So, you can just get off your high horse." He glanced down the hill, to where the crowd was dispersing. "And don't tell me you need to fix things for me. I can take care of myself. It may not be your way, but it's my way. You just worry about your life and let me live mine."

I didn't know what to say. All this time, I'd been trying to get my father to be normal. But he couldn't be; he didn't know how—and I was wrong to want him to change. If he were the father I sometimes wished he was, he wouldn't be all those other things I loved about him. And he wouldn't have taught me all that he had: to dream, to dare, to bounce back no matter what. To never take no for an answer and to always look for that rainbow. I would be forever grateful for those lessons. As I would be forever grateful that he was my father.

"Sorry, Dad. You're right. It *is* your life, not mine. And I wouldn't trade you for a whole herd of Shetland ponies."

He looked up sharply, but when he saw I was being sincere, his face relaxed. "Now, if you don't mind, I'm going to have some paperwork to fill out with that lovely lady in uniform."

"Dad, don't you dare chat her up."

In an odd way, the accident with the yachts freed me. I realized I couldn't always save my father from himself. Even if I wanted to, I couldn't be with him every minute of the day. And I didn't have to be. This was his life, not mine. And he was living it the only way he knew how.

I didn't know then where that revelation would take me, but I felt myself begin to let go of a burden I'd been carrying around for a long time. If I didn't have my father to take care of, I began to think that maybe I *could* move on one day.

The yachts also freed Brad and my father—from the store. The accident had finally given the city the grounds they were looking for. Citing my father for inadequate customer parking, they gave him one month to close the shop.

CHAPTER 35

THE YEAR OF DACKER

VICTORIA, 1983

MY ELECTRIC TYPEWRITER WHIRRED TO LIFE—but my fingers were stuck. The deadline for the University of British Columbia's creative writing degree was coming up fast. This was a master's program I was applying for, and I had no idea what to compose that would be good enough to get me in.

The ocean glimmered silver beyond the blank page sticking out of my typewriter. I had already moved one step away from my father, into my own place. I was living in an apartment near Mile Zero, the spot that had marked the beginning of our new life here on the West Coast. Now it was marking *my* new beginning—whatever that was going to be.

Just then, I heard a musical knock. *Rat-a-tat-tat.* I looked at my watch: right on time. I opened the door to the carpeted corridor that connected all the apartments in the building.

My father was standing there in his pajamas and slippers. He had moved in next door. "Do you want some french toast?"

"Sure, Dad."

After I got my BA, my father had encouraged my dream to do a postgraduate creative writing degree; I don't think he realized it would take me away from him.

The following week, I was driving by the warehouse containing the latest incarnation of my father's gold-extraction machine when I saw a flatbed truck. It was backed up to the hulking metal contraption he'd been tinkering with for months.

My father and brother were out by the jury-rigged machine, standing in the rain.

"This is going to be the Year of Dacker," my father was saying to Brad. "I thought it was last year, but I was wrong. This is definitely the year." He patted his invention like he would the flank of his old horse Bucky. Rough, welded seams made this one look Frankensteined together from different machines. Which probably was the case.

"Dad, you're getting wet." I held my umbrella over his head.

He had designed this prototype to extract literal gold dust. His pot at the end of the rainbow was the fine gold trapped in the black sands of riverbeds, too small to capture by gold panning or any other process. To increase his odds of success, my father had put together in one machine every placer mining technique he'd ever heard of, no matter how fringe or unproven: riffles, grizzly bars, mercury traps, a sluice box, a centrifuge, and who knows what else.

"One of these is sure as hell going to work."

"Yeah, Dad. You keep telling yourself that," Brad said. I wondered why my brother cared. He wouldn't be around for the fallout. Next week, he'd be living in the Okanagan Valley.

"When we get the gold, what kind of car do you two want?" It always annoyed me when my father asked us that.

"A Ferrari," Brad replied.

"Good choice," my father said.

I gave my brother a black look. "Don't encourage him."

"What about you, Lor?"

"Let's just see if the machine works."

"Your sister's a real downer." My father gave me a sidelong glance. "I hope you're not going to be like this when we're rich."

So far, my father had managed to avoid talking about the fact that Brad was moving away. Or that I was applying to a university that was also on the mainland.

The rain was letting up now, so I put my umbrella away. Just then, Kit, my father's latest welder, came up the street. Small and lithe, he was a former Vietnamese boat person who worked two other jobs besides this one. Kit spoke little, in contrast to my father and Brad, who argued loudly and prolifically. Today there was peace—with no customers to enjoy it.

"You need my help, Dad?" Brad asked. Kit and my father were now threading a cable under the gold-extraction machine so they could winch it up onto the back of the flatbed truck.

"No, son. I've got it under control."

Brad looked skeptical that anything here was under control. "Well, in that case, knock yourself out." He waved his arm expansively.

"Kit, not like that!" my father said.

Kit didn't look up. "I don't understand."

"You turn it the other way," my father said, demonstrating with his hands, even though he had zero mechanical knowledge, and Kit wasn't looking anyway. My father had invented the gold-extraction machine in his head and asked Kit to build it working from drawings he'd sketched on the backs of the envelopes all those bills came in.

Kit continued what he was doing. "You want to help, you pay me more money."

Before Kit had a chance to turn the winch on, my father slid his hands under the machine as if he couldn't wait for the motor to lift it up. His cap slipped forward, his arms trembled, but the machine didn't budge.

"Easy, killer," my brother said to our father. "Let the winch do the work." He climbed up onto the truck, where Kit had attached the cable. Then, with a flick of his finger, Brad turned the winch on. Slowly, the machine ascended into the air. Kit pushed and tugged it into the right spot on the vehicle.

"Thanks, son," my father said. "Why don't you come with us?"

"Nah, I've got some stuff to finish up. I don't want to leave you with a mess when I go to the Okanagan."

"I wish you'd stay, son."

"I can't, Dad. We talked about this."

My father turned to me. "Come with us. It'll be interesting."

I didn't admit how curious I was about the Sombrio area, where back in the 1700s, Spaniards discovered gold in the riverbed. But the grad school deadline was getting closer, while a story to bolster my application seemed to be farther away than ever.

"I've got work to do," I said.

"Bring your work with you. You won't want to miss this."

"I have to write a story for my application," I told him. "Maybe I should write about *you*."

"About me?" My father tried to hide his pleasure, but he wasn't a very good actor. "Why would you want to write about me?" He was on a fishing expedition.

"Dad, nothing you do is boring. You're like the gift that keeps on giving."

He seemed happy about this and clearly thought he could eke another compliment out of the situation. "You just think I'm interesting because you love me."

I didn't argue.

"Come on, then. Let's go."

"Oh, what the hell." Going to my car, I put my umbrella in the back seat and grabbed my notebook. Then I went to sit next to Kit. Being the smallest of the three of us, he had already shimmied into the middle of the cab, where the gearshift was.

We drove north along the Trans-Canada, then cut west to Sooke. The ocean shone sterling through gaps in the rainforest—dense stands of cedar, hemlock, and fir. Before long, my father was humming "If I Were a Rich Man." With his cap and gray beard, not to mention his eyes shining with hope, he did bear an uncanny resemblance to the protagonist of *Fiddler on the Roof*.

My father working on his gold machine, Victoria, 1983

Our destination was Loss Creek. The river emptied out into the wild west coast of Vancouver Island, though we were headed for a spot near the headwaters. I'd never heard of Loss Creek, but my father assured me that it was well known in mining circles: a hundred years ago, there was a gold rush right there. At least if things went wrong, someone might be able to find us.

After an hour and a half, it seemed like we would have reached the top of Vancouver Island. In fact, we were nowhere near. The whole island was almost three hundred miles from Victoria to the tip. With slow progress navigating the winding roads in that heavy truck, we'd gone only sixty miles. But that was far enough to bring us to what already seemed like a different world from my campus life.

"Hang on," my father said now, as we swerved onto a narrow logging road. We drove between ancient fir trees that were as somber as sentries, with long beards of moss. Abruptly, they gave way to the shock of clear-cutting. Logged out, the hillsides were covered in fresh, ugly stumps, still bleeding. Hacked branches cascaded down the muddy ground like matchsticks. You could see where whole slopes, denuded of their trees, had slid into the river. I was holding on to the dashboard while, below us, the water hurtled by, churned a silty brown.

Where the logging road ended, we turned onto an even narrower track and began to wind along its hairpin turns. I was relieved when we made it safely to the bottom. My father backed the truck to the river's edge with the wheels just touching the water.

A scrum of scruffy men were watching us from under a tarpaulin. They had long beards and matted hair, as if they'd taken their cue from the hoary trees. I felt as if we'd traveled not only to another world, but also back in time.

"Who are they?" I asked.

"Prospectors," my father said.

I wondered who they thought *we* were—my father in his trench coat and plaid cap; Kit in his orange-and-yellow safety vest; me with a notebook under my arm.

We were close enough to their encampment to smell the sausages and hear their sizzle on the open fire. The prospectors stayed in a wary group under their shelter, except for one. His hair was pulled back into a ponytail, making him look as if he had been trapped in this place since the sixties. He came toward us. I moved closer to my father. Just then, the prospector knocked one of the guylines holding the tarp, unleashing a stream of water onto his head.

"*Tabarnak.*" He had a French-Canadian accent just like my mother's husband. "'Allo, Dacker."

My head snapped to my father—he was *acquainted* with these people?

"This is my daughter, Lori, and my welder, Kit." He didn't even try to introduce the prospector: they could have been best friends, for all I knew, and still he would have forgotten the man's name. It was lucky he'd gotten both Kit's and mine on the first try.

"How are things?" my father asked companionably.

"Last night, Molly took a shot at me."

"You must've been near her claims," my father said, unfazed.

"Are *we* near her claims?" I whispered as the prospector walked away, glancing around to make sure no one had a hunting rifle trained on us.

"Don't worry," my father said under his breath. "Anyone can prospect a riverbed. But don't get too friendly with these guys. Not like you usually do. Prospectors are crazy as coots."

"You're telling me, Dad."

Kit had switched on the electric winch. After he lowered the gold machine onto the riverbed, he jumped down off the back of the truck and squatted next to it.

My father dragged the back of his hand across his wet forehead, leaving behind a smear of dirt. He pushed his cap back, then bent to make one more check of the grizzly bars at the bottom of the sluice box separating the rocks from the fine material. His long nose nearly touched them as he peered through to the mercury traps inside the steel pipe.

It had taken him years to get to this moment, yet I was the one who was impatient as he inspected, adjusted, checked for tension and tilt, and moved parts only to put them into the same spot. He tightened a screw on the sluice box and stepped back.

"Okay, Kit. Fire her up."

With his shovel, my father dug into the black sands of the riverbed. He filled the pail, then tipped it over the lip of the sluice box. The sands began to spread out over the grizzly bars. Next, they filtered through the sluice box screen.

I had always been a skeptic when it came to my father's inventions, but this time was different. The sand was passing through the sluice box and into the centrifuge, and the centrifuge was spinning like the barrel of a clothes dryer—which was probably what it had been made from. The gold-extraction machine seemed to be functioning as it was supposed to. I was impressed.

After the centrifuge had done its job, the mercury traps would catch the gold. My father scooped some of the silvery liquid into a glass jar and studied it.

"You know you've got gold when the mercury goes dull."

As a child—before we knew how dangerous it was—I'd played with the tiny, glittering balls of mercury from a broken thermometer. If memory served, those balls were shinier than this mercury, but I couldn't be sure.

A light rain had been falling since we left Victoria, as fine as an ocean spray. All at once, the drizzle turned to a downpour. I pulled my hood over my head and tucked my notebook under my shirt to prevent the ink from running. Kit squatted down and made adjustments to the motor to keep the centrifuge spinning at the right speed. My father took off his raincoat and held it over Kit's head to shelter him from the cloudburst. When Kit ran his arm over his eyes to wipe away the rain, my father bent closer to shield him.

Suddenly, Kit jumped back. My father's raincoat had started flapping though the air. My father tried to hold on to it, but it was twisting around and around. The sleeve was caught in the fan belt. The raincoat was wrenched out of his hand. It whipped about wildly while a burning smell came from the machine. The timing chain snapped. The centrifuge stopped spinning. The motor died.

My father was too shocked to say a word. The prospectors under their tarpaulin just stared.

Kit was the first one to speak. "Too much to fix."

"Are you sure?"

Kit nodded.

My father was silent. "Then let's go," he said, finally. "No point standing around in the rain."

"But what about your machine, Dad?"

"We leave it here."

"What? Why?"

"I already knew it wasn't getting any gold. I just didn't want to tell you. I was still hoping, you know. But when I looked at the mercury, the writing was on the wall."

As we drove away, I looked back and saw that the prospectors were already moving toward the broken machine as if to cannibalize it for parts.

We dropped Kit off at his place. Then we continued to the warehouse, where Brad had just finished stacking tools in preparation for his departure.

"How'd it go?" he asked, wiping his hands on a cloth he took from a nail on the wall.

The light went out of my father's eyes, and he looked down. "Sometimes I think I'm just not going to make it." He shook his head slowly, defeated.

Brad and I shared a look of alarm. No matter how much we both criticized our father, the defeat in his voice was something neither one of us could take.

"You don't believe that for a second," I chided him. "You'll figure something out. You always do."

"Yeah, Dad," Brad said. "You taught us never to give up."

"Well, when I was looking at the mercury trap, it did occur to me that there could be a better way to go." The tiniest spark had returned to our father's eyes. He pulled an envelope out of his pocket to write on.

"Yeah, that's what we're talking about," Brad said in an encouraging voice.

It was going to be hard when my brother moved away.

With Brad standing there, so lean and tall and handsome, I thought how sad it was that we were losing him. But then I heard my father say that this was going to be the Year of Dacker after all, and that made me smile.

And now I had my submission for the writing program.

CHAPTER 36

THE RESCUE

VANCOUVER, 1984–1986

IN EARLY SPRING, WHILE Victoria was doing its annual flower count to lord over the rest of Canada, a letter arrived in my mailbox bearing the crest of the University of British Columbia. I tore it open with trepidation. But inside was the glorious news I was hoping for: the short story about my father's gold machine had earned me a spot in the master's program.

That summer, I moved from Victoria, on Vancouver Island, to the city of Vancouver, on the mainland. With Brad in the Okanagan Valley, the Strait of Georgia now separated my father from both his children.

Only 250 miles stretched between the Okanagan and the coast, yet it was as if Brad and I inhabited different countries. My brother was so over Victoria's clement microclimate that he'd found himself a town with honest-to-God winters. It wasn't Kirkland Lake, but it was close enough. He bought himself a snowmobile and a ski pass and never looked back.

My father called me not even a full day after I moved. "You must be missing your old dad." From his voice, I could tell he meant it the other way around.

"You're just a ferry ride away," I reassured him.

To stretch my savings, I'd rented a room in a basement apartment near the university. There was one high, small window and a bed that took up almost the entire space. I'd thought it would be okay sharing an apartment with a journalism student I didn't know, but my roommate was slovenly and depressed and smoked a lot of weed. So far, I hadn't seen him out of his pajamas.

I was still adjusting to my new, and diminished, living conditions a couple of days later when the hall phone rang.

"Guess what?" It was my father again.

"I'm afraid to ask."

"I'm moving to the mainland."

"Dad, no. You can't come over here." I had an image of him taking up residence in the bedroom next door, which gave me a sudden appreciation for my stoner roomie. "Vancouver rents are crazy."

"Oh, I don't have to worry about rent. A guy I know bought a power station. He removed all the equipment—now it's as big inside as a football field. I'm going to live there for free, as a security guard."

"But where will you sleep?"

"In the lunchroom. On the table. It's warmer than the floor."

I had to make an effort not to feel sorry for my father. After all, he was living life on his terms.

The following day, halfway into my creative nonfiction class, where a dozen of us were critiquing a piece around a conference table, a new student burst through the door.

"Sorry, the plane from Paris was late," she said.

Maxine wore a scarf tied around her neck European style, with a triangle at the front. Her freckled nose was burned a deep Moroccan red. Wispy tendrils of brown hair flew out from under her headband. Her pants, Continental chic, stopped partway down her bare calf. Her shoes were flat and simple, which somehow made her ensemble seem like something she radiated, rather than something she thought about before putting on.

I looked around the table. It was like she was a gleaming quarter and the rest of us dull pennies. I made a place for her beside me.

At the end of the class, Bob Harlow, our instructor, assigned us pages for the next week.

"What do we write?" one of the students asked.

"Just write."

"What word count do you want us to hit?" Maxine sounded like a professional.

Bob took off his square-framed glasses to focus on her. "If I know you, you'll be aiming at magazine length."

Maxine, I found out, was a working adventure travel journalist. She was successful, worldly, and courageous. All my life, I had been looking for a role model. When I was a girl, it was to answer the question "Who am I?" But now I wanted to know "Who can I be?"

In Maxine, I saw the answer.

Anything.

As the classroom emptied that day, I reached the door at the same time she did, making for a shuffle as we decided who would go through first. (She would, always.)

"I'd love to hear more about your travel writing." I tried not to gush. "Do you want to go for a drink sometime?"

"Let's have dinner tonight," she said, and took my arm. "I haven't got a thing in the fridge, and no one knows I'm back yet."

Later, while eating tacos, Maxine and I bonded over our love of writing. I found out that she was a Montrealer who spoke fluent Quebec French; that she was a world-class skier, a climber, a mountain biker, and an equestrian whose horse had been chosen for the Olympics. She'd traveled the world as a journalist. At twenty-six, she was just a few months older than me.

My early admiration for Maxine only grew as I got to know her better. Like my father, she dreamed big. But unlike him, she managed to have an adventurous life without things going wrong.

As fall approached winter, we discovered we both had been keeping journals since our early teens. One day, we sat side by side on her floor, our backs against the sofa, and began reading each other's secrets.

As a proponent of the sexual liberation of women, I had never had a hard time getting dates. Now Maxine was reading all those secrets about me that no one else knew.

"Wow, Lori."

My words also revealed my self-doubts, which seemed more extensive than the ones she wrote about in her journals.

Showing each other our vulnerabilities deepened our friendship. Maxine saw my contradictions: the confidence of a fiercely loved daughter and the insecurity of an abandoned child. She seemed to like me anyway.

Meanwhile, in his power station, my father had started taking cold showers.

"They don't have hot water?"

"I have to toughen myself up," he said. "If I get all warm in the shower, it'll make it harder to stand the cold."

"Why on earth do you stay there?"

"Didn't I tell you? They don't call us Hollywood North for nothing. I'm renting the place out as a film set. That Mr. MacGyver, what a nice guy."

"That's not his real name, Dad."

A few months later, *MacGyver* switched production locations, and my father gave up on the power station. With the TV money, he bought a small motor home and parked it on the banks of the Fraser River. He was moving ever closer to me.

Directly outside his new front door, tugboats drew log booms upriver. One day, he saw a log roll free of the boom. Then he started noticing logs everywhere: littering the shoreline, rubbing up against the barnacle-encrusted docks, deadheading dangerously in front of boats. Figuring they had to be worth something to someone, he got himself an old salvage boat and started selling the logs back to the sawmills that had lost them in the first place. Trees that would have been worth one hundred dollars inside the booms now, water-logged, were worth about twelve. But salvaging those logs gave him the same joy as he got from picking up a bottle in the street: it was money for nothing.

That winter, Maxine was staying in Vancouver to study at UBC. Usually the first snows found her in the French Alps, in Chamonix—her friends there were jet-set ski bums, along with some world champion skiers—but she had started a relationship with Alain, another transplanted Montrealer. When they met, she described him in a letter with just six words and three exclamation points: "He skis! He climbs! He's Jewish!" Dark-haired and stunningly handsome, Alain was the glamorous one of the pair.

When they moved in together the following spring, Maxine insisted I leave my basement room and take her apartment. She had been renting the top floor of a house in Kitsilano, a bike ride from the university. The kitchen looked out over the spectacular North Shore Mountains, while off the living room was a little alcove where I could gaze out over the chestnut trees while I wrote.

Diana, my new landlady, was an Englishwoman raising two young boys on her own. She was asking twice as much in rent as I'd been paying, but Maxine was right: I couldn't afford not to take that apartment. I was hired for a job at the university library that my new boss assured me would be the best one I would ever have in my life. She was right. To find titles for the library to purchase, I was reading *The New York Review of Books* and *The Times Literary Supplement*—and getting paid for it.

Maxine had moved to Southlands, a unique area within Vancouver city limits with actual farms. She'd phone me every day and hold the receiver out the window. "Lor, you have to hear this." On the other end of the line, a donkey would be braying.

Early one morning, when the phone rang, I expected to hear the now-familiar *hee-haw*. But this time it was my father. "Lor, I'm going to need you to come and get me."

That was the problem with having my father on the same side of the Strait of Georgia. I had been planning to have lunch at the Cannery with Maxine, but now I would have to play rescue again. Whatever junker he was driving must have broken down.

I sighed into the phone to let him know he was inconveniencing me. "All right. I'll come get you, Dad—just tell me where you are."

"I'm at the hospital."

"The hospital? Are you okay?"

"I'm okay. I just need you to come—and maybe buy some clothes on the way over. Mine are burned." He gave a sheepish chuckle that sounded as if it were hurting him to move his lips. "I blew up my motor home."

"What? But you're fine, right?"

"Yes. Well, not *fine* fine, but fine. It was the damnedest thing. I turned on the stove to cook my breakfast, but when I turned it on, I was actually turning it off. The gas must have been on all night. Then I lit a match."

"Oh my god, Dad."

"Blew out the windows, the doors, the whole shebang."

"I'll be right there."

"Do you want to hear the good news?"

"There's good news?"

"The doctor said that when my face heals, it'll be as smooth as a baby's bottom."

"Dare I ask if your motor home was insured?"

"Oh, yeah. I insured it."

"You did?"

"Well, just for damage I might do to a third party. I learned my lesson with the yachts. But I don't think it's going to cover me for this."

"Oh, Dad." With his home blown to smithereens, he'd have nowhere else to go. "Of course I'll be right there. I guess you're homeless now."

"I'm not homeless as long as I've got you."

At the hospital, I parked in the employee lot and ran into the emergency department. He was sitting in a wheelchair, his face covered in bandages. There were suppurating burn strips crisscrossing his cheeks and nose. His forehead had been spared, but his eyebrows and eyelashes were singed off.

"Lucky I was at the epicenter," he said as I wheeled him to the car. "I learned that in the war—safest place to be."

"Lucky?" I was furious. "You were at the bloody epicenter because you were the one who caused the explosion!" He said nothing, but I felt the recrimination of the yellowish liquid seeping out from under his bandages.

We sat in angry, guilty silence the rest of the way back to my apartment.

I helped him up the stairs, his chastened demeanor making me feel worse about my outburst. While I pulled out the hide-a-bed for him, in case he wanted to rest, he looked at the Chamonix ski poster on the opposite wall. Maxine had left it behind when she gave me her apartment—maybe to inspire me to travel. "How's your friend?"

I put a pillow behind my father's back. "She just climbed to the top of the Lions Gate Bridge." The Lions Gate spanned the Burrard Inlet from Stanley Park to North Vancouver. I was pretty much in awe of everything Maxine did, but this was on a whole other level.

"Isn't that hundreds of feet high?"

"Yeah, four hundred. She used mountain-climbing gear."

"Is it legal to scale a bridge like that?"

"No, definitely not. The police were waiting for her when she climbed back down. But then again, so was the press."

I didn't say it, but I suspected Maxine of having alerted the newspapers herself.

"No publicity is bad publicity," my father said, nodding sagely.

I thought then how much he and Maxine had in common: for one thing, they were both *un*common. And they both wanted me to dream more adventurously. Maxine didn't fly by the seat of her pants like my father, but she did fly. And now she had made me feel like I could, too. She was reminding me how I was once a girl who sat on a ridge and dreamed of a bigger life.

For our next writing class, Maxine brought in a piece entitled "My Horse Is Going to Die." It was about Gray, her old horse who had once been in the Olympics.

Usually in workshops, you try to focus on what's good, but Maxine's piece took some tough critiques that day. The consensus was that the story was sentimental and predictable, especially when her horse died at the end. Bob suggested a complete rewrite.

"Do you mind if I don't change it? I've already sold the story." There was genuine apology in her voice. "To *Reader's Digest*."

"To *Reader's Digest*?"

"Yes. For seventeen hundred dollars."

We all went silent. With the exception of Bob, none of us had yet to publish a word.

Maxine's career was heating up. She often missed classes now so she could jet somewhere for a story. One week, she was horseback riding in the Rockies; the next, heli-skiing in Northern BC. I hadn't seen her in a while because she'd been on a reporting trip to Tonga, but when she got back to town, we made a date to go to Granville Island. That morning, I watched out the window of my writing nook as she pulled up in her red VW Beetle. When I let her in, she kissed me on both cheeks, French style.

My father, on his way to the shower, raised his eyebrows.

Maxine took in the open hide-a-bed where he had been recovering for weeks. Unmade, as it had been since he'd moved in, the bed was strewn with tissues, candy wrappers, and one of my books, lying flat with its spine split.

"I love what you've done with the place," she said.

"Yes, it's true." I shrugged. "I always did have a flair for decorating."

The Granville Island Public Market was bustling when we got there. People milled past displays of Okanagan fruit, maple-flavored salmon, chocolaty Nanaimo bars. We were meandering among the food stalls when Maxine asked me for some suggestions to spice up her sex life with Alain. He'd asked her to marry him, so she needed to make some improvements before they settled down. I had painted myself as an expert, which might have been a bit of an oversell, but sex was the one area where she looked up to me.

I cast around for an answer to give her. It was hard to prescribe something for someone else's sex life—you kind of had to be there. "Have you tried whipped cream?" I'd never done anything with whipped cream myself, because of the calories, but I was grasping for inspiration, and we were standing in front of a small dairy stand.

"No, how does it work?"

Maxine returned from the dairy stand holding a brown paper bag. "I can't believe how expensive a can is," she said, "so I got this instead." She pulled out a carton of whipping cream. "I'll whip it myself."

By November, my father's face had healed, and the doctor's silver-lining prediction had come true: my father had turned into a wrinkle-free sixty-year-old. The only problem was that he was getting awfully comfortable on my hide-a-bed.

One morning, I caught him staring out the kitchen window that faced north. The mountains were dusted with snow. "I can't stand this weather," he said to me. "It's time for your old man to get the hell outta Dodge."

"To go where?" I tried not to sound excited at the prospect of losing my roommate.

"I'm going to go live in a tent in Hawaii."

True to his word, my father went to Hawaii, and soon after, Maxine began planning a reporting trip to Guatemala. I tried not to feel like they were both abandoning me.

Before her big trip, I invited Maxine over for dinner. I was trying to make a vinaigrette the way she had taught me. She'd lit a fire in me for everything French; I suppose I wanted to be like her, maybe one day even live in France like her. But this evening, I had overdone the mustard, and the dressing burned my tongue, so I overcompensated with the vinegar, which made it too acidic. I was still trying to figure out how to save my salad dressing when she knocked on the door.

"What's the latest news of your father?" He had been writing me letters daily as he took his red pup tent from Honolulu to Maui and then, finally, back to Oahu, and she'd been following his adventures with me.

"I can only sleep five days in a row for free," he had written at Christmas. "So before I can go back to the park, I have to spend one night under a bridge."

The bridge was near the Kokokahi Pier, which had started appearing regularly in his letters. "They should fix it up and give it back to the fishermen," his last letter had said.

I got up from the table to retrieve the packet that had arrived in the post that morning. "Wait till you see this," I said to Maxine. I turned the manila envelope upside down, shaking out the *Windward Sun Press* clipping that my father had sent. Under a picture of him with his gray beard and mariner's cap was the headline "Canadian Seeks Support for Area Pier." I started to read aloud:

"'Dacker Thicke had come to share his dream of sprucing up the Kokokahi Pier.'"

"The what?"

"Just listen. It's about a city council meeting where my dad made a presentation. 'I want to build you a pier,' said the Canadian visitor, who looks like he stepped out of a Herman Melville novel.'"

"Herman Melville?" Maxine snorted. "I wish I'd thought of that description for your father. It's perfect!"

"There's more: 'Until recently, Thicke said, he was head of a large glass company in Canada. But he got tired of the rat race, and his daughter encouraged him to move to Hawaii.'"

"What large glass company?" Maxine had come around the table to read the article over my shoulder.

"Windshields. Don't ask." I continued reading aloud: "'An old salt, he said he would like to rebuild the Kokokahi Pier.'"

"He wants to rebuild their pier?"

"Wait. Here's the best part." I skipped to the end of the article, where a local had addressed the room: "'It sounds like a lot of hooey. Do you know where the guy lives? He lives in a tent under the bridge.'"

Maxine hooted. "That's the Dacker we know and love," she said. "Seeing himself as a property developer while living under a bridge."

She was still laughing as she showed me how they really made vinaigrette in France.

Six weeks after my father went to Hawaii, Maxine set off for her reporting trip in Guatemala. I drove her to the airport. Alain would be catching up with her later. I was wearing a winter coat; Maxine, a light windbreaker.

"I love you, Shreep," she said, using the nickname she had given me.

"I love you, Shreep," I said back.

She kissed me on both cheeks, then grabbed her pack and hoisted it up. At the automatic doors, she turned and waved goodbye.

With Maxine away again, the January doldrums took over me. One day after classes, I stopped at a bike shop on Tenth to get a fender to keep the rain from soaking my bum. While I waited inside the shop, I started a conversation with another customer. He was nice-enough-looking, but not my type. Still, with Maxine gone, I was lonely, so when he asked me out, I agreed.

That night, Rick picked me up in front of my house, and we went down Broadway to the Fraser Arms. Whether it was because I missed Maxine and wanted to talk about her or because I really believed that all mountain bikers knew each other, I asked him if he had ever biked with her.

"Yeah, I went biking with Maxine a couple of times. She a friend of yours?"

"Yeah, my best friend," I said.

"The last time I saw Maxine, a group of us caught a lift up the mountain to do some riding. She was the only girl. One of the guys said maybe she couldn't keep up with us. And that was it. Man, she was breathing fire. When we stopped that van, she flew out of there on her bike and never once let us get ahead of her."

I smiled. "Yeah, that's Maxine."

After that, we didn't have much to say to each other, so I begged off early. He looked surprised but dropped me back at my place without protest.

I let myself in the front door quietly so I wouldn't wake up my landlady's family. When I got to the top of the stairs, I saw a note taped to my door.

"Sit down before you read this," my landlady had written on the outside of the envelope.

Dread filled me. I peeled the letter off the door, went in, and laid it on the table. Whatever was inside, I had a feeling there was going to be a life before that letter and a life after it.

I left the letter unopened. I took my makeup off and brushed my teeth. I washed the dishes that were in the sink. I turned down the sheets on my bed. Then, when I couldn't put it off any longer, I went back to the table, feeling a band of apprehension around my heart. I sat down, as my landlady had instructed, and extracted the letter from the envelope. Slowly, I unfolded it.

Maxine died in a plane crash today. I'm so sorry.

I threw down the letter. I didn't believe it for an instant. Someone like Maxine wouldn't just die in a plane crash. She was too alive. She skied and climbed and rode with the best athletes in the world. Nothing could keep her down.

I turned on the radio. If there really was a crash, I'd hear about it.

At two a.m. the news came on.

"Journalist Maxine Sevack was killed in Guatemala today when a Venezuelan Airlines plane crashed into a mountain with ninety-three people on board. There were no survivors." Alain had been with her on that flight.

I crumpled to the floor, keening uncontrollably. My breath came out in great, wrenching sobs. Eventually, I became aware of a banging at my door.

It was my landlady. "We can hear you all the way downstairs," she said. I think she meant to be kinder, but it was the middle of the night, and she had children. I had been crying by the open heating vent.

It was January 18, 1986. Even if I could have reached my father at his campsite, I didn't want to call him. It was his birthday.

And it was too late to call anyone else. Alone in the dark, I listened to the radio all night, waiting for the hourly news to tell me that one survivor had walked out of the jungle. I must have slept, because I woke up thinking Maxine would soon be calling me. Even as my head cleared, I continued to believe that she was still alive. How could I survive losing her, too?

I left a message at one of the campsites I knew my father stayed at. Then I phoned my mother. She was living about two hours away, in a town called Hope.

"Mom, Maxine's dead." I cried as I told her about the crash. "Can you come?"

"Do you really need me, Lor?" I could hear her reluctance. "It's just the bus is expensive, and I'm the only one of us that's working."

"Yeah, I know, Mom." She worked at a gas station.

"But I'll come if you want me to."

I *did* want her to, but I didn't say that. "It's okay, Mom. Don't worry. I'm all right."

Looking back now, I blame myself for not pressing her to come. It wasn't that I wanted to prove I could take care of myself, not like when I walked home without my shoes. It was something else. I didn't want her to be able to make amends. Unlike Maxine, she'd had a choice about leaving me. I didn't want to forgive her for that.

"Are you sure you don't want me to come, Lor?" she asked again, her voice uncertain, as if she'd just realized I was giving her a chance.

"No. I'm fine, Mom."

I wasn't fine. I couldn't eat. For the first time in my life, I would grow thin, though I wouldn't realize how thin until I saw the pictures. Months later, a couple of my fellow grad students would waylay me in the mimeograph room, where I was making copies. They would tell me I needed a bereavement counselor, and *she* would tell me I wasn't just grieving Maxine; I was also grieving my mother.

Less than twenty-four hours after Maxine's plane crashed, I said goodbye to my mother on the phone. Then I tried my father again at his campsite, and this time I reached him. The next day, he bought a ticket and flew back from Hawaii.

Journalist Maxine Sevack (1957–1986), Vancouver, 1984

CHAPTER 37

FATHER-DAUGHTER DANCE

VANCOUVER, 1986

A SUMMER BREEZE WAS blowing salty air from the harbor as we stood on the steps of the Bayshore, Vancouver's swankiest hotel. I was carrying on the argument we had started in the lobby.

"It's a waste of money." I didn't mean the cost of this mining convention, where he hoped to sell his new gold-extraction machine. Instead, we were in a dustup about a taxi. "You're being ridiculous." My words came out louder than I intended, catching the attention of the uniformed doorman. On his shoulders were gold epaulets like the ones I imagined my father wearing when he met my mother—who, since Maxine's death, I'd been trying to open my heart to.

Beside us, a taxi idled expectantly, waiting to waste my father's money.

"Would you *just* get in the cab?" My father's whisper sounded like his speaking voice forced through a wind tunnel.

"We are not taking a taxi to go two blocks."

He tipped his head in the direction of the doorman. "Keep your voice down." As if my father didn't enjoy an audience as much as I did.

Other people from the convention were starting to line up behind us for taxis of their own. "Lor, get inside." He was pleading now. "I don't want to look like a piker."

So that he wouldn't look like a "piker," he was wearing his best pin-striped suit, while I, a graduate student with two jobs, was wearing blue jeans and a red plaid shirt. I bent down to address the driver through the open door. "Thank you, sir, but we're going to walk." Then I glared at my father. "The restaurant is so close I can practically read the menu from here."

"You're making a scene."

"*I'm* making a scene?"

I got into the cab, but I wasn't giving up. "*You're* the one who's being unreasonable." The driver stared at us in the rearview mirror. "We're only going two blocks," I said to the reflection of his eyes.

He shrugged and turned the meter on.

This wasn't what I'd come to discuss with my father, but the battle of wills was our usual pattern. Bickering was our love language.

The taxi ride cost $1.80. I felt vindicated that the meter had added just 20 cents since we left the Bayshore Hotel. My father tipped the driver another $2 bill. When he noticed me watching, he shrugged. "It's only money." Growing up, I must have heard that a thousand times.

"Yeah, right. It's only money." On the ferry last week, I'd seen him fish a newspaper out of the garbage can rather than purchase a fresh one.

The restaurant I'd picked was nice but not too expensive. Beams, bricks, and barrels gave it a woodsy, West Coast atmosphere. The hostess led us to a booth in the back where the families were and handed us both a menu.

"Money is no object," my father said, right on cue.

"I'm not that hungry," I lied. I didn't feel comfortable being on the disposing end of his disposable income. Since he'd come back from Hawaii, he had been sharing a basement apartment. Not that he minded the cramped quarters: his roommate was a beautiful young woman, *and* his rent was being subsidized by her grateful parents. (Their daughter had a tendency to come in late, forget her insulin shots, and pass out. My father had saved her life on two occasions.)

"I'll just take the salad bar," I said. I caught his eyes, hazel like mine, over the menu.

"Go on, order a steak," he insisted. Like me, he was more comfortable in conflict.

"No, it's okay." I laid down my menu. "I feel like a salad."

"She'll have a steak," he said to the server when she came to take our order. "*And* a salad."

The server tucked her pencil into her apron pocket. "I'll come back when you've decided."

"No, we've decided," my father said. "We'll have two filets mignons, medium rare. Do you want to top that with a lobster tail, Lori?"

I shook my head violently, fearing he'd order one for me anyway. He didn't.

He tucked his napkin under his chin so that it fell like a diamond over his suit and tie. I put mine on my lap. When the waitress came back with our steak dinners, my father touched his plate to see if it was hot. I was relieved to see it was heated to his satisfaction: he could be living in a tent under a bridge and still return a cold plate to the kitchen.

"How's the convention going?" I asked as he reached out his hand to test the rolls. "Closed any deals?"

"The deals all get done on the last day." Breaking open a bun, he slathered on the butter. "But don't you worry. I'll find some buyers." His eyes had that distant look, as if he were counting up the deals he was going to sign.

I didn't ask if this machine was any better than his earlier inventions. He'd be seeing what he wanted to see, so his answer would leave me no wiser.

After dinner, we stopped on the sidewalk and looked across the harbor to the North Shore. The sky was black now, except for the necklace of lights draped around the peak of Grouse Mountain. He'd followed me here to the mainland, just like he'd followed me every time I tried to move away.

"Are you stinking thinking?" My father handed me my doggie bag from the restaurant.

I shook my head. "I was just remembering when I got my place on Bay Street, and you said you were going to live in your car. Then I came home to find out that after five hours, you'd moved into my house. And you chased my roommates out."

"Did I do that?" He chuckled.

"Yeah, Dad. You did the same thing when I got my own place after Meadowlily Road, and you moved in with me."

"I don't remember. Here, let me get you a cab home." He stepped into the road to flag down a taxi.

"Dad, wait. I've got something to tell you." He put his hand down and came back to me with a quizzical look. I took a deep breath. "You remember how Maxine spent every winter in France?"

He nodded.

"Well, she always used to tell me I should go there, see the world, try new things, have adventures. And with my two jobs, now I've saved enough."

"Good for you! You'll have a wonderful holiday."

"Dad, it's not a holiday. I'm moving to Paris."

His head jerked up. "The hell you are."

"Dad, I'm twenty-seven. It's time for me to move away from home."

"Of course. It's just that—" He didn't finish his sentence.

"I'll come back every year."

"Every year! If I only see you once a year, how many times will I see you before I die? Twenty? You're telling me I'll only see my daughter twenty more times?"

We were both silent. In the dark expanse of sea between Gastown and North Vancouver, brightly lit windows were bobbing, the SeaBus crossing the harbor.

"Come on, Dad. Be happy for me."

"First, Brad moves away. Now you." He crossed his arms over his chest. "If you're going, I am, too."

"Dad, you're not coming!" At that moment, I realized how much I wanted to get away. To become whoever I was supposed to be. I wonder now if I'd looked for a place so far away that he couldn't follow me there—not like the other times. "You don't even have a visa. You don't speak French. You can't move to Paris!"

"Paris?" He looked puzzled. "Why would I move to Paris? I was thinking of Mexico."

"Mexico?"

"Yes, Mexico. Why not? I can drive down and live in my van."

My head was spinning. "How long have you been thinking about this?"

"About five minutes," he said. "Since I realized you and Brad don't need me anymore."

"You mean you've been sticking around for us?"

"Isn't that what a dad does?"

I smiled. Ever since my mother left, we'd both thought we were taking care of each other.

The next afternoon, the mining executives were lined up in front of the Bayshore, waiting for their airport limousines. My father came out after them, shoulders down, footsteps slow, telling me everything I needed to know. I wondered how much money he'd spent to end up worse off. I asked the doorman for a taxi and took my father's arm.

"Let's go to Stanley Park," I said.

I told the driver to drop us off at a spot by the seawall. To the right, there was only ocean blue; to the left, a sea of green. "Come on, Dad." I tugged my father in the direction of the park. "We're going to rent some roller skates."

"We're going to do what?"

"Roller skates. You know, those things with wheels you put on your feet. We can get some over there." I pointed across the grass. "And then we can skate around the seawall."

"You do realize that I am a sixty-two-year-old man, don't you?"

"Yeah, so?"

"Oh well. What the hell." He sighed. "I'm no party pooper."

We picked up our skates and then strapped them on at the park entrance, despite the signs forbidding us to wear them inside the gates.

"Rules are for other people," I said.

"That's my girl."

Later on, we took our skates off and sat on a bench at the water's edge. Across the inlet, the mountains began on the North Shore and didn't stop until they got to the Arctic. While Kirkland Lake came to me as a canvas of trees and rocks, greens and browns, the view in front of us was pure blue. Even the mountains were blue, turning to purple the farther away they moved from us.

"I'll never get over how beautiful this is," my father said.

"Aren't you glad we left Kirkland Lake?" I was thinking that our farm burning down and all the other stuff that had happened really had been for the best: it had freed us to move to the most stunning city in the world. Part of me wondered why anyone would ever want to leave this place. Why I would.

Just then, we heard the distinctive hum of a floatplane as it dropped down to land in the harbor. "One day, I'm going to get myself a little pontoon plane," my father said.

"I know, Dad."

"I learned to fly on pontoons."

"I know, Dad."

"All I need is a new angle, an idea no one has tried. Then I'll make it."

"I know, Dad."

I felt relieved to hear him rally again. Just as he had always done. Once, when we were kids, he came home with a vinyl superhero for Brad and me. It was a boxing bag a couple of feet tall, weighted with sand on the bottom. No matter how hard you hit it, it always bounced back. That was him.

In the end, my father set out before I did. He drove his rust-brown Toyota van over to my house in Kitsilano to say goodbye. He had replaced the trilby hat that had never served him very well in business with a sporty cap. He wore a small stud in his freshly pierced ear. That had been my idea: I was hoping an earring could provide cover for his behavior. (It would: people in Mexico would take him for a hippie, even though he had never tried drugs, had never had long hair, and, to his probable chagrin, had missed out on all that free love.)

"Are you sure you don't need any money?" I asked him.

"I have that war veteran's pension you got me, and I'll make money while I'm down there." (He wouldn't.)

Behind him in the van, boxes were piled to the ceiling, filling every inch of space. They were children's clothes, eyeglasses, and hearing aids that he'd distribute for free once he got to Mexico. Later, I would see a photo of him in the newspaper in the same van with the same cap, but his beard would be snowy white. The headline would refer to him as a Canadian Santa Claus.

"You'll be okay in Mexico?"

"Why wouldn't I be?"

"Well, for one thing, you don't speak Spanish."

"You know your old daddy. It'll all work out." (It would.)

It was hard letting him go. But I had to. Even though we'd never mentioned that argument after his truck crashed into the yachts, I still remembered his words, *You're not responsible for me.* But I would always feel responsible for him.

His window was rolled down, and he rested his thick forearm on the frame. Around his wrist he wore a large watch with a band made to look like gold nuggets. He had removed the watch face and inserted under the glass two school pictures of Brad and me, side by side.

"I want to be able to look at you kids every day," he said, catching my eye. I felt the tears come.

He took my hand and kissed it. Then he reached under his seat for a screwdriver to start the engine. "Don't forget to look in on your brother," he said. As he drove away from the curb, I heard, "Ah-ooh-ga!"

My father and me, Kitsilano, 1986

After he had gone, I sat on the front steps for I don't know how long. I was filled with a strange sadness at seeing him go, even though I myself would be leaving soon. It seemed like everyone I loved had gone away.

That night, Maxine came to me in a dream. "I'm okay, Lor," she said. "You don't have to worry about me." It was the most vivid dream I'd ever had. I saw her, I heard her. It was like she had come back from the dead to tell me I didn't need to grieve so much.

Four weeks later, I flew to London, then took a ferry across the English Channel. On the other side, I boarded a train for Paris.

The evening sky was a royal blue as my train slid under the glass roof of the Gare du Nord. Not even perched on those rocks above our old farm had I been able to imagine the grandeur of Paris. The train squealed to a stop. I threw open the door. Then I stepped out onto the platform and into my new life.

I swung my pack up onto my back. It was so heavy, I had to position it so it rested on my hips. Everything I owned was inside. I thought how small our life would have been if we hadn't lost everything.

Well, kids, now we're free!

I tapped the money belt around my waist to make sure the envelope was still there. It held eight typewritten pages, the letters black and red where the ribbon had gotten twisted. "Dear Daughter and Son." It was the first of many my father would send us from Mexico. He was living with a fisherman and his family, he wrote, in a village called Boca de Tomatlán, on the Pacific Coast. Every morning, he went out with Luis to fish in a wooden panga. He had plans to open a little fish and chips stand on the beach. In the picture he'd sent me, he was shirtless and honey brown, one tattooed arm crooked around a fishing rod while the other held up an enormous fish.

I let the wave of people on the platform sweep me out to the front of the station. The crowd deposited me on a cobblestone street corner. As my wonder at my surroundings died down, the full weight of my situation hit me. I didn't have a plan, I didn't know anyone, and I had nowhere to go that night. I'd figured that once I got here, it would all work out.

I'd arrived on the last train from Calais. Now it was dark. My shoulders were aching from the weight of all the books in my backpack. I didn't know which way to go. Outside the train station, the hotels that minutes before had seemed so charming and European now looked seedy and scary. Their awnings were ripped and dirty. Neon signs were missing letters. From the shadows, I could feel eyes on me: it seemed every doorway held a man who was smoking a Gauloise while watching me.

I decided to go back where I'd come from. Inside the train station, there was a bank of pay phones. Next to my father's letter was a piece of paper. I fished it out. On it were three phone numbers, friends of friends. I went to a phone and picked up the receiver. I didn't know where I was going to sleep that night or how I would manage to live in Paris, but I did have a pocketful of one-franc coins. And I was my father's daughter.

I made it to Europe!

ACKNOWLEDGMENTS

I AM GRATEFUL BEYOND words to my father for encouraging me to follow my dreams. Bringing this book to life is truly a dream come true; my heartfelt thanks to those who helped make it a reality. To Mollie Glick, who was literally my first choice as an agent (and turned out to be a great editor as well). And to everyone else at CAA, especially Gabrielle Fetters, Olivia Romano, Jamie Stockton, Molly Schwartzberg—and Lola Bellier, who plucked the manuscript for *Dreamer's Daughter* out of the slush pile.

My dream team at Simon & Schuster Canada begins with executive editor Adrienne Kerr, who has graced me with her vision, thoughtful edits, and, above all, infectious enthusiasm: an author could do no better than to have Adrienne in their corner. Thanks also to the S&S team: publisher Nicole Winstanley, VP of sales Michael Guy-Haddock, VP of marketing and communications Dan French, director of sales Shara Alexa, senior designer Sebastian Frye, editorial intern Sabrina Futia, and copy editor Jenna Dolan, whose talents helped make my story clearer. Senior publicity manager Lisa Wray and marketing manager Rebecca Snoddon took me on the adventure of a lifetime getting me ready for the book's launch.

They say it takes a village. My village is my fellow writers. Year after year, draft after draft, my Paris writers' group helped me hone my book and my craft. There are not enough thanks in the world for Laurel Zuckerman, Anca Metiu, Craig Carlson, Marissa McCants, Yara Zgheib, and especially Janet Skeslien Charles. With a big shout-out to Jake Lamar.

I also want to celebrate my Vancouver writers' group: Ellen Schwartz, Chris Petty, Morna McLeod, Heather Duff, and Scott Yates—still writing together since our days in the inspiring Creative Writing Program at the University of British Columbia.

My beta readers went above and beyond, giving me feedback on chapters and sometimes entire drafts of my memoir. Thanks to Heather Jackson, Ros Smith-Thomas, Stewart Pfisterer, Randy Klarenbach, Catherine Mortier, Patrick Hamm, Don DePalma, and the writers Jane Silcott, Connie Bradburn, Kathryn Clutz, and Kathryn Thomson.

Thank you as well to the other members of the village. To Marites Joveres David (1974–2020), who had a heart as big as the ocean: I will always miss you. Also to Jo Vella, Karla de la Peña, Ivan Applegate, Juan Estrada, Larry Mcpherson, Rebecca Petras, Haze Manuel, Elaine Kasket, Aimee Ansari, Henry Dotterer, Susan Bryant, Lisa Bryant, William Cowie, Heather Virtue-Lapierre, Derrick Healey, Laure Trémeau, Renaud Sebbah, Laurent Mamou, Raphaël Piotraut, Dr. Stephen Macdonald, and Keahna Gonzalez (love my website!). Thanks especially to Graham Bretton Bibby, whose amusing stories about my father are worth a book of their own.

Speaking of books, thanks to the authors who wrote about those fascinating years in Kirkland Lake and the North: Michael Barnes (*Fortunes in the Ground: Cobalt, Porcupine and Kirkland Lake*), Douglas O. Baldwin (*Cobalt: Canada's Forgotten Silver Boom Town*), André Wetjen and L. H. T. Irvine (*The Kirkland Lake Story*), and the Little Claybelt Homesteaders Museum (*Claybelt Chronicles*).

I will never forget the writing teachers who believed in me when I didn't believe in myself: Warren Munch, Bob Harlow, and Jake Zilber, who told me I was a diamond in the rough at a time when all I could hear was "rough."

ACKNOWLEDGMENTS

Thanks also to the Canada Council for the Arts (and, in particular, Richard Holden), the government of British Columbia, and the CBC for their awards and financial support.

This book portrays people and events as I remember them. Conversations have been re-created, based on ones I recall, or taken verbatim from my journals. Timelines have been altered only when they made the sequence of events clearer. No one in the book is a composite: everyone is themselves, though I've changed a few names. My warmest thanks to those who were willing to populate these pages, including the Rev. Gord Williams, Susan Hannah, Jacqueline Czernin von Chudenitz, and Lukia Czernin von Chudenitz. And my love, as always, to the late Maxine Sevack. I owe an especially large debt of gratitude to Bev Thicke Wilson, who meant so much to me growing up, and still does.

I may have moved to Europe, but writing this book showed me how much my family remains at the heart of my life, and my story. I'm deeply grateful to Shelley Wilson, Cal Thicke, Joanne Thicke, Don Thicke, and Dr. Brian Thicke. I will always appreciate Robin Thicke for prompting me to go deeper, and Alan Thicke for being my dad's cheerleader. I myself couldn't have asked for a better champion than Todd Thicke. Nor could I have asked for a better son: thanks to Farrell Thicke Farquhar for accepting all these messy revelations about his mother's life with his usual good humor.

A special thank-you to my partner, Andreas Vossler, for his love, wisdom, and support—and the insightful suggestions that helped make this book better.

But most of all, I thank my brother, Brad Thicke. I cannot express how grateful I am that he let me tell his story along with mine.

My final words are for my mother. Writing this book has brought me a deeper understanding of how it hurt her to give up her children and how she never forgave herself. Her own dreams were so small, but the love she gave my son, her grandson, was boundless. I thank my mother for that love, which in the end allowed us to heal.

ABOUT THE AUTHOR

LORI THICKE is a Canadian author, founder, and speaker. She was born in Toronto and raised in the northern mining town of Kirkland Lake. She earned an MFA in creative writing from the University of British Columbia, where she was awarded the CBC Writing Prize for "exceptional promise," followed by a grant from the Canada Council for the Arts. She moved to Paris and founded a language company and the world's largest translation charity, Translators Without Borders, whose work has taken her to five continents. She now lives and writes in the South of France. *Dreamer's Daughter* is her first book.

Visit Lori at her website, LoriThicke.com, to access a reading group guide for *Dreamer's Daughter*.